S0-AWD-943

It must be something in the ink.

by Cathy Guisewite

Selected Cartoons from
Thin thighs in thirty years
Volume I

FAWCETT CREST • NEW YORK

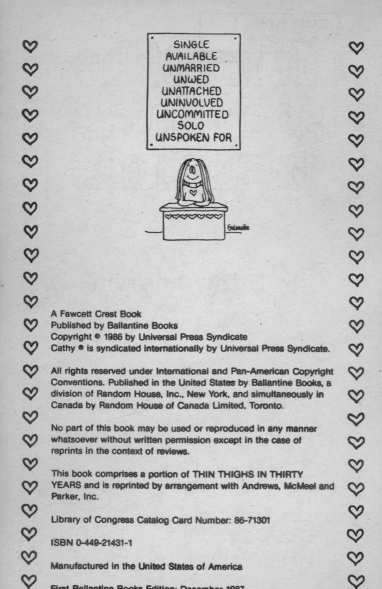

SINGLE
AVAILABLE
UNMARRIED
UNWED
UNATTACHED
UNINVOLVED
UNCOMMITTED
SOLO
UNSPOKEN FOR

A Fawcett Crest Book
Published by Ballantine Books
Copyright © 1986 by Universal Press Syndicate
Cathy ® is syndicated internationally by Universal Press Syndicate.

This book comprises a portion of THIN THIGHS IN THIRTY
YEARS and is reprinted by arrangement with Andrews, McMeel and
Parker, Inc.

Library of Congress Catalog Card Number: 86-71301

ISBN 0-449-21431-1

Manufactured in the United States of America

First Ballantine Books Edition: December 1987

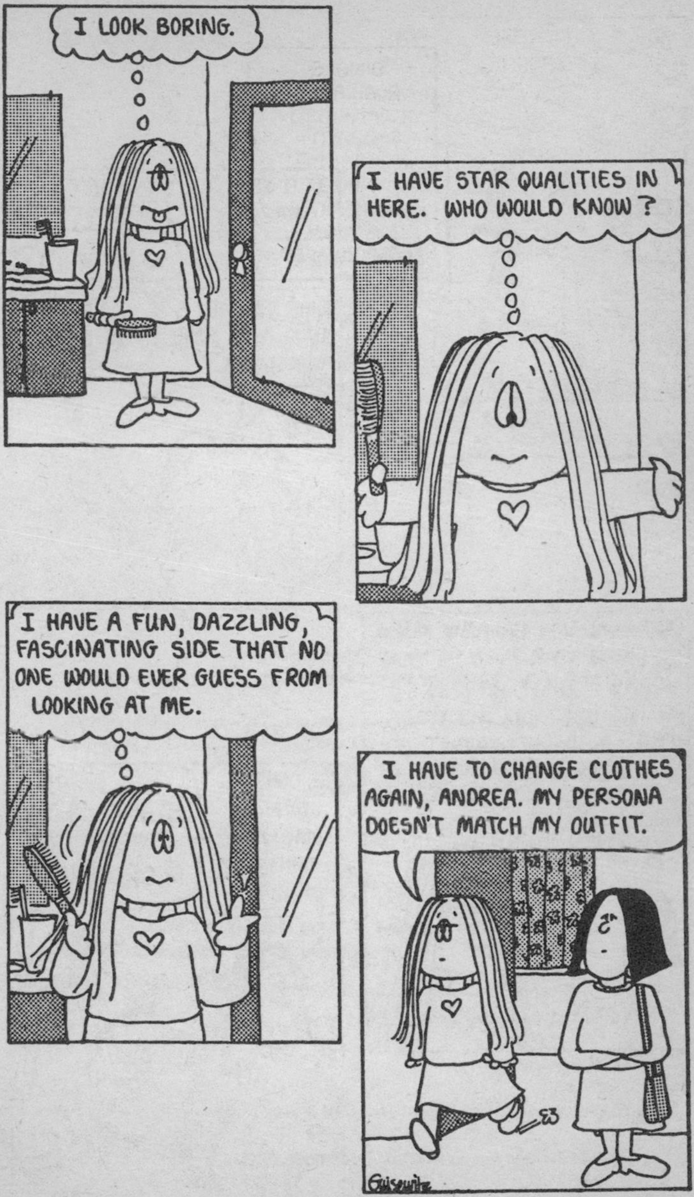
I LOOK BORING.
I HAVE STAR QUALITIES IN HERE. WHO WOULD KNOW?
I HAVE A FUN, DAZZLING, FASCINATING SIDE THAT NO ONE WOULD EVER GUESS FROM LOOKING AT ME.
I HAVE TO CHANGE CLOTHES AGAIN, ANDREA. MY PERSONA DOESN'T MATCH MY OUTFIT.
Guisewite

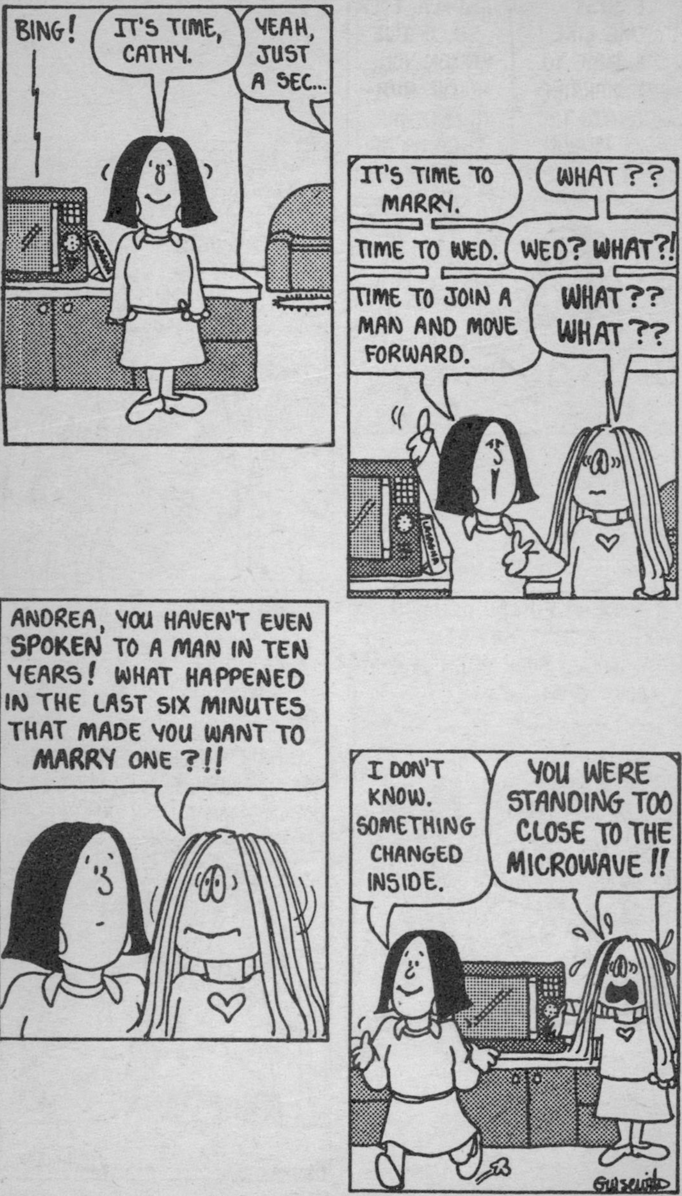
BING!
IT'S TIME, CATHY.
YEAH, JUST A SEC...
IT'S TIME TO MARRY.
WHAT??
TIME TO WED.
WED? WHAT?!
TIME TO JOIN A MAN AND MOVE FORWARD.
WHAT?? WHAT??
ANDREA, YOU HAVEN'T EVEN SPOKEN TO A MAN IN TEN YEARS! WHAT HAPPENED IN THE LAST SIX MINUTES THAT MADE YOU WANT TO MARRY ONE?!!
I DON'T KNOW. SOMETHING CHANGED INSIDE.
YOU WERE STANDING TOO CLOSE TO THE MICROWAVE!!
Guisewite

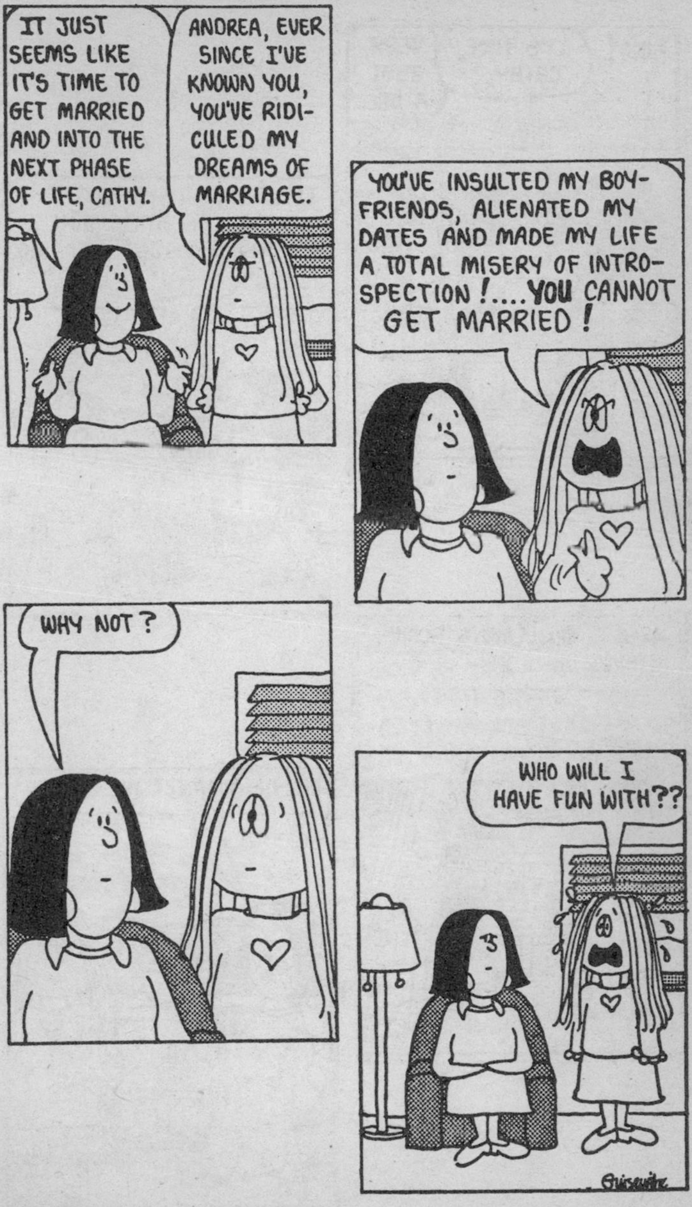

IT JUST SEEMS LIKE IT'S TIME TO GET MARRIED AND INTO THE NEXT PHASE OF LIFE, CATHY.
ANDREA, EVER SINCE I'VE KNOWN YOU, YOU'VE RIDICULED MY DREAMS OF MARRIAGE.
YOU'VE INSULTED MY BOYFRIENDS, ALIENATED MY DATES AND MADE MY LIFE A TOTAL MISERY OF INTROSPECTION !.... YOU CANNOT GET MARRIED !
WHY NOT ?
WHO WILL I HAVE FUN WITH??

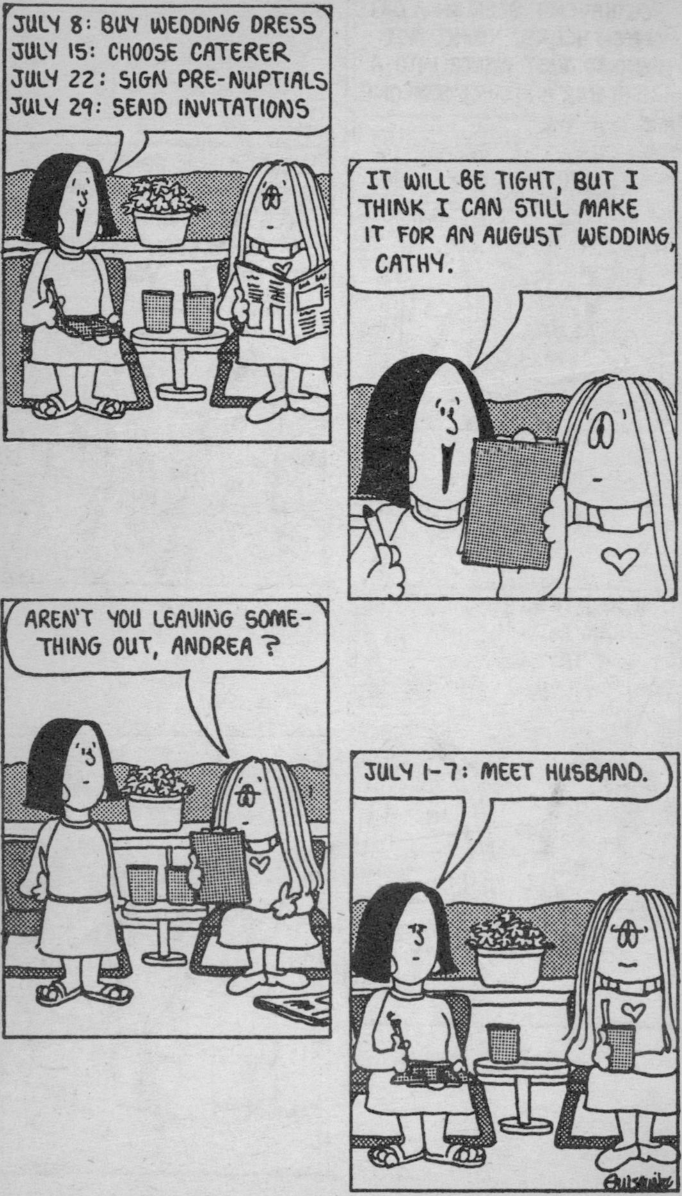
JULY 8: BUY WEDDING DRESS
JULY 15: CHOOSE CATERER
JULY 22: SIGN PRE-NUPTIALS
JULY 29: SEND INVITATIONS
IT WILL BE TIGHT, BUT I THINK I CAN STILL MAKE IT FOR AN AUGUST WEDDING, CATHY.
AREN'T YOU LEAVING SOME-THING OUT, ANDREA?
JULY 1-7: MEET HUSBAND.

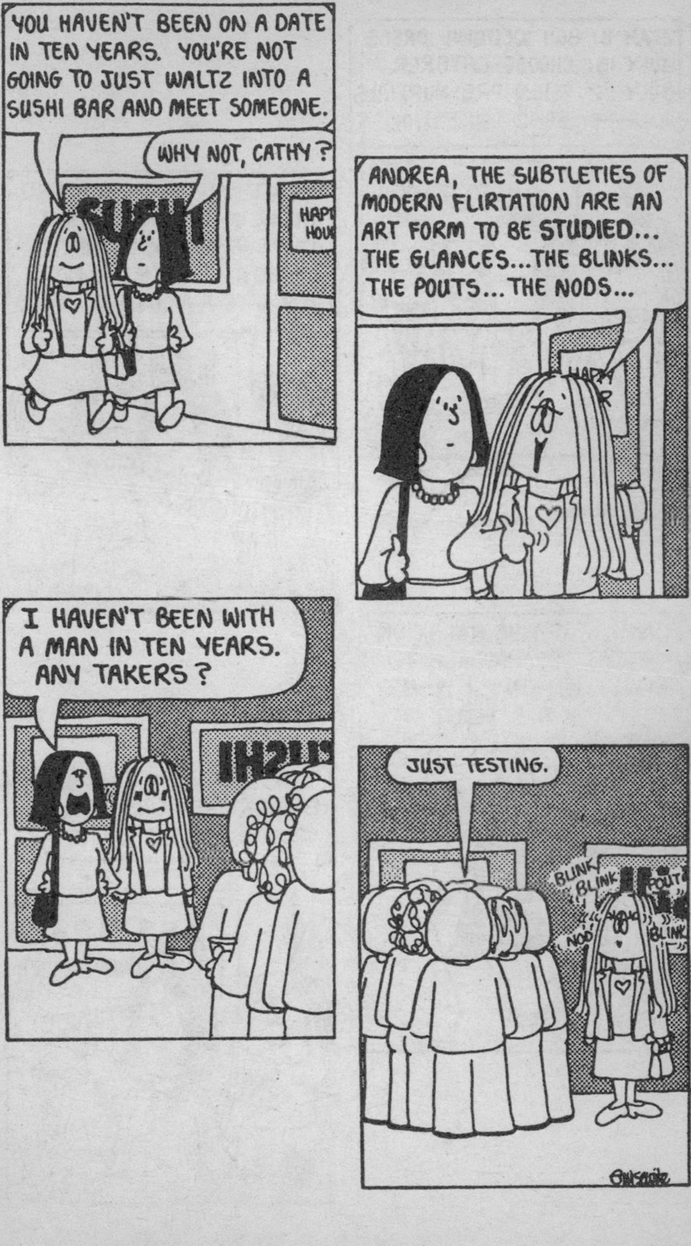
YOU HAVEN'T BEEN ON A DATE IN TEN YEARS. YOU'RE NOT GOING TO JUST WALTZ INTO A SUSHI BAR AND MEET SOMEONE.
WHY NOT, CATHY?
ANDREA, THE SUBTLETIES OF MODERN FLIRTATION ARE AN ART FORM TO BE STUDIED... THE GLANCES...THE BLINKS... THE POUTS... THE NODS...
I HAVEN'T BEEN WITH A MAN IN TEN YEARS. ANY TAKERS?
JUST TESTING.
BLINK
BLINK
NOD
BLINK
Guisewite

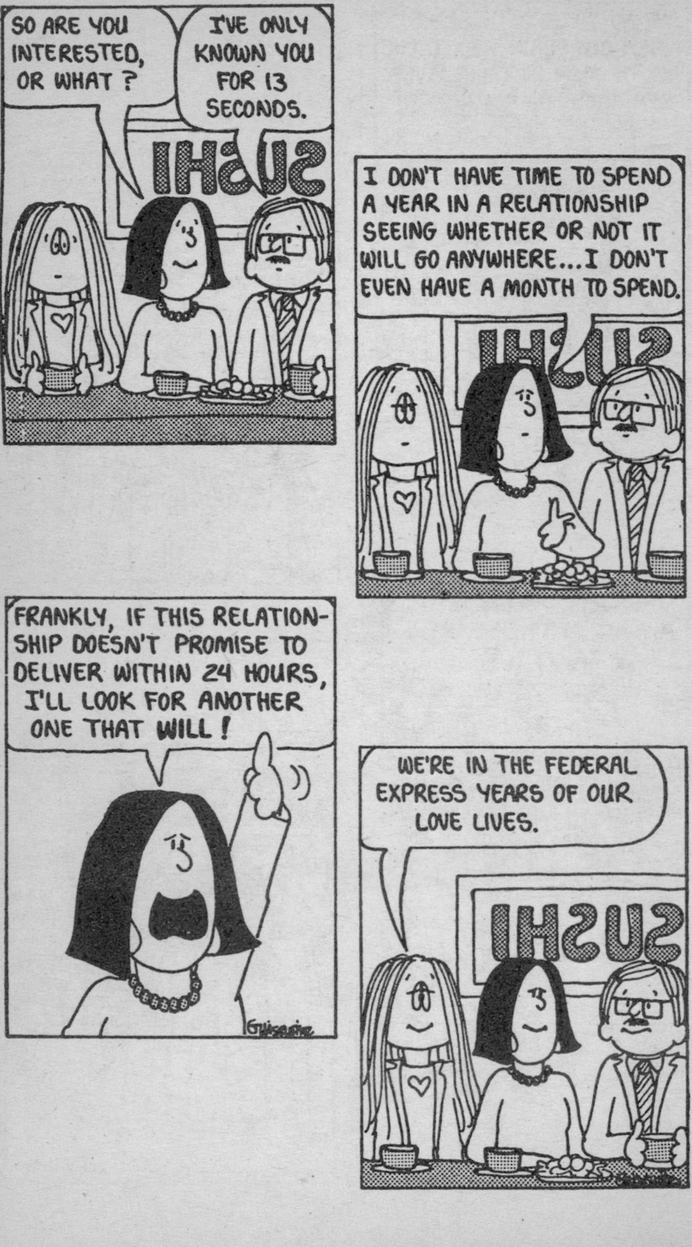
SO ARE YOU INTERESTED, OR WHAT?
I'VE ONLY KNOWN YOU FOR 13 SECONDS.
SUSHI
I DON'T HAVE TIME TO SPEND A YEAR IN A RELATIONSHIP SEEING WHETHER OR NOT IT WILL GO ANYWHERE... I DON'T EVEN HAVE A MONTH TO SPEND.
SUSHI
FRANKLY, IF THIS RELATIONSHIP DOESN'T PROMISE TO DELIVER WITHIN 24 HOURS, I'LL LOOK FOR ANOTHER ONE THAT WILL!
Guisewite
WE'RE IN THE FEDERAL EXPRESS YEARS OF OUR LOVE LIVES.
SUSHI

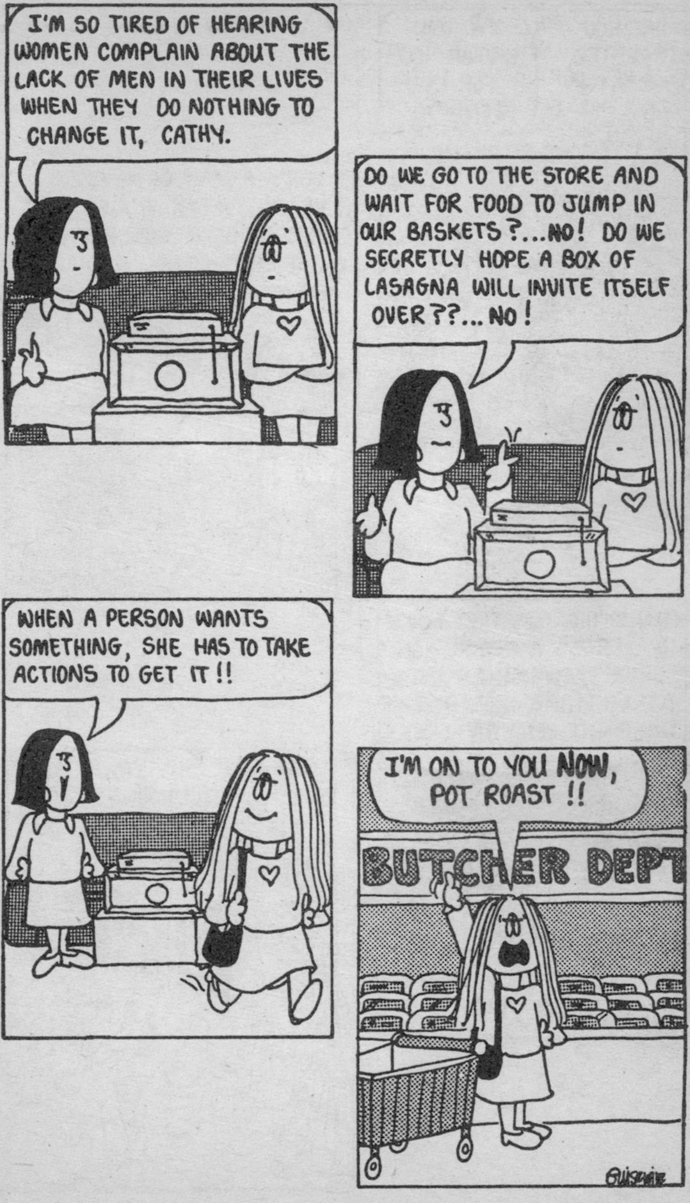
I'M SO TIRED OF HEARING WOMEN COMPLAIN ABOUT THE LACK OF MEN IN THEIR LIVES WHEN THEY DO NOTHING TO CHANGE IT, CATHY.
DO WE GO TO THE STORE AND WAIT FOR FOOD TO JUMP IN OUR BASKETS?...NO! DO WE SECRETLY HOPE A BOX OF LASAGNA WILL INVITE ITSELF OVER??...NO!
WHEN A PERSON WANTS SOMETHING, SHE HAS TO TAKE ACTIONS TO GET IT!!
I'M ON TO YOU NOW, POT ROAST!!
BUTCHER DEPT

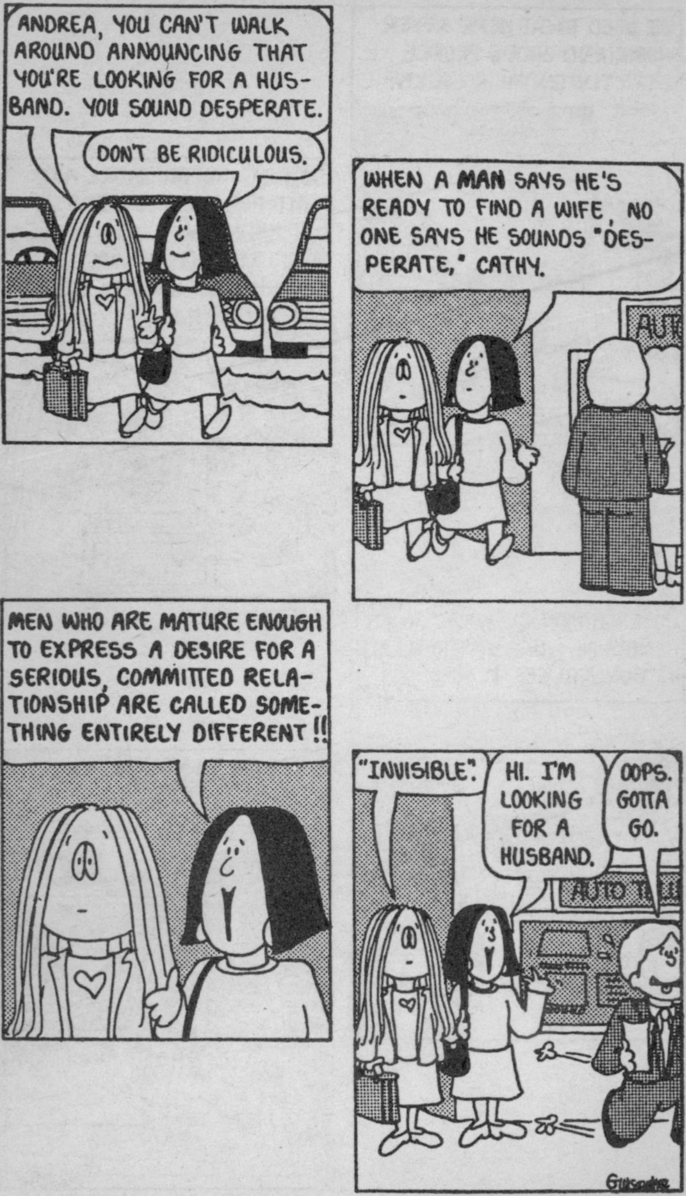
ANDREA, YOU CAN'T WALK AROUND ANNOUNCING THAT YOU'RE LOOKING FOR A HUSBAND. YOU SOUND DESPERATE.
DON'T BE RIDICULOUS.
WHEN A MAN SAYS HE'S READY TO FIND A WIFE, NO ONE SAYS HE SOUNDS "DESPERATE," CATHY.
MEN WHO ARE MATURE ENOUGH TO EXPRESS A DESIRE FOR A SERIOUS, COMMITTED RELATIONSHIP ARE CALLED SOMETHING ENTIRELY DIFFERENT!!
"INVISIBLE".
HI. I'M LOOKING FOR A HUSBAND.
OOPS. GOTTA GO.

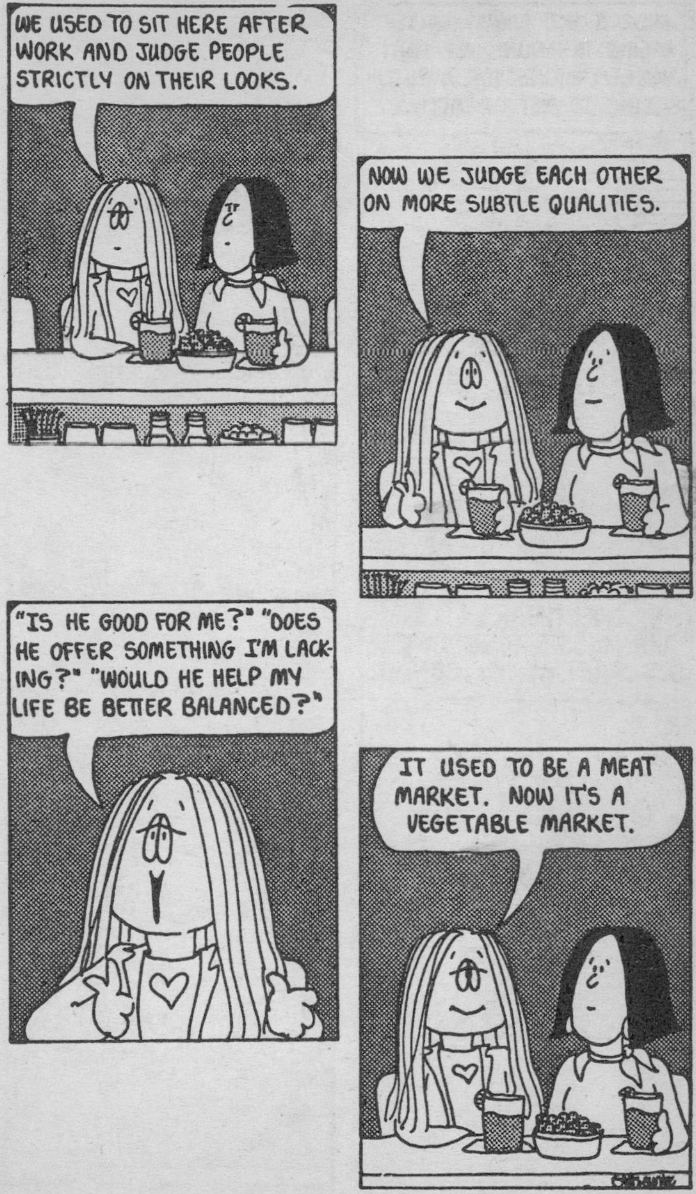
WE USED TO SIT HERE AFTER WORK AND JUDGE PEOPLE STRICTLY ON THEIR LOOKS.
NOW WE JUDGE EACH OTHER ON MORE SUBTLE QUALITIES.
"IS HE GOOD FOR ME?" "DOES HE OFFER SOMETHING I'M LACKING?" "WOULD HE HELP MY LIFE BE BETTER BALANCED?"
IT USED TO BE A MEAT MARKET. NOW IT'S A VEGETABLE MARKET.

THESE ARE THE QUALITIES I'D LIKE TO FIND IN A MAN... THESE ARE THE QUALITIES I'M WILLING TO PUT UP WITH....

AND THESE ARE THE QUALITIES I FIND UTTERLY REPULSIVE AND THAT I WOULD NOT TOLERATE UNDER ANY CONDITION.

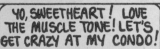

YO, SWEETHEART! LOVE THE MUSCLE TONE! LET'S GET CRAZY AT MY CONDO!

LIKE A BUG TO FLYPAPER.

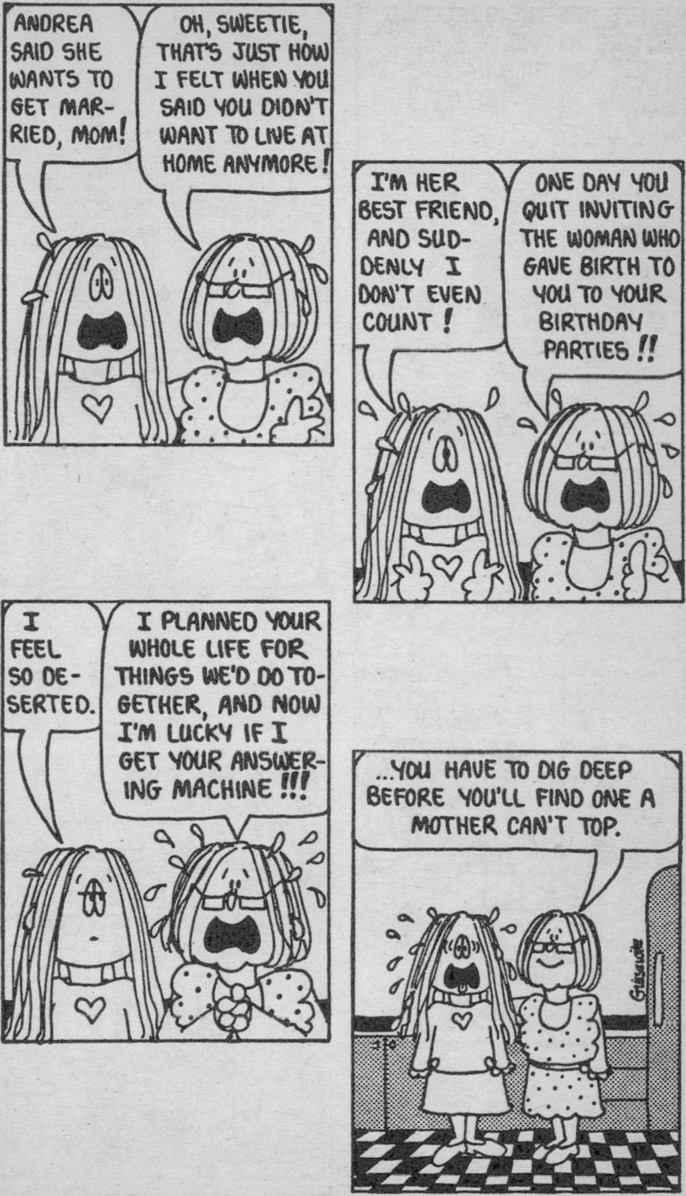
ANDREA SAID SHE WANTS TO GET MAR-RIED, MOM!
OH, SWEETIE, THAT'S JUST HOW I FELT WHEN YOU SAID YOU DIDN'T WANT TO LIVE AT HOME ANYMORE!
I'M HER BEST FRIEND, AND SUD-DENLY I DON'T EVEN COUNT!
ONE DAY YOU QUIT INVITING THE WOMAN WHO GAVE BIRTH TO YOU TO YOUR BIRTHDAY PARTIES!!
I FEEL SO DE-SERTED.
I PLANNED YOUR WHOLE LIFE FOR THINGS WE'D DO TO-GETHER, AND NOW I'M LUCKY IF I GET YOUR ANSWER-ING MACHINE!!!
...YOU HAVE TO DIG DEEP BEFORE YOU'LL FIND ONE A MOTHER CAN'T TOP.

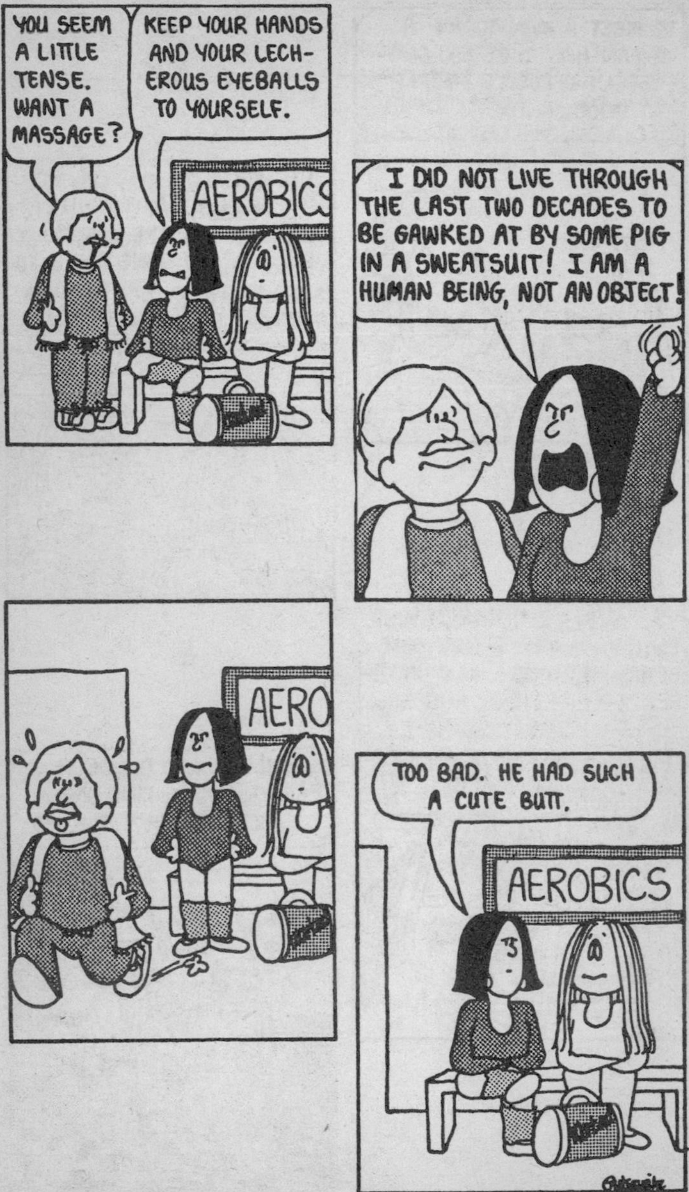
YOU SEEM A LITTLE TENSE. WANT A MASSAGE?
KEEP YOUR HANDS AND YOUR LECHEROUS EYEBALLS TO YOURSELF.
AEROBICS
I DID NOT LIVE THROUGH THE LAST TWO DECADES TO BE GAWKED AT BY SOME PIG IN A SWEATSUIT! I AM A HUMAN BEING, NOT AN OBJECT!
AERO
TOO BAD. HE HAD SUCH A CUTE BUTT.
AEROBICS

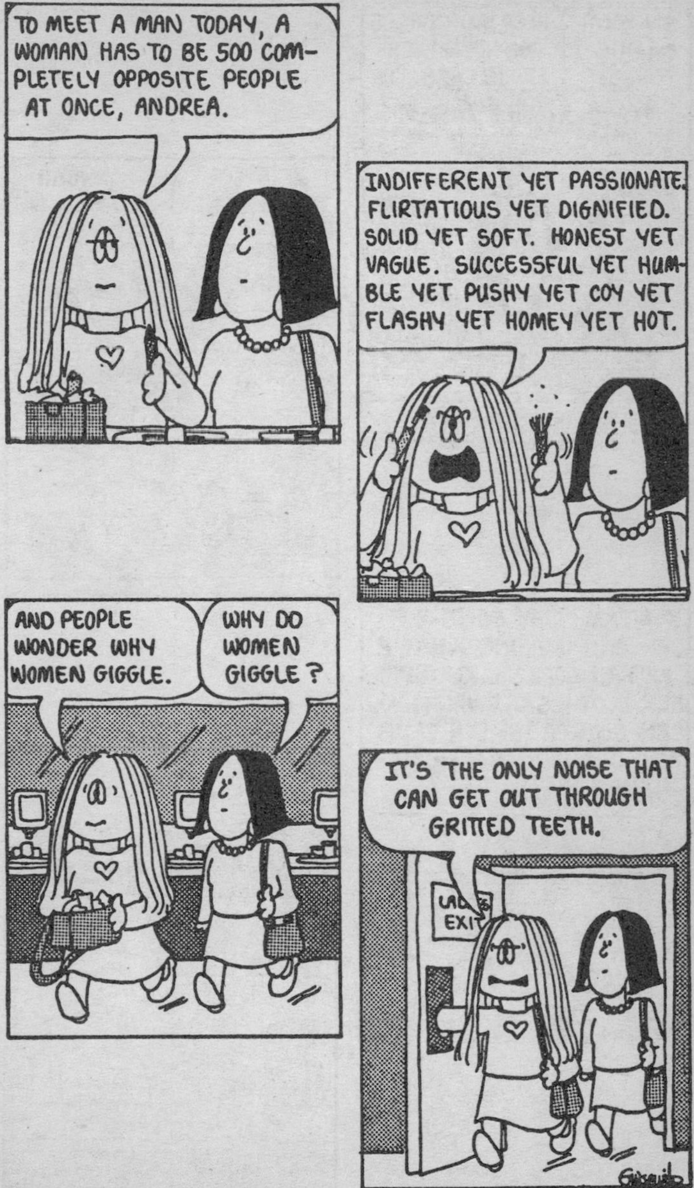
TO MEET A MAN TODAY, A WOMAN HAS TO BE 500 COMPLETELY OPPOSITE PEOPLE AT ONCE, ANDREA.
INDIFFERENT YET PASSIONATE. FLIRTATIOUS YET DIGNIFIED. SOLID YET SOFT. HONEST YET VAGUE. SUCCESSFUL YET HUMBLE YET PUSHY YET COY YET FLASHY YET HOMEY YET HOT.
AND PEOPLE WONDER WHY WOMEN GIGGLE.
WHY DO WOMEN GIGGLE?
IT'S THE ONLY NOISE THAT CAN GET OUT THROUGH GRITTED TEETH.
EXIT
Guisewite

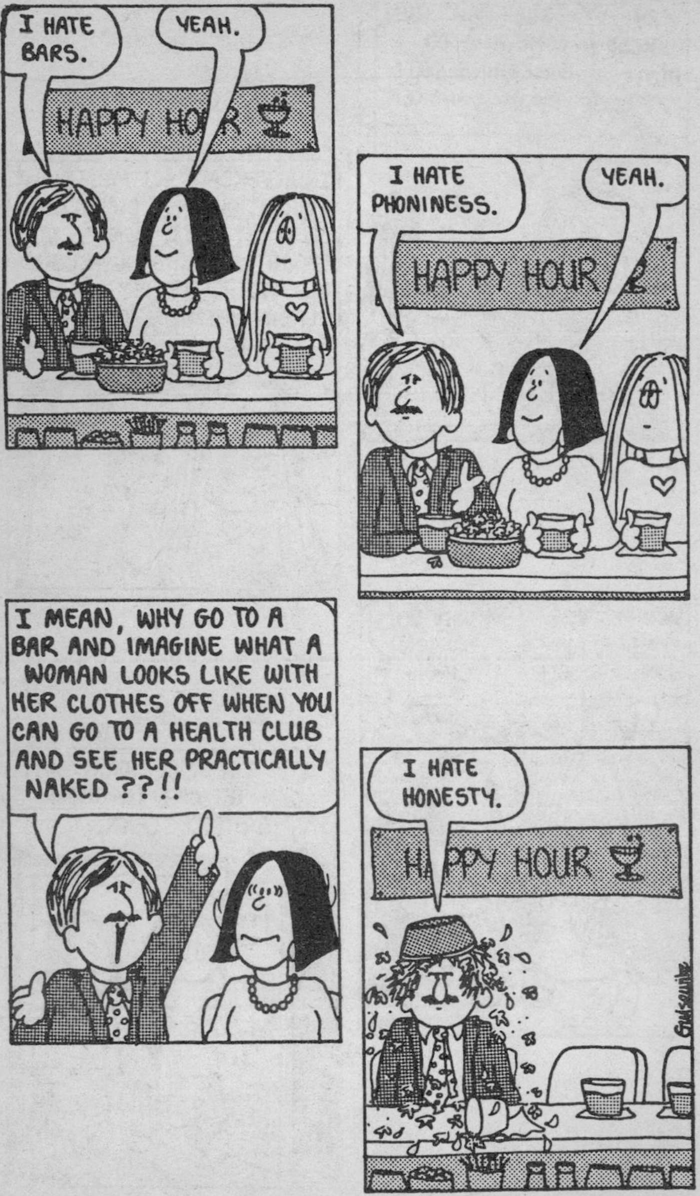
I HATE BARS.
YEAH.
I HATE PHONINESS.
YEAH.
I MEAN, WHY GO TO A BAR AND IMAGINE WHAT A WOMAN LOOKS LIKE WITH HER CLOTHES OFF WHEN YOU CAN GO TO A HEALTH CLUB AND SEE HER PRACTICALLY NAKED ??!!
I HATE HONESTY.

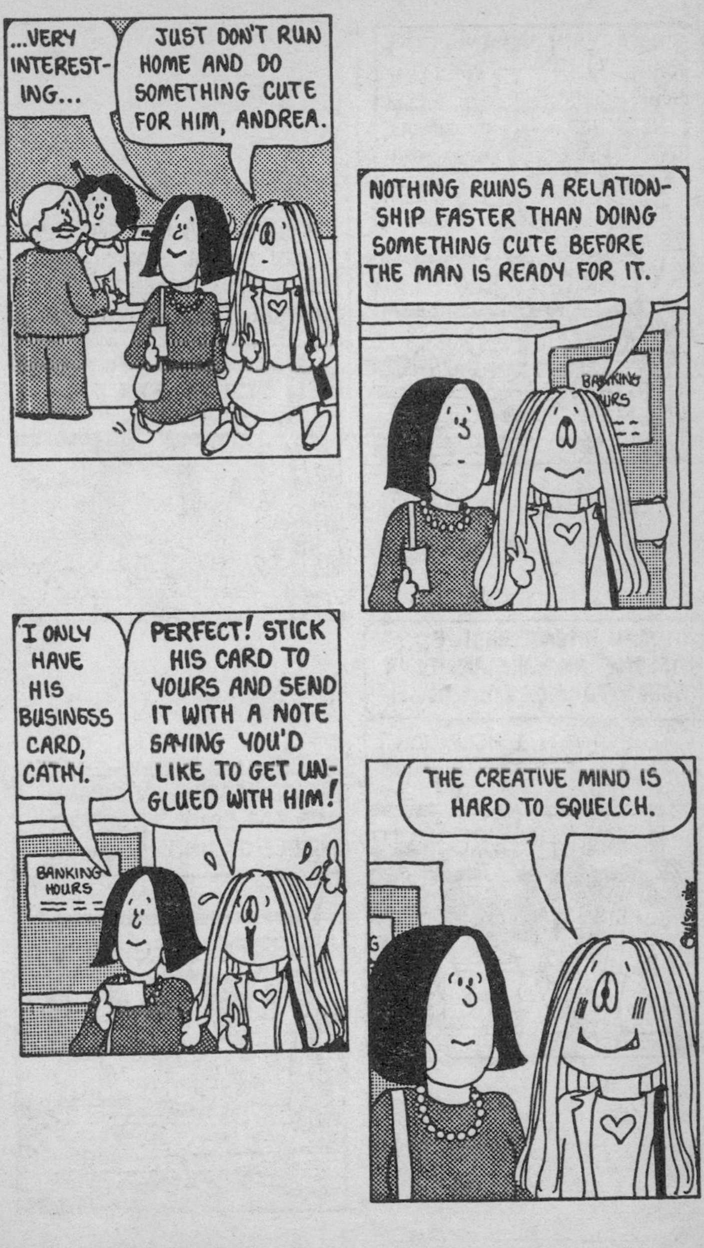
...VERY INTERESTING...
JUST DON'T RUN HOME AND DO SOMETHING CUTE FOR HIM, ANDREA.
NOTHING RUINS A RELATIONSHIP FASTER THAN DOING SOMETHING CUTE BEFORE THE MAN IS READY FOR IT.
I ONLY HAVE HIS BUSINESS CARD, CATHY.
PERFECT! STICK HIS CARD TO YOURS AND SEND IT WITH A NOTE SAYING YOU'D LIKE TO GET UNGLUED WITH HIM!
BANKING HOURS
THE CREATIVE MIND IS HARD TO SQUELCH.

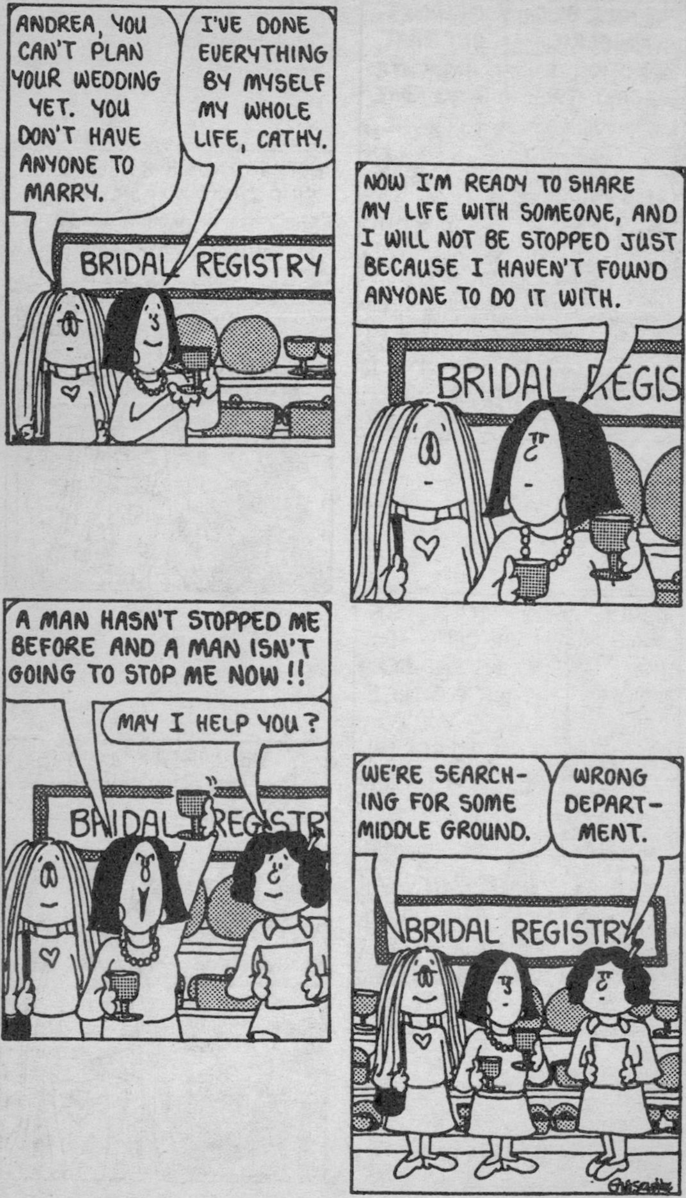
ANDREA, YOU CAN'T PLAN YOUR WEDDING YET. YOU DON'T HAVE ANYONE TO MARRY.
I'VE DONE EVERYTHING BY MYSELF MY WHOLE LIFE, CATHY.
BRIDAL REGISTRY
NOW I'M READY TO SHARE MY LIFE WITH SOMEONE, AND I WILL NOT BE STOPPED JUST BECAUSE I HAVEN'T FOUND ANYONE TO DO IT WITH.
A MAN HASN'T STOPPED ME BEFORE AND A MAN ISN'T GOING TO STOP ME NOW!!
MAY I HELP YOU?
WE'RE SEARCHING FOR SOME MIDDLE GROUND.
WRONG DEPARTMENT.
BRIDAL REGISTRY

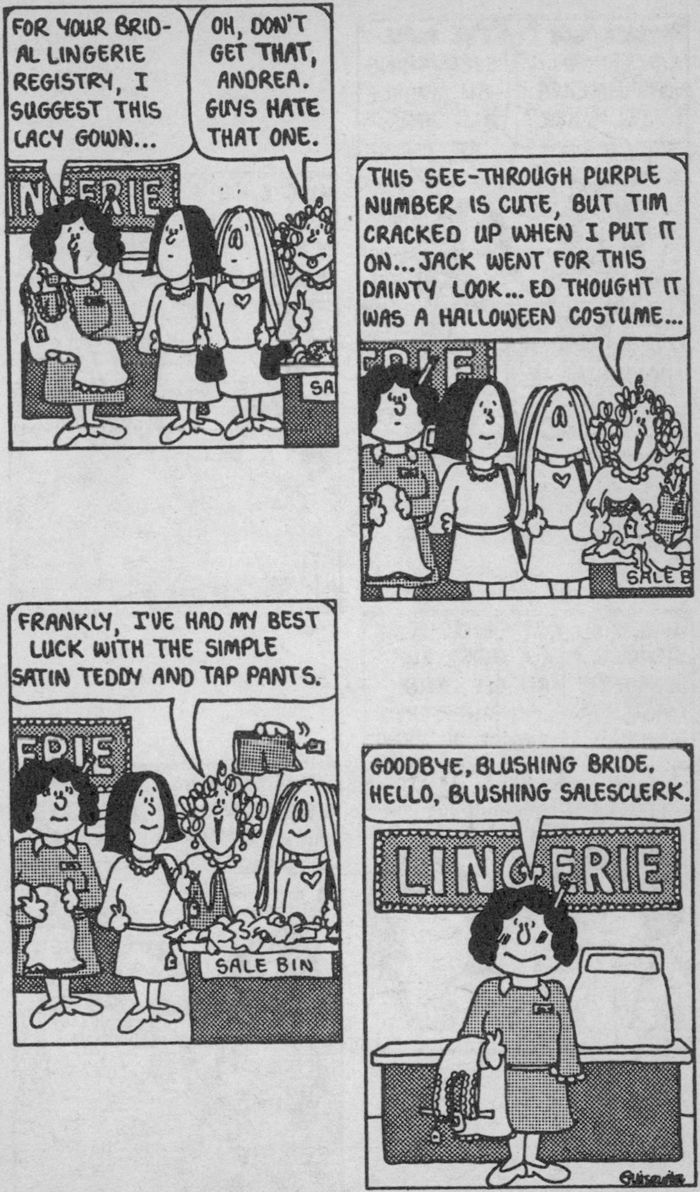
FOR YOUR BRID-AL LINGERIE REGISTRY, I SUGGEST THIS LACY GOWN...
OH, DON'T GET THAT, ANDREA. GUYS HATE THAT ONE.
THIS SEE-THROUGH PURPLE NUMBER IS CUTE, BUT TIM CRACKED UP WHEN I PUT IT ON... JACK WENT FOR THIS DAINTY LOOK... ED THOUGHT IT WAS A HALLOWEEN COSTUME...
FRANKLY, I'VE HAD MY BEST LUCK WITH THE SIMPLE SATIN TEDDY AND TAP PANTS.
SALE BIN
GOODBYE, BLUSHING BRIDE. HELLO, BLUSHING SALESCLERK.
LINGERIE

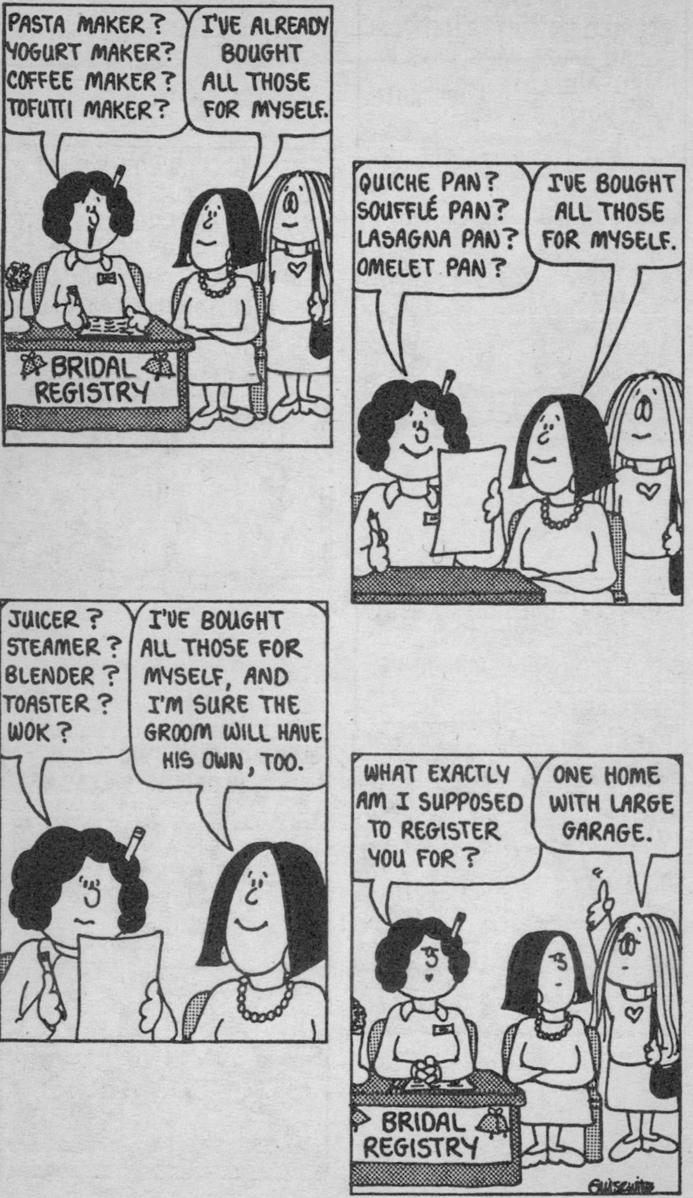
PASTA MAKER? YOGURT MAKER? COFFEE MAKER? TOFUTTI MAKER?
I'VE ALREADY BOUGHT ALL THOSE FOR MYSELF.
BRIDAL REGISTRY
QUICHE PAN? SOUFFLÉ PAN? LASAGNA PAN? OMELET PAN?
I'VE BOUGHT ALL THOSE FOR MYSELF.
JUICER? STEAMER? BLENDER? TOASTER? WOK?
I'VE BOUGHT ALL THOSE FOR MYSELF, AND I'M SURE THE GROOM WILL HAVE HIS OWN, TOO.
WHAT EXACTLY AM I SUPPOSED TO REGISTER YOU FOR?
ONE HOME WITH LARGE GARAGE.
BRIDAL REGISTRY

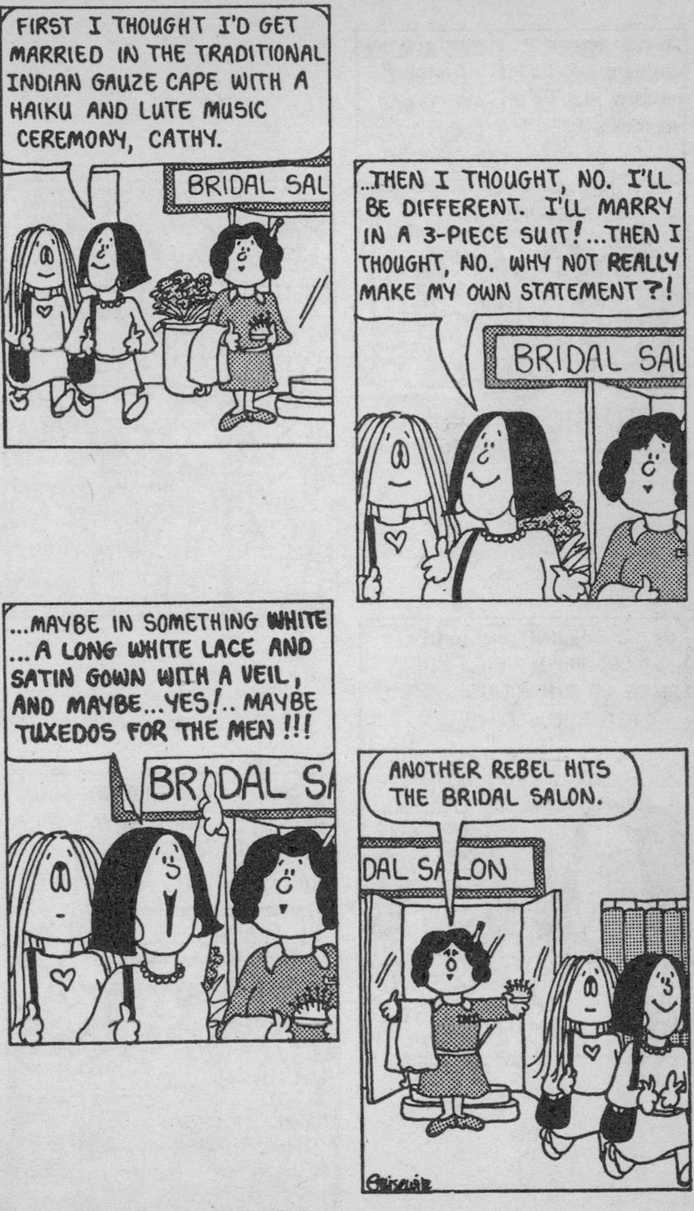

FIRST I THOUGHT I'D GET MARRIED IN THE TRADITIONAL INDIAN GAUZE CAPE WITH A HAIKU AND LUTE MUSIC CEREMONY, CATHY.
BRIDAL SAL
...THEN I THOUGHT, NO. I'LL BE DIFFERENT. I'LL MARRY IN A 3-PIECE SUIT!...THEN I THOUGHT, NO. WHY NOT REALLY MAKE MY OWN STATEMENT?!
BRIDAL SAL
...MAYBE IN SOMETHING WHITE ...A LONG WHITE LACE AND SATIN GOWN WITH A VEIL, AND MAYBE...YES!.. MAYBE TUXEDOS FOR THE MEN!!!
BRIDAL SA
ANOTHER REBEL HITS THE BRIDAL SALON.
DAL SALON

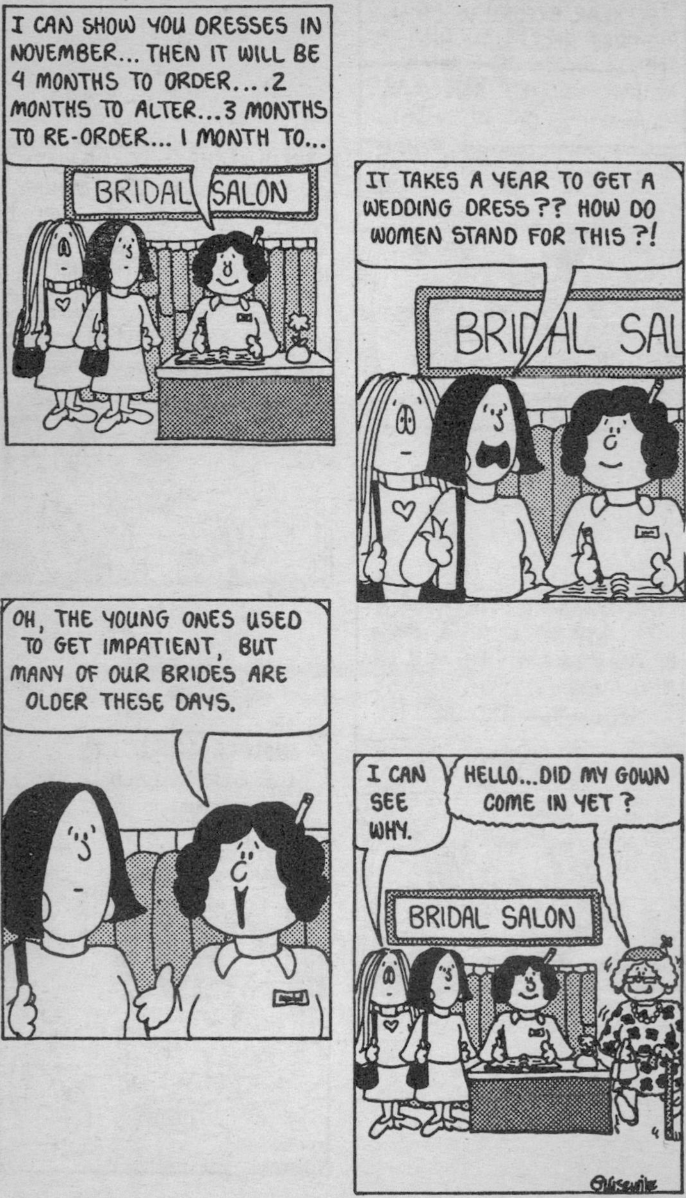
I CAN SHOW YOU DRESSES IN NOVEMBER... THEN IT WILL BE 4 MONTHS TO ORDER....2 MONTHS TO ALTER...3 MONTHS TO RE-ORDER... I MONTH TO...
BRIDAL SALON
IT TAKES A YEAR TO GET A WEDDING DRESS?? HOW DO WOMEN STAND FOR THIS?!
OH, THE YOUNG ONES USED TO GET IMPATIENT, BUT MANY OF OUR BRIDES ARE OLDER THESE DAYS.
I CAN SEE WHY.
HELLO...DID MY GOWN COME IN YET?
BRIDAL SALON

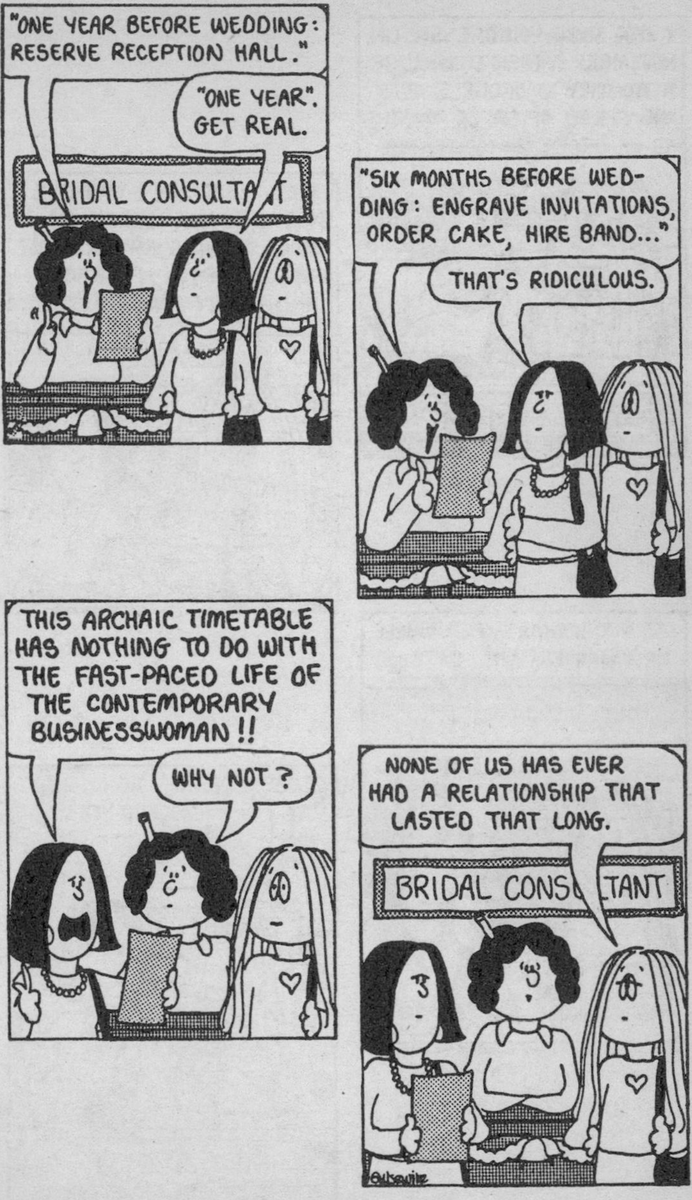
"ONE YEAR BEFORE WEDDING: RESERVE RECEPTION HALL."
"ONE YEAR". GET REAL.
BRIDAL CONSULTANT
"SIX MONTHS BEFORE WEDDING: ENGRAVE INVITATIONS, ORDER CAKE, HIRE BAND..."
THAT'S RIDICULOUS.
THIS ARCHAIC TIMETABLE HAS NOTHING TO DO WITH THE FAST-PACED LIFE OF THE CONTEMPORARY BUSINESSWOMAN!!
WHY NOT?
NONE OF US HAS EVER HAD A RELATIONSHIP THAT LASTED THAT LONG.
BRIDAL CONSULTANT

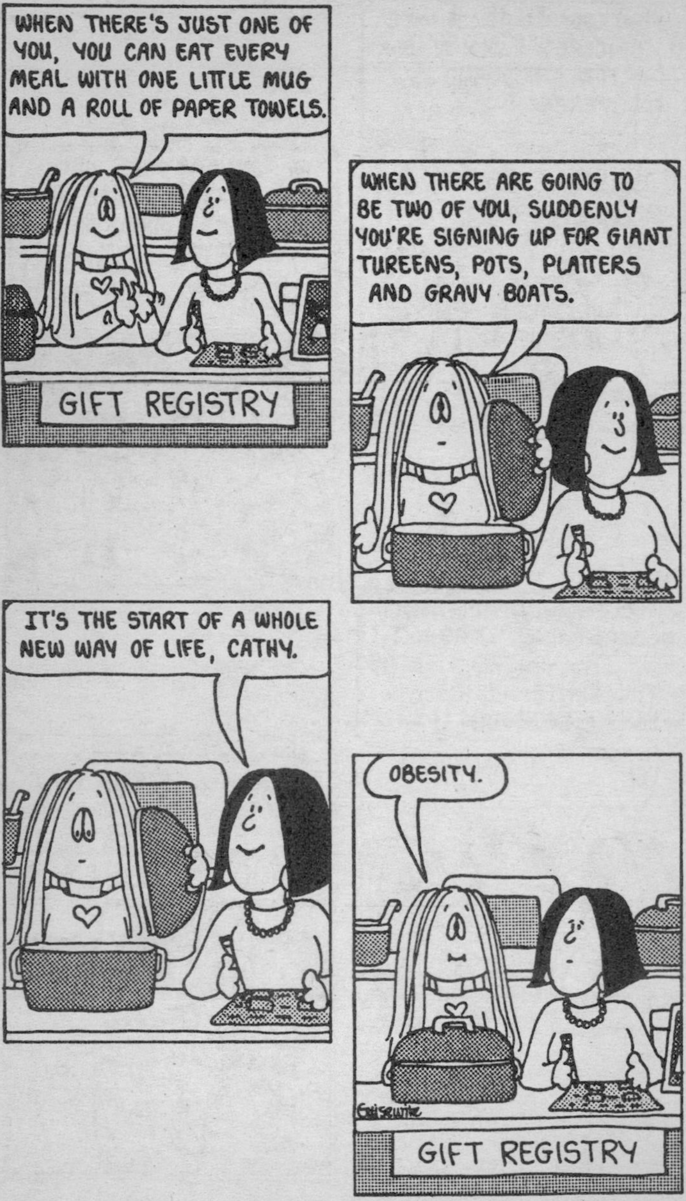
WHEN THERE'S JUST ONE OF YOU, YOU CAN EAT EVERY MEAL WITH ONE LITTLE MUG AND A ROLL OF PAPER TOWELS.
GIFT REGISTRY
WHEN THERE ARE GOING TO BE TWO OF YOU, SUDDENLY YOU'RE SIGNING UP FOR GIANT TUREENS, POTS, PLATTERS AND GRAVY BOATS.
IT'S THE START OF A WHOLE NEW WAY OF LIFE, CATHY.
OBESITY.
Guisewite
GIFT REGISTRY

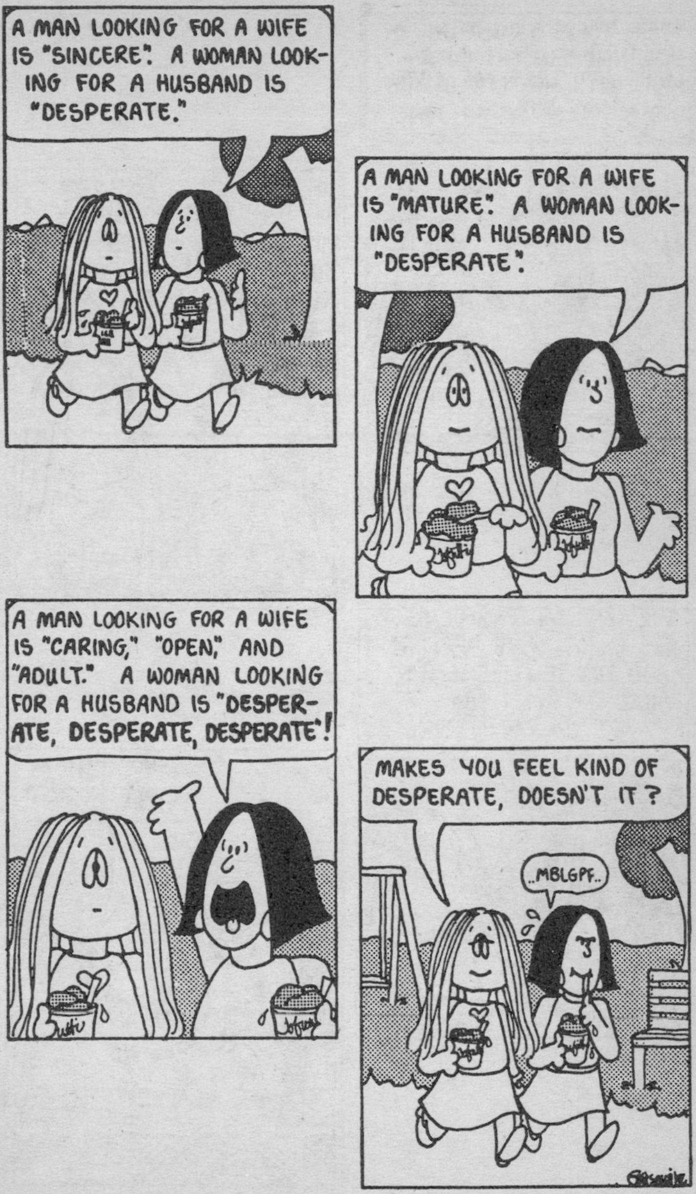

A MAN LOOKING FOR A WIFE IS "SINCERE". A WOMAN LOOKING FOR A HUSBAND IS "DESPERATE."
A MAN LOOKING FOR A WIFE IS "MATURE". A WOMAN LOOKING FOR A HUSBAND IS "DESPERATE".
A MAN LOOKING FOR A WIFE IS "CARING," "OPEN," AND "ADULT." A WOMAN LOOKING FOR A HUSBAND IS "DESPERATE, DESPERATE, DESPERATE"!
MAKES YOU FEEL KIND OF DESPERATE, DOESN'T IT?
..MBLGPF..

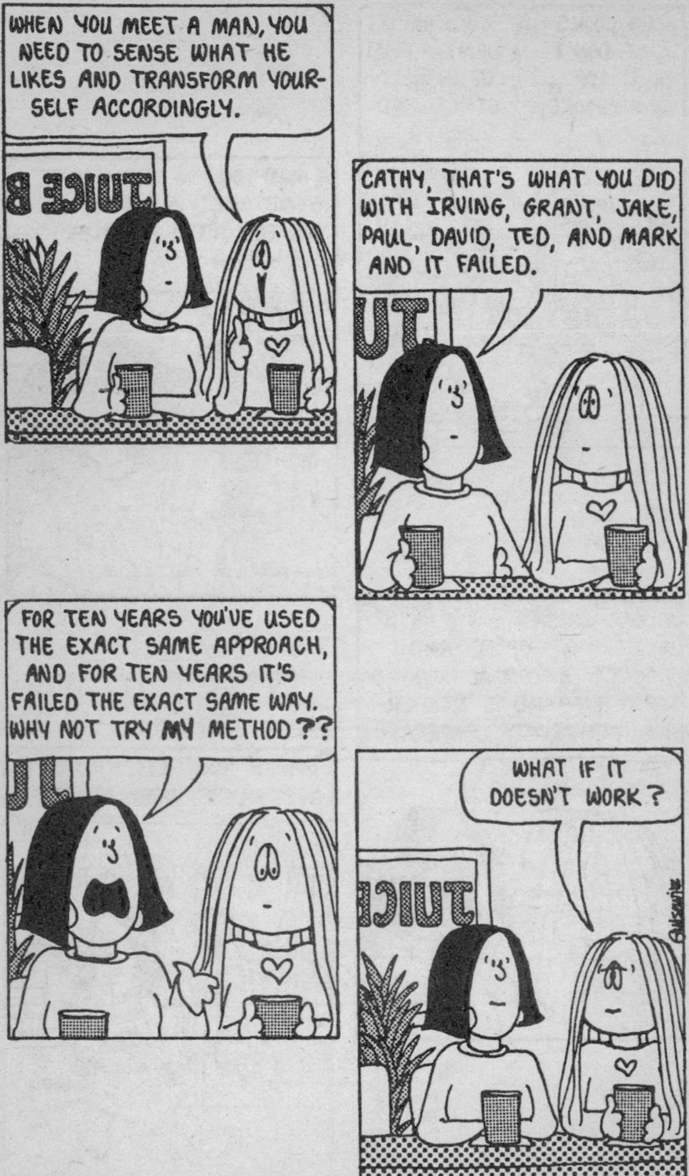
WHEN YOU MEET A MAN, YOU NEED TO SENSE WHAT HE LIKES AND TRANSFORM YOURSELF ACCORDINGLY.
JUICE B
CATHY, THAT'S WHAT YOU DID WITH IRVING, GRANT, JAKE, PAUL, DAVID, TED, AND MARK AND IT FAILED.
FOR TEN YEARS YOU'VE USED THE EXACT SAME APPROACH, AND FOR TEN YEARS IT'S FAILED THE EXACT SAME WAY. WHY NOT TRY MY METHOD??
WHAT IF IT DOESN'T WORK?
JUICE

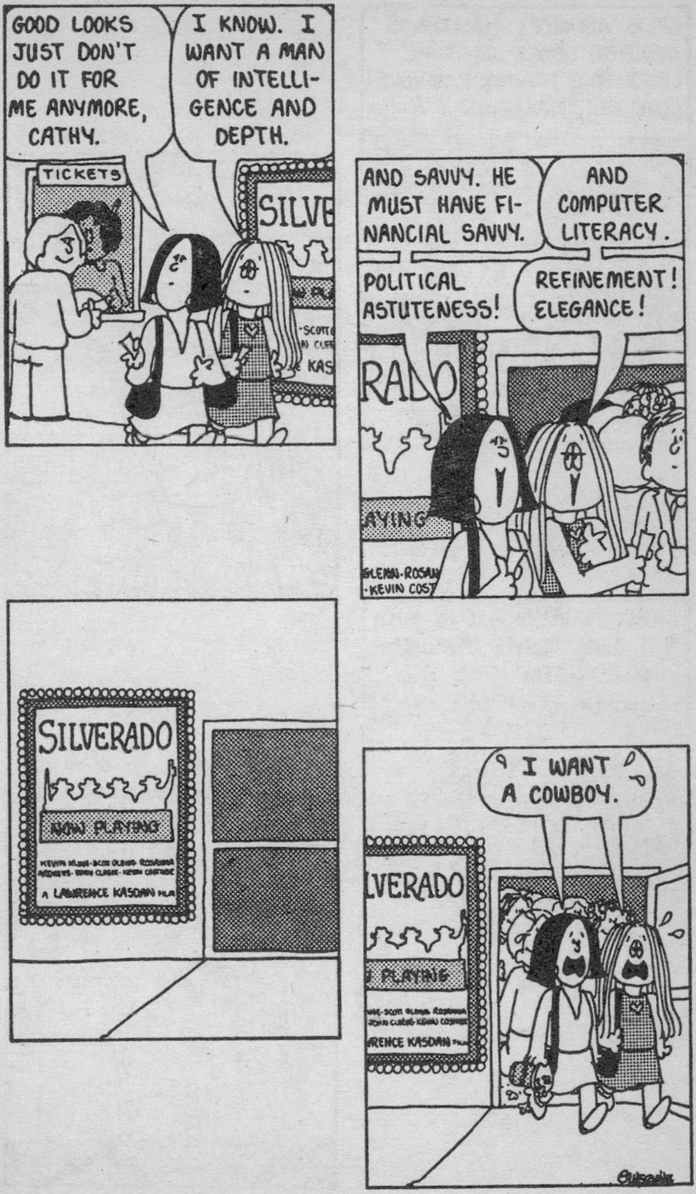
GOOD LOOKS JUST DON'T DO IT FOR ME ANYMORE, CATHY.
I KNOW. I WANT A MAN OF INTELLI-GENCE AND DEPTH.
TICKETS
AND SAVVY. HE MUST HAVE FI-NANCIAL SAVVY.
AND COMPUTER LITERACY.
POLITICAL ASTUTENESS!
REFINEMENT! ELEGANCE!
SILVERADO
NOW PLAYING
A LAWRENCE KASDAN
I WANT A COWBOY.

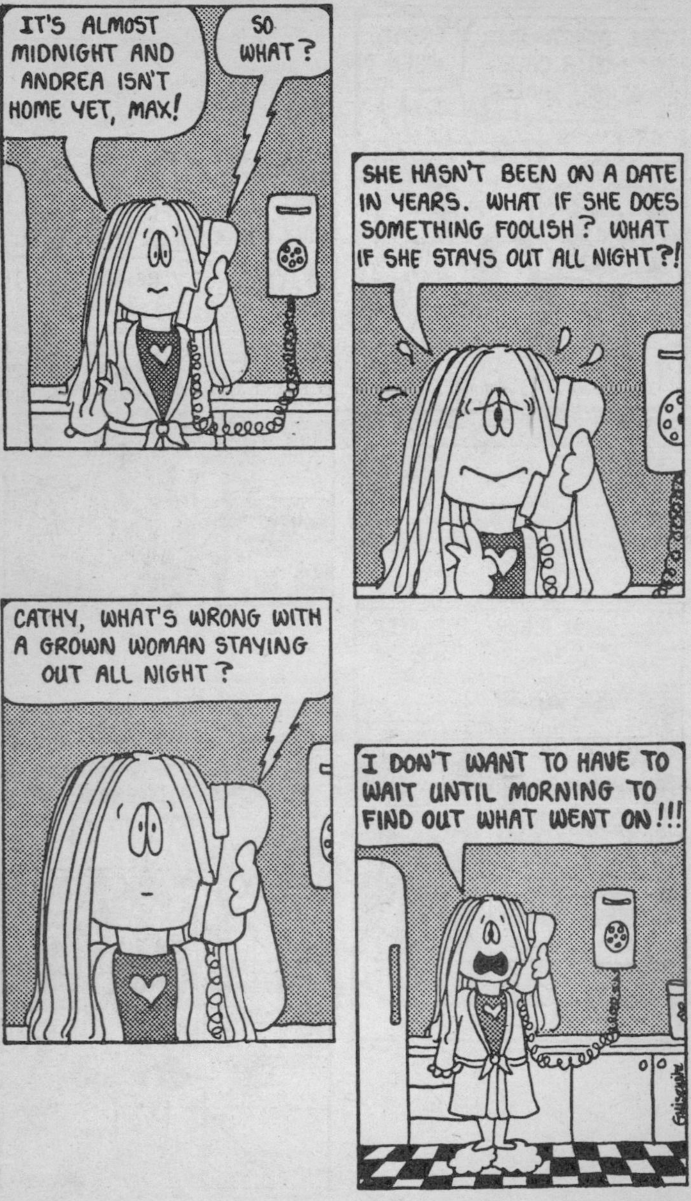
IT'S ALMOST MIDNIGHT AND ANDREA ISN'T HOME YET, MAX!
SO WHAT?
SHE HASN'T BEEN ON A DATE IN YEARS. WHAT IF SHE DOES SOMETHING FOOLISH? WHAT IF SHE STAYS OUT ALL NIGHT?!
CATHY, WHAT'S WRONG WITH A GROWN WOMAN STAYING OUT ALL NIGHT?
I DON'T WANT TO HAVE TO WAIT UNTIL MORNING TO FIND OUT WHAT WENT ON!!!

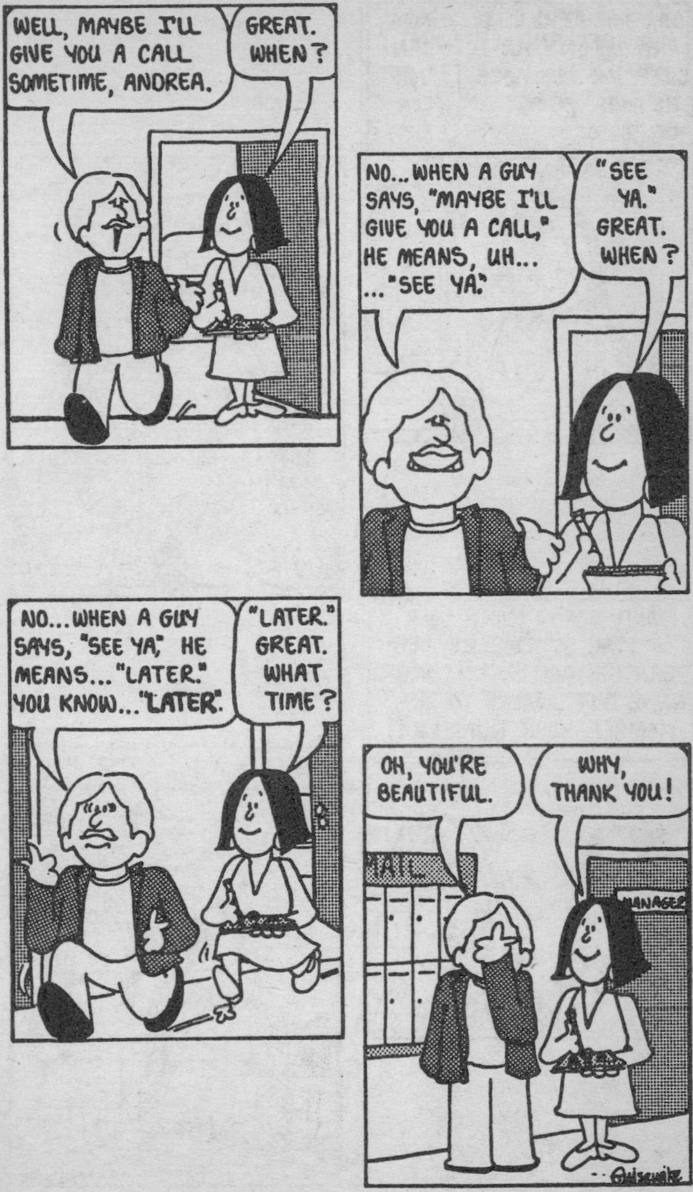
WELL, MAYBE I'LL GIVE YOU A CALL SOMETIME, ANDREA.
GREAT. WHEN?
NO... WHEN A GUY SAYS, "MAYBE I'LL GIVE YOU A CALL," HE MEANS, UH... ..."SEE YA."
"SEE YA." GREAT. WHEN?
NO... WHEN A GUY SAYS, "SEE YA," HE MEANS... "LATER." YOU KNOW... "LATER."
"LATER." GREAT. WHAT TIME?
OH, YOU'RE BEAUTIFUL.
WHY, THANK YOU!
MAIL
MANAGER
Guisewite

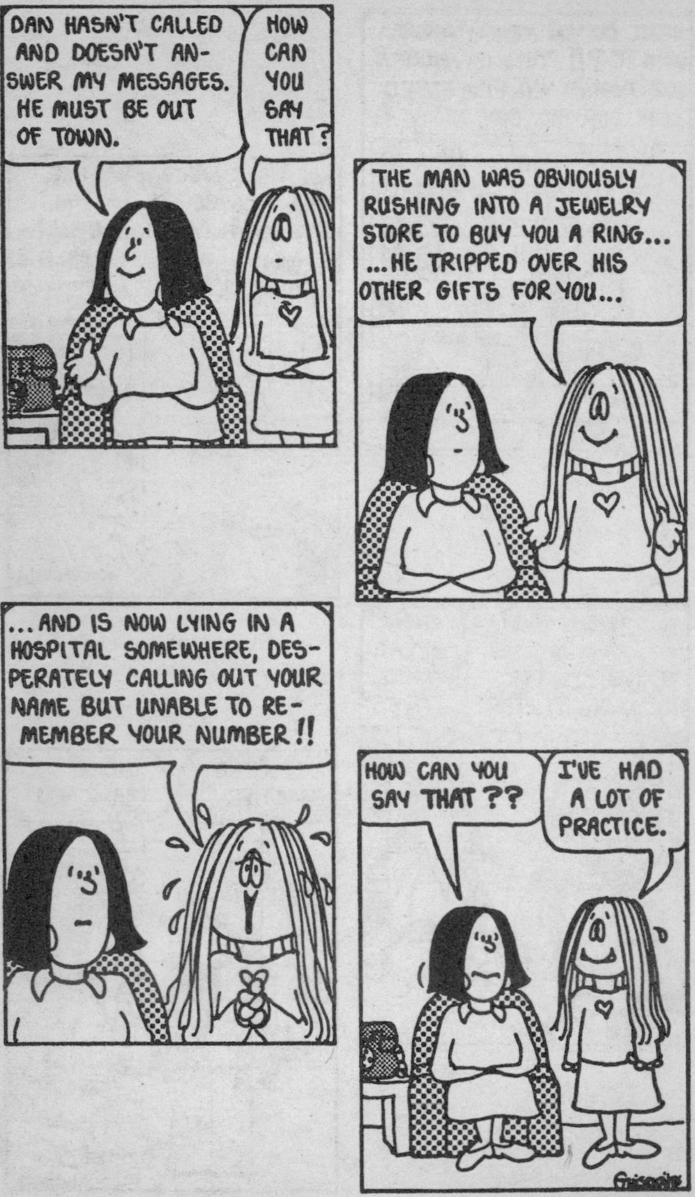
DAN HASN'T CALLED AND DOESN'T ANSWER MY MESSAGES. HE MUST BE OUT OF TOWN.
HOW CAN YOU SAY THAT?
THE MAN WAS OBVIOUSLY RUSHING INTO A JEWELRY STORE TO BUY YOU A RING... ...HE TRIPPED OVER HIS OTHER GIFTS FOR YOU...
...AND IS NOW LYING IN A HOSPITAL SOMEWHERE, DESPERATELY CALLING OUT YOUR NAME BUT UNABLE TO REMEMBER YOUR NUMBER!!
HOW CAN YOU SAY THAT??
I'VE HAD A LOT OF PRACTICE.

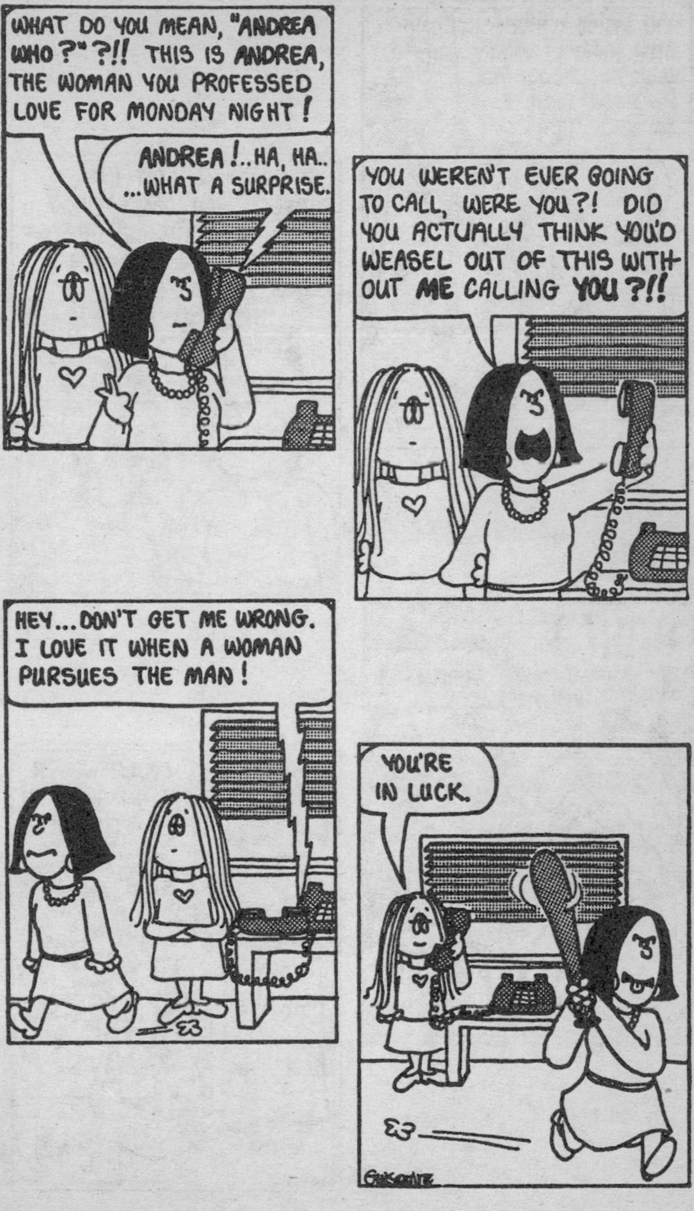
WHAT DO YOU MEAN, "ANDREA WHO?"?!! THIS IS ANDREA, THE WOMAN YOU PROFESSED LOVE FOR MONDAY NIGHT!
ANDREA!..HA, HA.. ...WHAT A SURPRISE.
YOU WEREN'T EVER GOING TO CALL, WERE YOU?! DID YOU ACTUALLY THINK YOU'D WEASEL OUT OF THIS WITHOUT ME CALLING YOU?!!
HEY...DON'T GET ME WRONG. I LOVE IT WHEN A WOMAN PURSUES THE MAN!
YOU'RE IN LUCK.

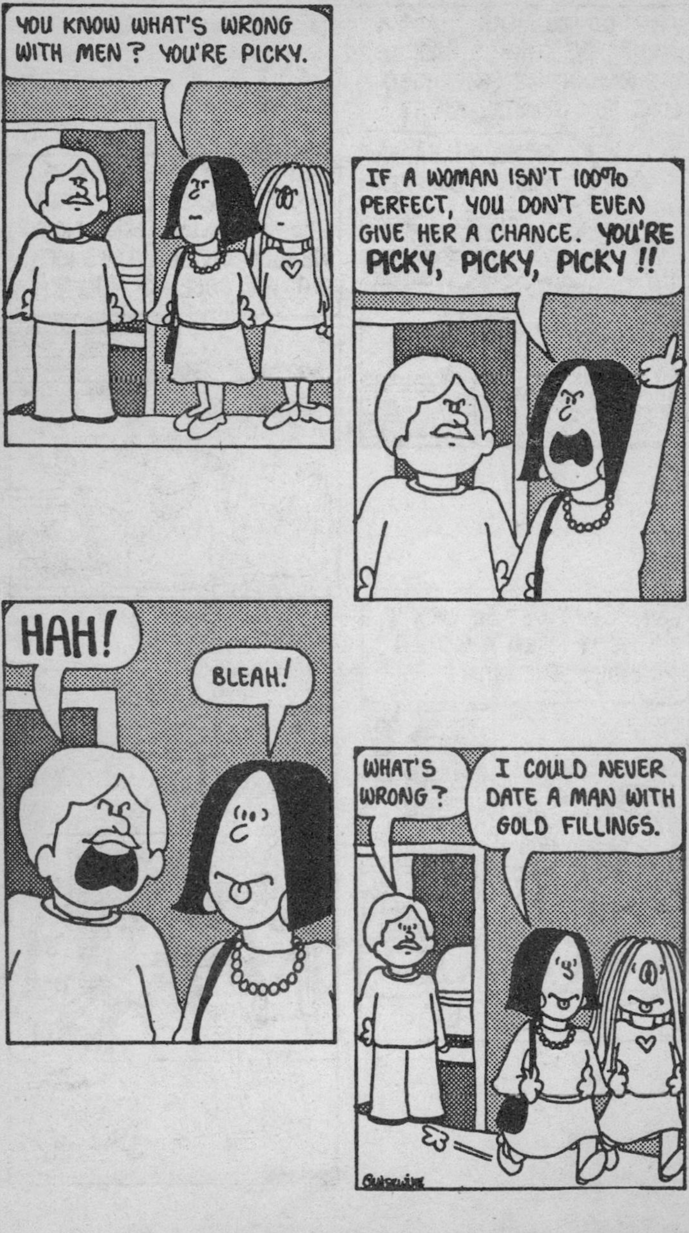
YOU KNOW WHAT'S WRONG WITH MEN? YOU'RE PICKY.
IF A WOMAN ISN'T 100% PERFECT, YOU DON'T EVEN GIVE HER A CHANCE. YOU'RE PICKY, PICKY, PICKY!!
HAH!
BLEAH!
WHAT'S WRONG?
I COULD NEVER DATE A MAN WITH GOLD FILLINGS.

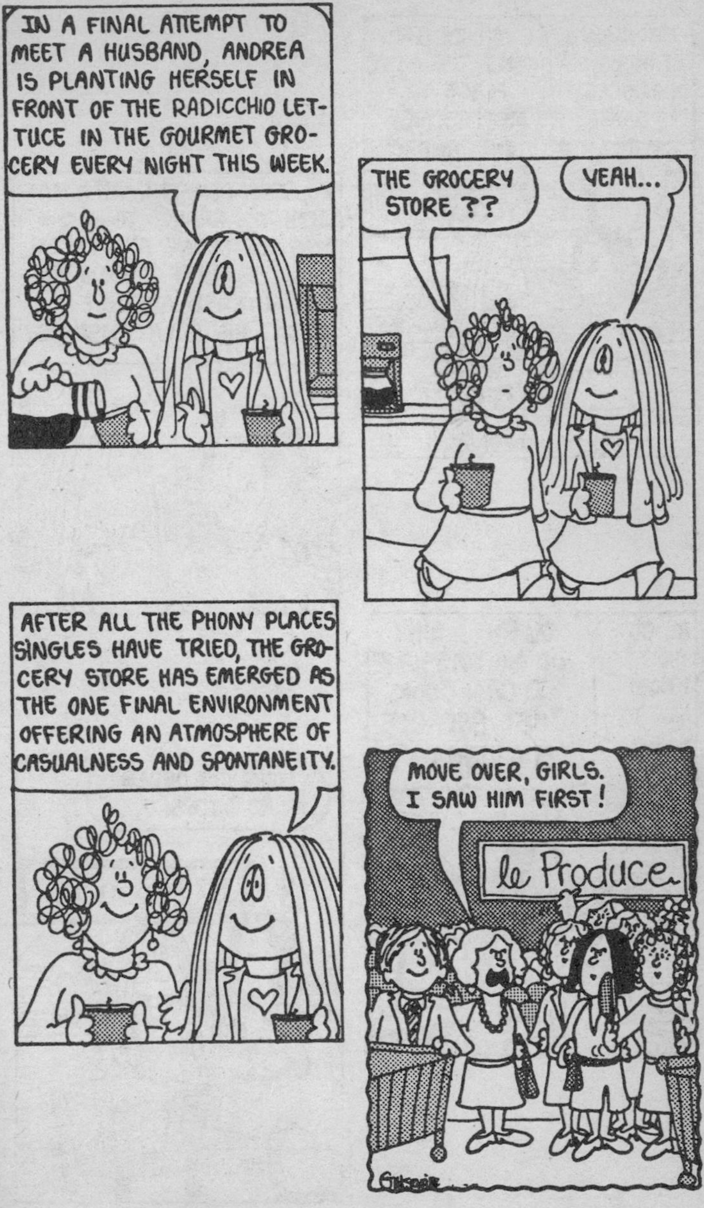
IN A FINAL ATTEMPT TO MEET A HUSBAND, ANDREA IS PLANTING HERSELF IN FRONT OF THE RADICCHIO LETTUCE IN THE GOURMET GROCERY EVERY NIGHT THIS WEEK.
THE GROCERY STORE ??
YEAH...
AFTER ALL THE PHONY PLACES SINGLES HAVE TRIED, THE GROCERY STORE HAS EMERGED AS THE ONE FINAL ENVIRONMENT OFFERING AN ATMOSPHERE OF CASUALNESS AND SPONTANEITY.
MOVE OVER, GIRLS. I SAW HIM FIRST!
le Produce

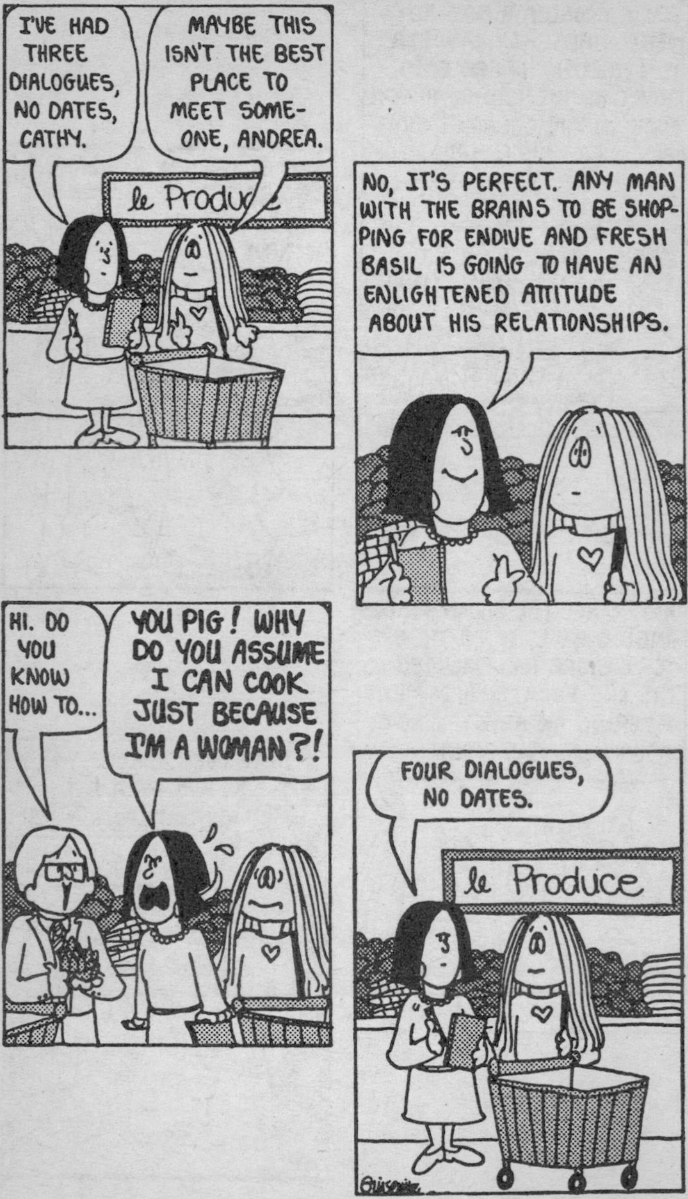
I'VE HAD THREE DIALOGUES, NO DATES, CATHY.
MAYBE THIS ISN'T THE BEST PLACE TO MEET SOMEONE, ANDREA.
NO, IT'S PERFECT. ANY MAN WITH THE BRAINS TO BE SHOPPING FOR ENDIVE AND FRESH BASIL IS GOING TO HAVE AN ENLIGHTENED ATTITUDE ABOUT HIS RELATIONSHIPS.
HI. DO YOU KNOW HOW TO...
YOU PIG! WHY DO YOU ASSUME I CAN COOK JUST BECAUSE I'M A WOMAN?!
FOUR DIALOGUES, NO DATES.
le Produce

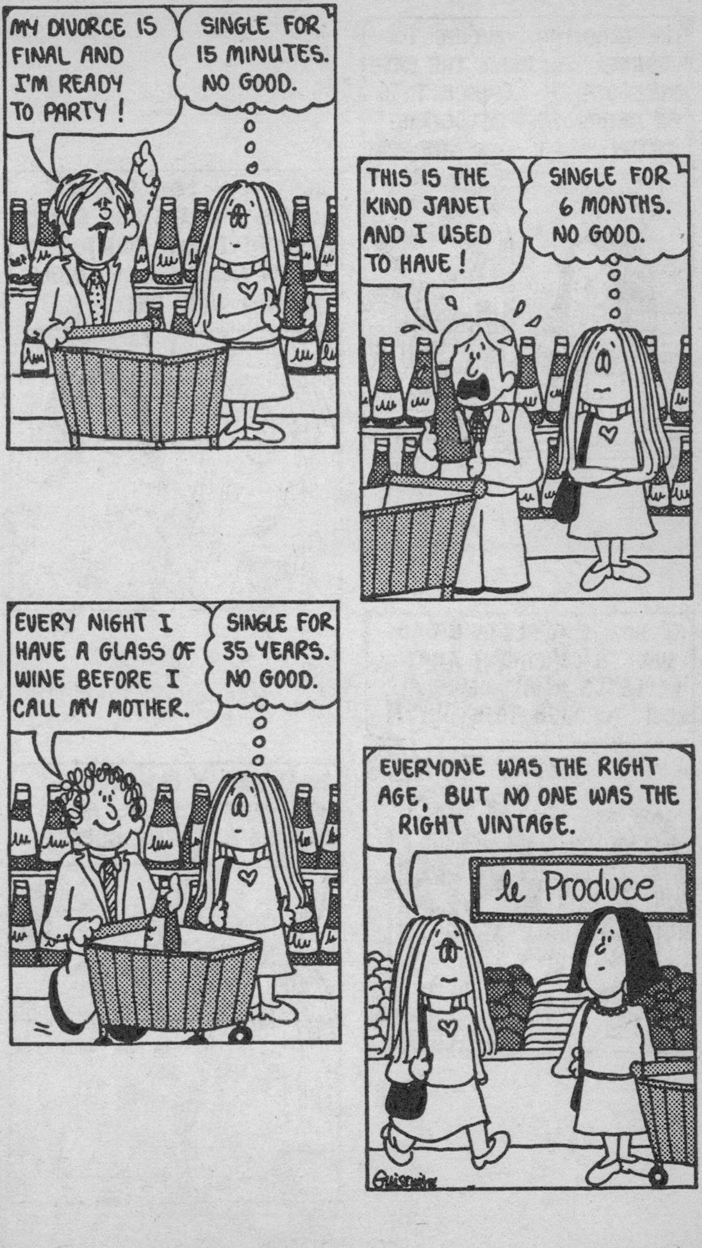
MY DIVORCE IS FINAL AND I'M READY TO PARTY !
SINGLE FOR 15 MINUTES. NO GOOD.
THIS IS THE KIND JANET AND I USED TO HAVE !
SINGLE FOR 6 MONTHS. NO GOOD.
EVERY NIGHT I HAVE A GLASS OF WINE BEFORE I CALL MY MOTHER.
SINGLE FOR 35 YEARS. NO GOOD.
EVERYONE WAS THE RIGHT AGE, BUT NO ONE WAS THE RIGHT VINTAGE.
le Produce

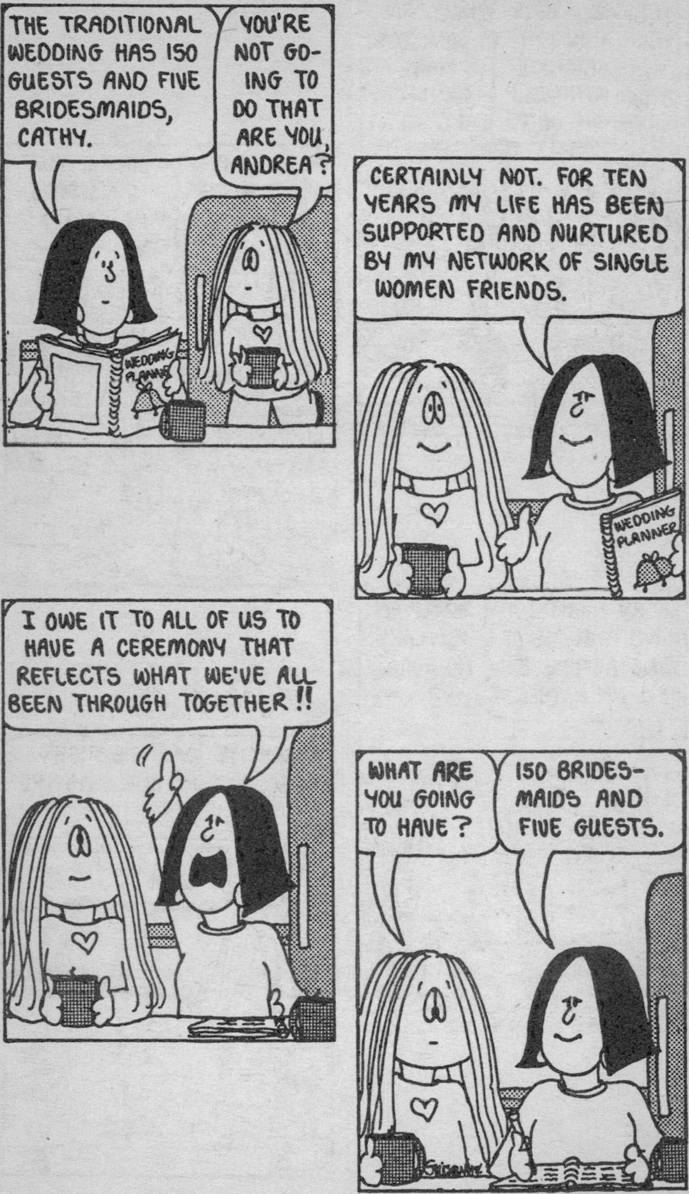
THE TRADITIONAL WEDDING HAS 150 GUESTS AND FIVE BRIDESMAIDS, CATHY.
YOU'RE NOT GOING TO DO THAT ARE YOU, ANDREA?
WEDDING PLANNER
CERTAINLY NOT. FOR TEN YEARS MY LIFE HAS BEEN SUPPORTED AND NURTURED BY MY NETWORK OF SINGLE WOMEN FRIENDS.
WEDDING PLANNER
I OWE IT TO ALL OF US TO HAVE A CEREMONY THAT REFLECTS WHAT WE'VE ALL BEEN THROUGH TOGETHER!!
WHAT ARE YOU GOING TO HAVE?
150 BRIDESMAIDS AND FIVE GUESTS.

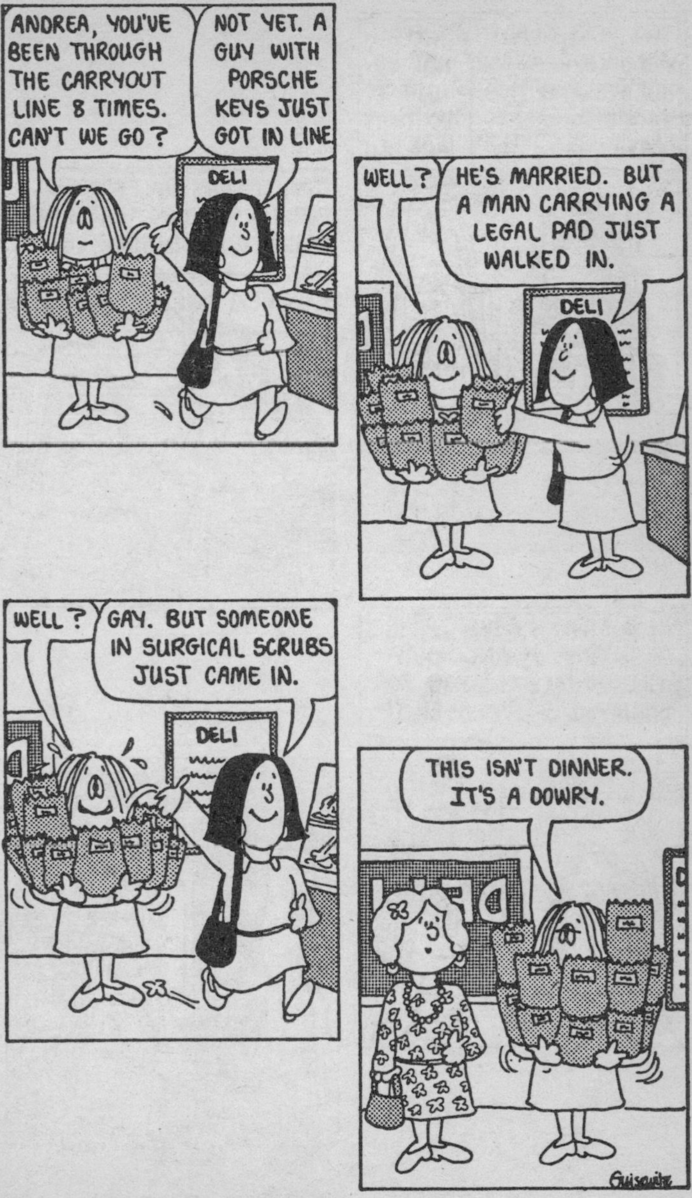
ANDREA, YOU'VE BEEN THROUGH THE CARRYOUT LINE 8 TIMES. CAN'T WE GO?
NOT YET. A GUY WITH PORSCHE KEYS JUST GOT IN LINE.
DELI
WELL?
HE'S MARRIED. BUT A MAN CARRYING A LEGAL PAD JUST WALKED IN.
DELI
WELL?
GAY. BUT SOMEONE IN SURGICAL SCRUBS JUST CAME IN.
DELI
THIS ISN'T DINNER. IT'S A DOWRY.
Guisewite

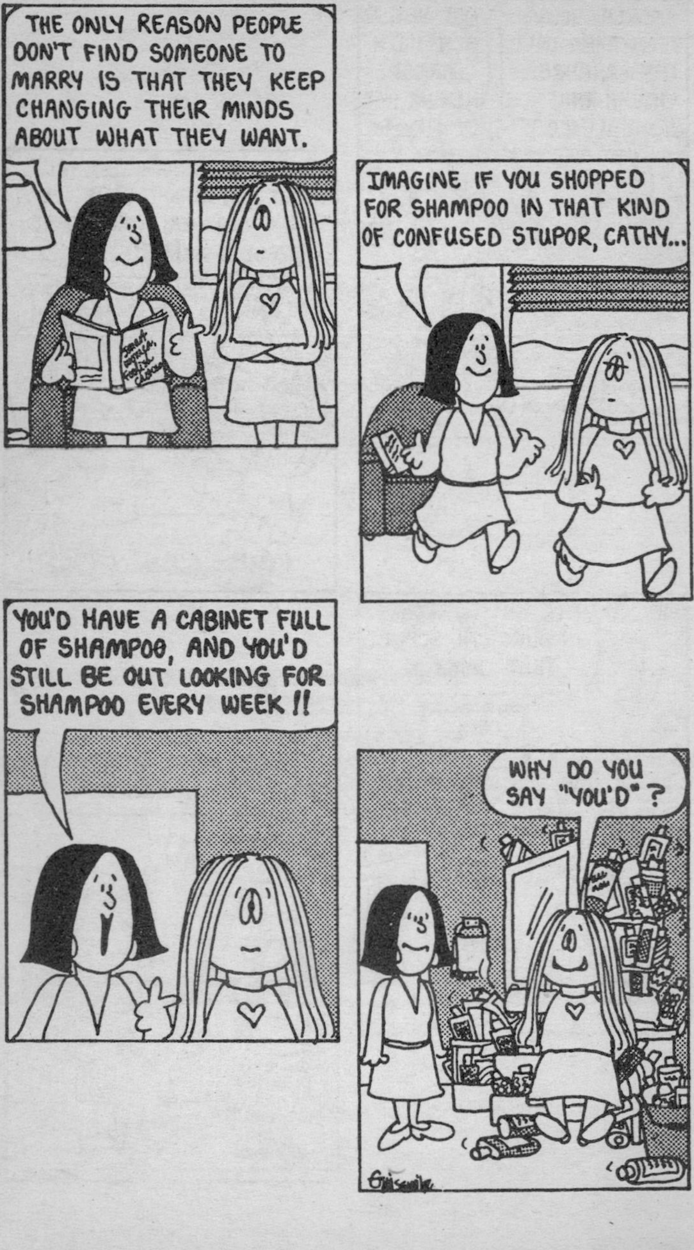
THE ONLY REASON PEOPLE DON'T FIND SOMEONE TO MARRY IS THAT THEY KEEP CHANGING THEIR MINDS ABOUT WHAT THEY WANT.
IMAGINE IF YOU SHOPPED FOR SHAMPOO IN THAT KIND OF CONFUSED STUPOR, CATHY...
YOU'D HAVE A CABINET FULL OF SHAMPOO, AND YOU'D STILL BE OUT LOOKING FOR SHAMPOO EVERY WEEK !!
WHY DO YOU SAY "YOU'D"?
Guisewite

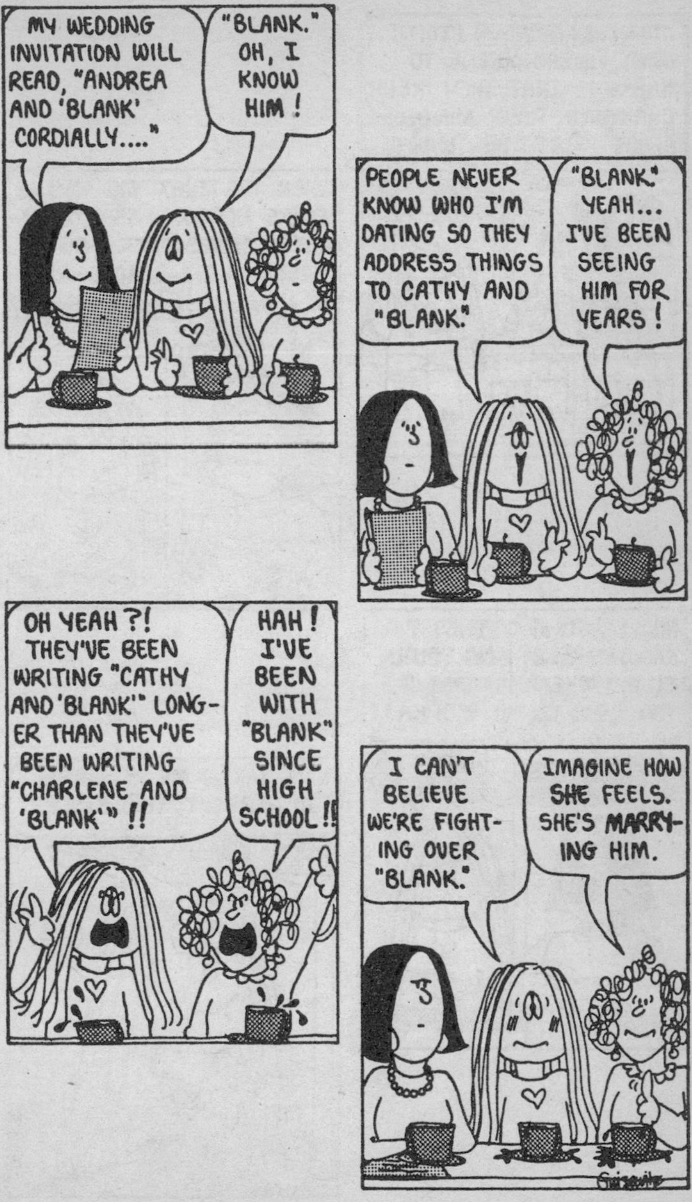
MY WEDDING INVITATION WILL READ, "ANDREA AND 'BLANK' CORDIALLY...."
"BLANK." OH, I KNOW HIM!
PEOPLE NEVER KNOW WHO I'M DATING SO THEY ADDRESS THINGS TO CATHY AND "BLANK."
"BLANK." YEAH... I'VE BEEN SEEING HIM FOR YEARS!
OH YEAH?! THEY'VE BEEN WRITING "CATHY AND 'BLANK'" LONGER THAN THEY'VE BEEN WRITING "CHARLENE AND 'BLANK'" !!
HAH! I'VE BEEN WITH "BLANK" SINCE HIGH SCHOOL!!
I CAN'T BELIEVE WE'RE FIGHTING OVER "BLANK."
IMAGINE HOW SHE FEELS. SHE'S MARRYING HIM.
Guisewite

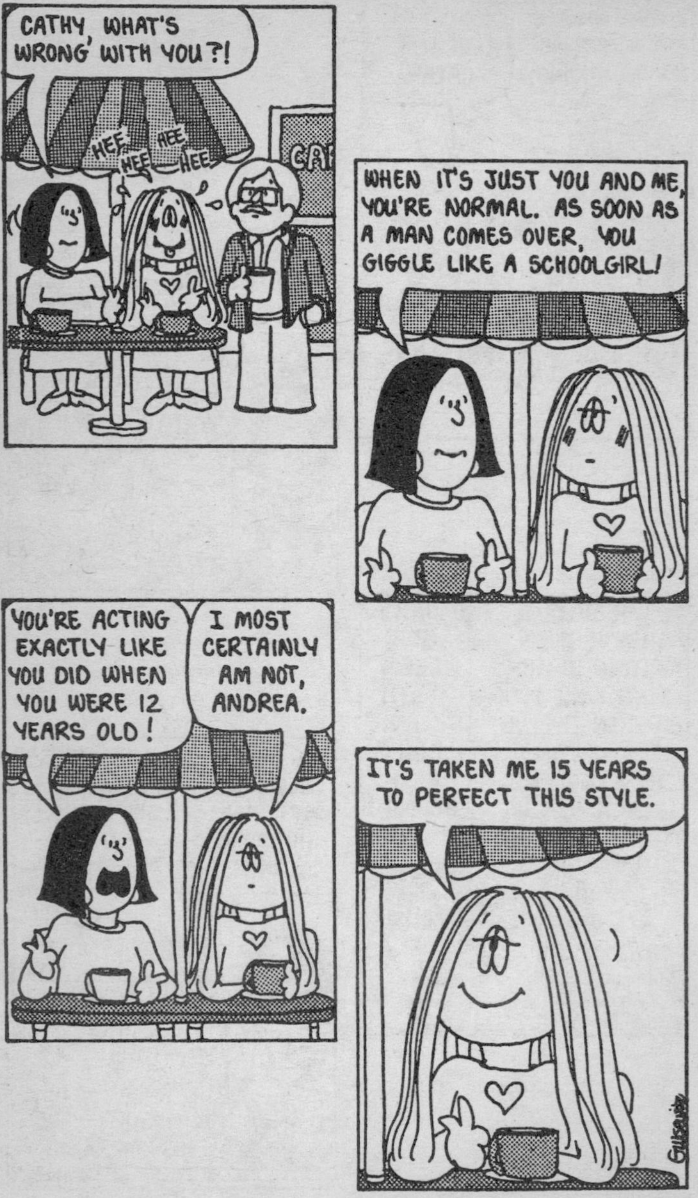
CATHY, WHAT'S WRONG WITH YOU?!
HEE HEE HEE HEE
WHEN IT'S JUST YOU AND ME, YOU'RE NORMAL. AS SOON AS A MAN COMES OVER, YOU GIGGLE LIKE A SCHOOLGIRL!
YOU'RE ACTING EXACTLY LIKE YOU DID WHEN YOU WERE 12 YEARS OLD!
I MOST CERTAINLY AM NOT, ANDREA.
IT'S TAKEN ME 15 YEARS TO PERFECT THIS STYLE.

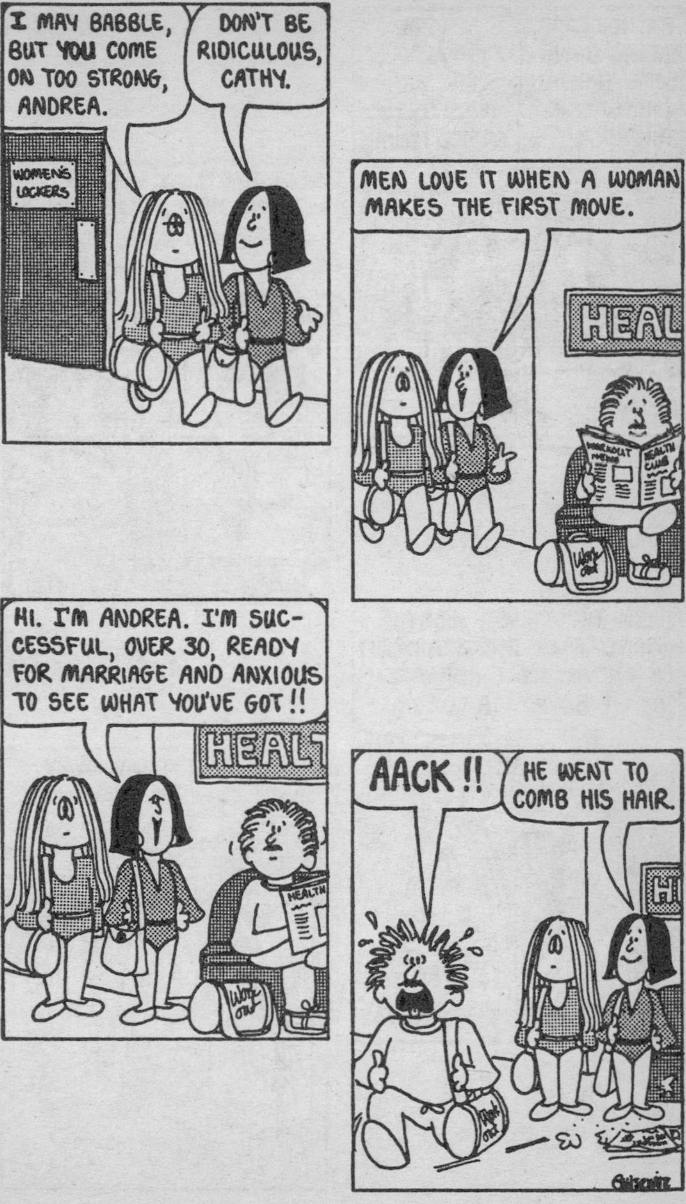
I MAY BABBLE, BUT YOU COME ON TOO STRONG, ANDREA.
DON'T BE RIDICULOUS, CATHY.
WOMEN'S LOCKERS
MEN LOVE IT WHEN A WOMAN MAKES THE FIRST MOVE.
HEAL
HI. I'M ANDREA. I'M SUCCESSFUL, OVER 30, READY FOR MARRIAGE AND ANXIOUS TO SEE WHAT YOU'VE GOT!!
HEALT
HEALTH
AACK!!
HE WENT TO COMB HIS HAIR.

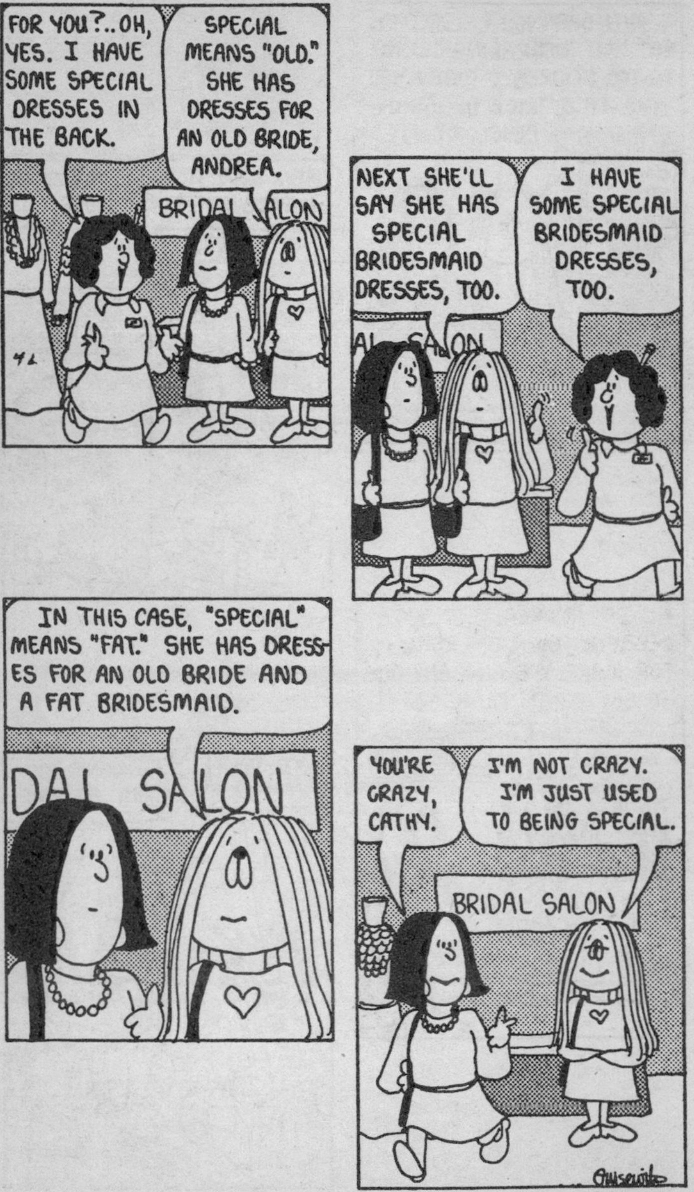
FOR YOU?..OH, YES. I HAVE SOME SPECIAL DRESSES IN THE BACK.
SPECIAL MEANS "OLD." SHE HAS DRESSES FOR AN OLD BRIDE, ANDREA.
BRIDAL SALON
NEXT SHE'LL SAY SHE HAS SPECIAL BRIDESMAID DRESSES, TOO.
I HAVE SOME SPECIAL BRIDESMAID DRESSES, TOO.
IN THIS CASE, "SPECIAL" MEANS "FAT." SHE HAS DRESSES FOR AN OLD BRIDE AND A FAT BRIDESMAID.
YOU'RE CRAZY, CATHY.
I'M NOT CRAZY. I'M JUST USED TO BEING SPECIAL.
BRIDAL SALON
Guisewite

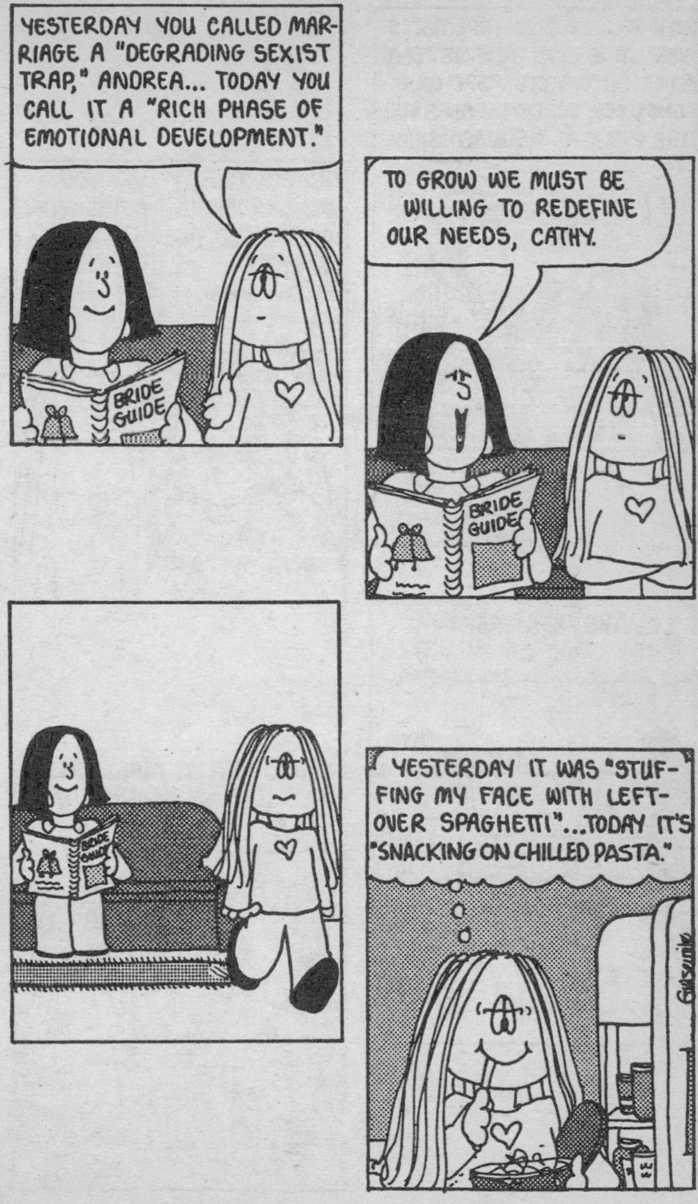
YESTERDAY YOU CALLED MARRIAGE A "DEGRADING SEXIST TRAP," ANDREA... TODAY YOU CALL IT A "RICH PHASE OF EMOTIONAL DEVELOPMENT."
BRIDE GUIDE
TO GROW WE MUST BE WILLING TO REDEFINE OUR NEEDS, CATHY.
BRIDE GUIDE
YESTERDAY IT WAS "STUFFING MY FACE WITH LEFTOVER SPAGHETTI"...TODAY IT'S "SNACKING ON CHILLED PASTA."
Guisewite

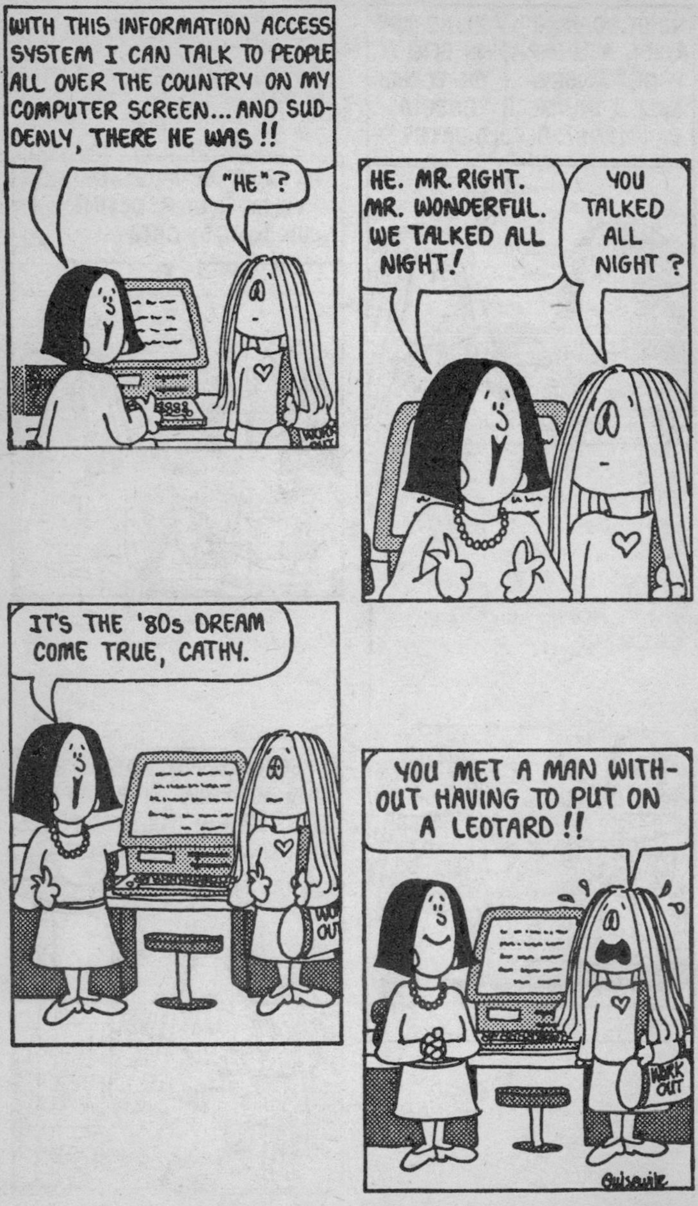
WITH THIS INFORMATION ACCESS SYSTEM I CAN TALK TO PEOPLE ALL OVER THE COUNTRY ON MY COMPUTER SCREEN... AND SUDDENLY, THERE HE WAS !!
"HE"?
HE. MR. RIGHT. MR. WONDERFUL. WE TALKED ALL NIGHT!
YOU TALKED ALL NIGHT?
IT'S THE '80s DREAM COME TRUE, CATHY.
YOU MET A MAN WITHOUT HAVING TO PUT ON A LEOTARD !!
WORK OUT
Guisewite

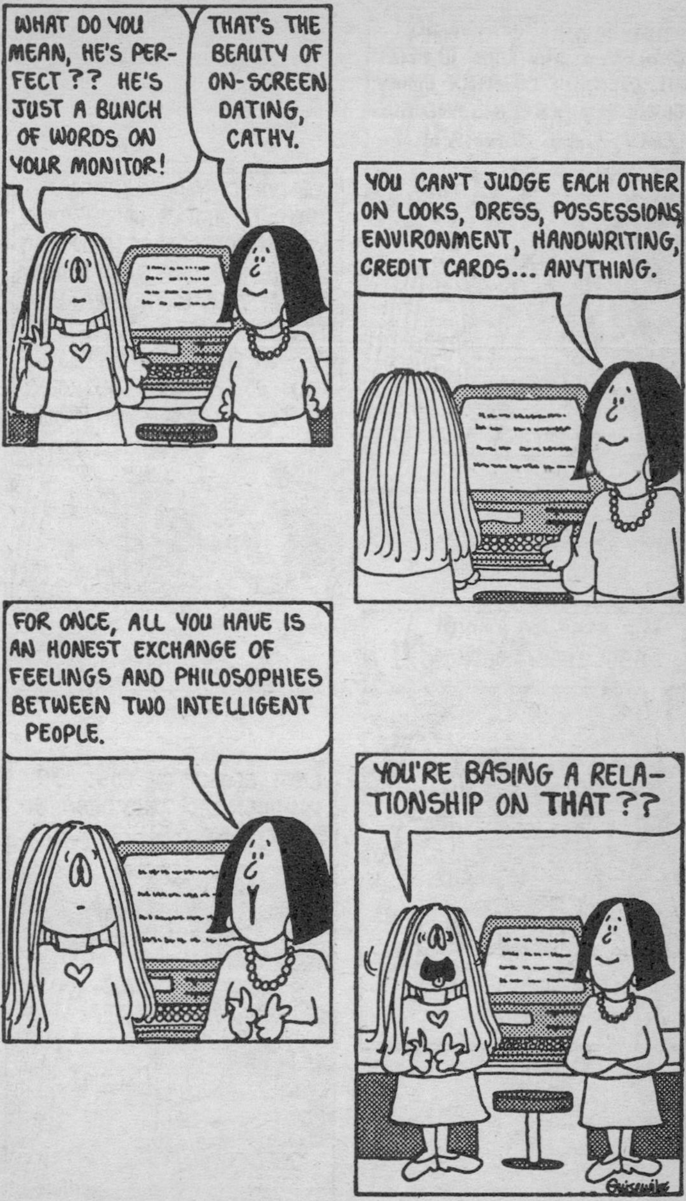
WHAT DO YOU MEAN, HE'S PERFECT?? HE'S JUST A BUNCH OF WORDS ON YOUR MONITOR!
THAT'S THE BEAUTY OF ON-SCREEN DATING, CATHY.
YOU CAN'T JUDGE EACH OTHER ON LOOKS, DRESS, POSSESSIONS, ENVIRONMENT, HANDWRITING, CREDIT CARDS... ANYTHING.
FOR ONCE, ALL YOU HAVE IS AN HONEST EXCHANGE OF FEELINGS AND PHILOSOPHIES BETWEEN TWO INTELLIGENT PEOPLE.
YOU'RE BASING A RELATIONSHIP ON THAT??
Guisewite

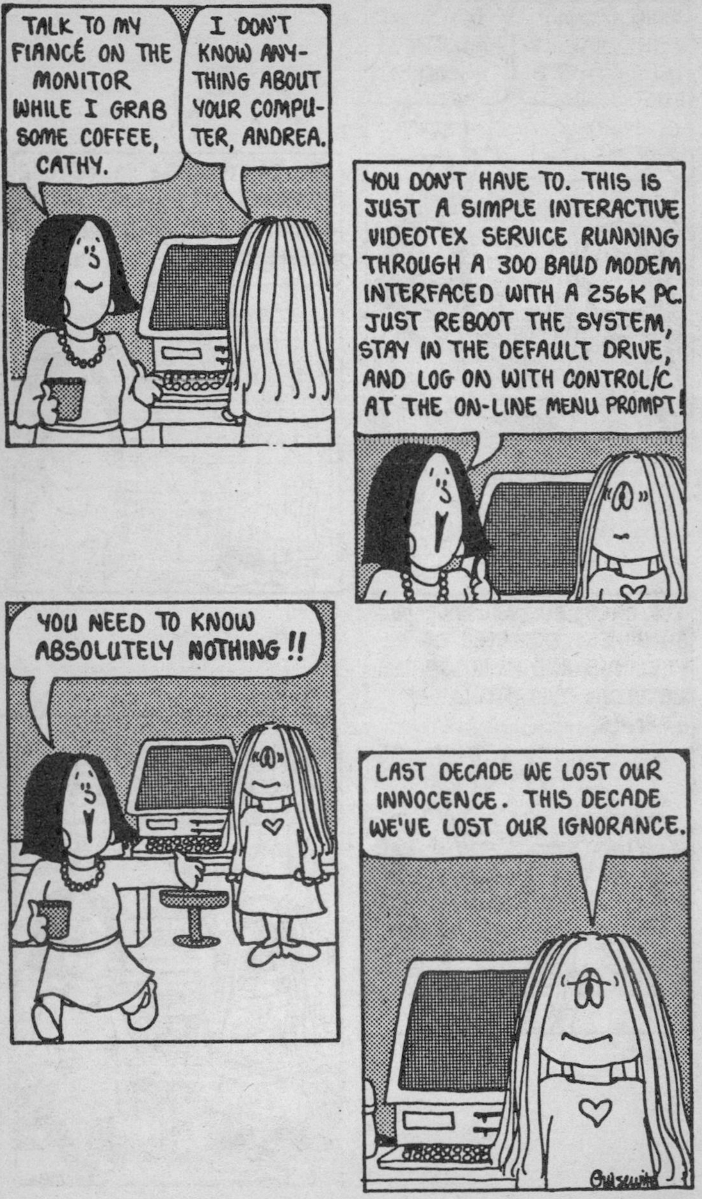

TALK TO MY FIANCÉ ON THE MONITOR WHILE I GRAB SOME COFFEE, CATHY.
I DON'T KNOW ANYTHING ABOUT YOUR COMPUTER, ANDREA.
YOU DON'T HAVE TO. THIS IS JUST A SIMPLE INTERACTIVE VIDEOTEX SERVICE RUNNING THROUGH A 300 BAUD MODEM INTERFACED WITH A 256K PC. JUST REBOOT THE SYSTEM, STAY IN THE DEFAULT DRIVE, AND LOG ON WITH CONTROL/C AT THE ON-LINE MENU PROMPT!
YOU NEED TO KNOW ABSOLUTELY NOTHING!!
LAST DECADE WE LOST OUR INNOCENCE. THIS DECADE WE'VE LOST OUR IGNORANCE.

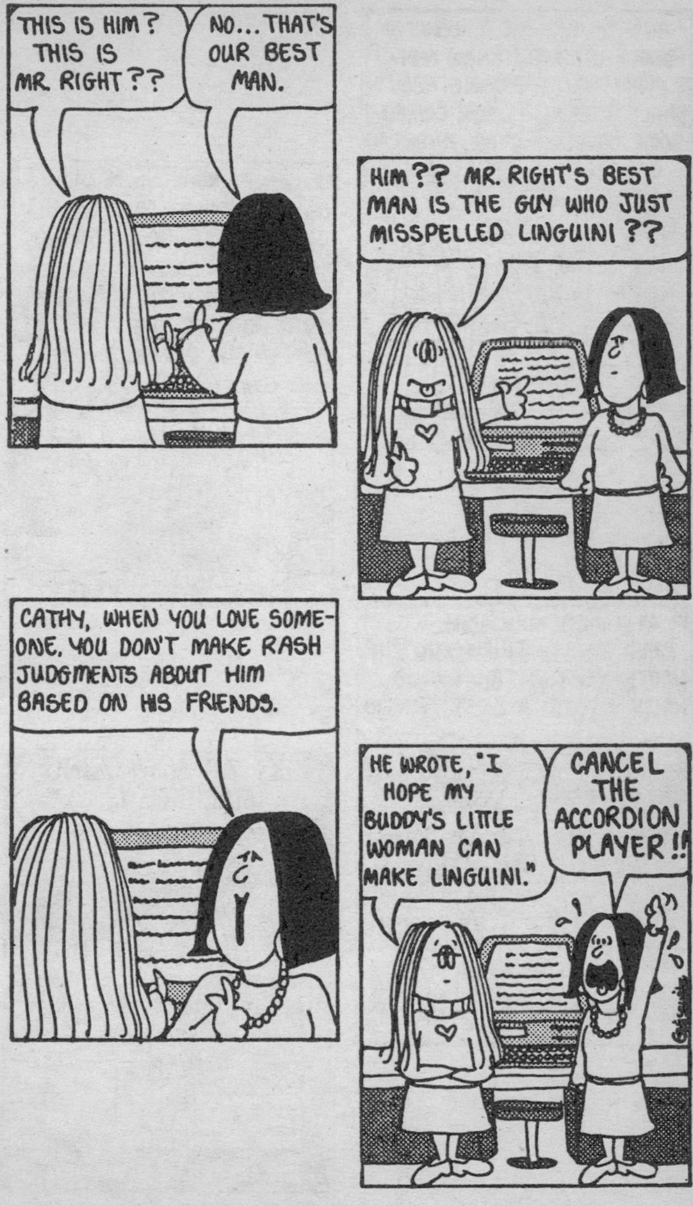
THIS IS HIM? THIS IS MR. RIGHT??
NO... THAT'S OUR BEST MAN.
HIM?? MR. RIGHT'S BEST MAN IS THE GUY WHO JUST MISSPELLED LINGUINI??
CATHY, WHEN YOU LOVE SOMEONE, YOU DON'T MAKE RASH JUDGMENTS ABOUT HIM BASED ON HIS FRIENDS.
HE WROTE, "I HOPE MY BUDDY'S LITTLE WOMAN CAN MAKE LINGUINI."
CANCEL THE ACCORDION PLAYER!!

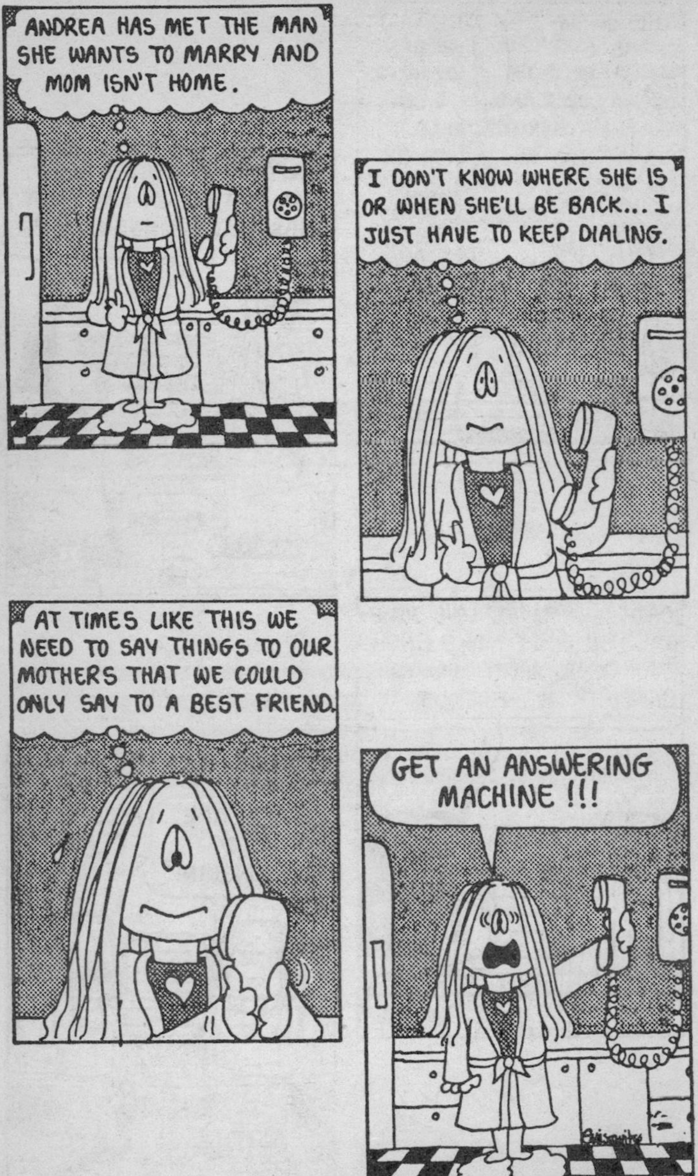
ANDREA HAS MET THE MAN SHE WANTS TO MARRY AND MOM ISN'T HOME.
I DON'T KNOW WHERE SHE IS OR WHEN SHE'LL BE BACK... I JUST HAVE TO KEEP DIALING.
AT TIMES LIKE THIS WE NEED TO SAY THINGS TO OUR MOTHERS THAT WE COULD ONLY SAY TO A BEST FRIEND.
GET AN ANSWERING MACHINE !!!

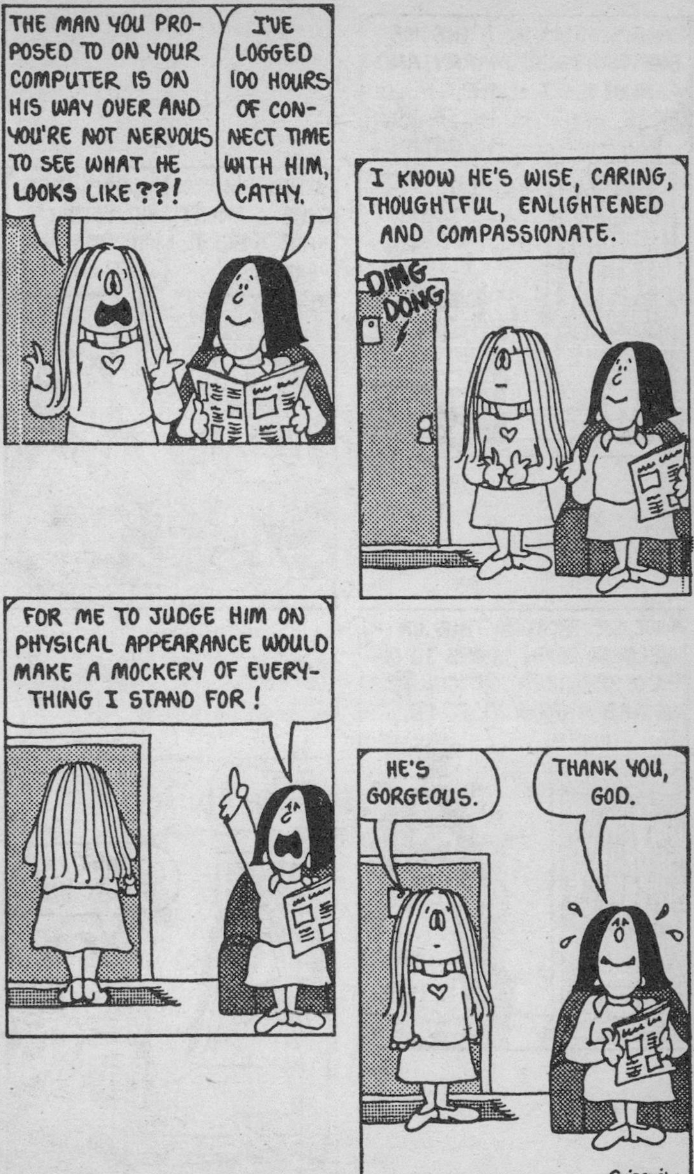
THE MAN YOU PROPOSED TO ON YOUR COMPUTER IS ON HIS WAY OVER AND YOU'RE NOT NERVOUS TO SEE WHAT HE LOOKS LIKE??!
I'VE LOGGED 100 HOURS OF CONNECT TIME WITH HIM, CATHY.
I KNOW HE'S WISE, CARING, THOUGHTFUL, ENLIGHTENED AND COMPASSIONATE.
DING DONG
FOR ME TO JUDGE HIM ON PHYSICAL APPEARANCE WOULD MAKE A MOCKERY OF EVERYTHING I STAND FOR!
HE'S GORGEOUS.
THANK YOU, GOD.

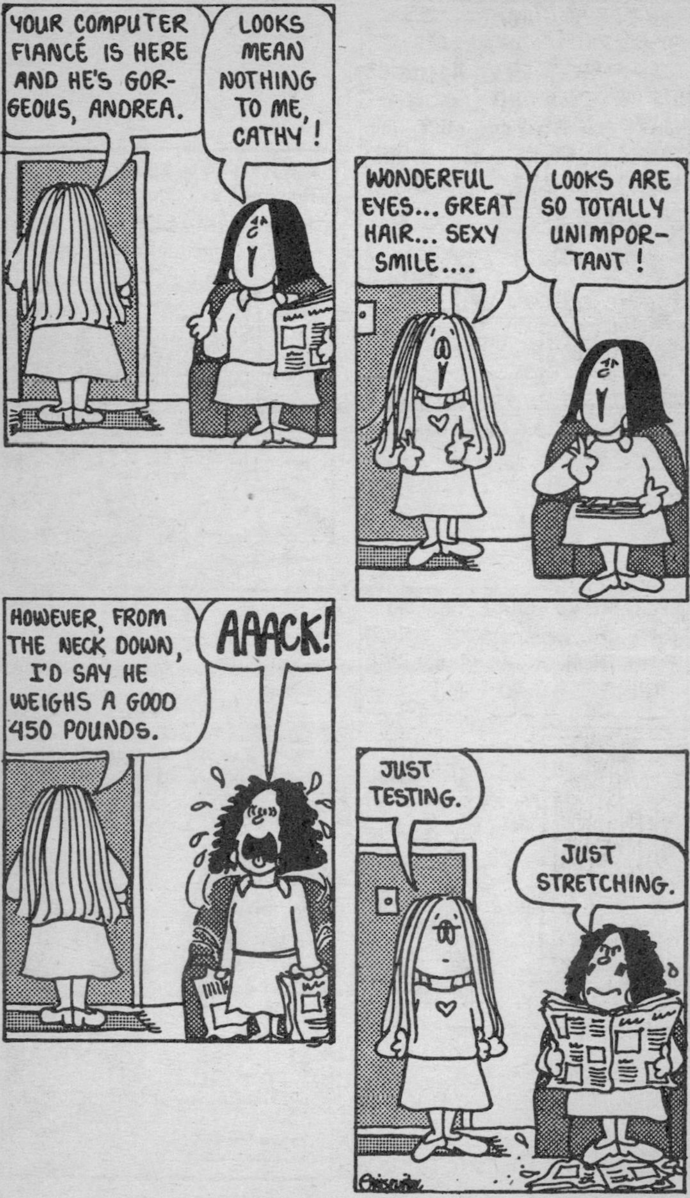
YOUR COMPUTER FIANCÉ IS HERE AND HE'S GOR-GEOUS, ANDREA.
LOOKS MEAN NOTHING TO ME, CATHY!
WONDERFUL EYES... GREAT HAIR... SEXY SMILE....
LOOKS ARE SO TOTALLY UNIMPOR-TANT!
HOWEVER, FROM THE NECK DOWN, I'D SAY HE WEIGHS A GOOD 450 POUNDS.
AAACK!
JUST TESTING.
JUST STRETCHING.

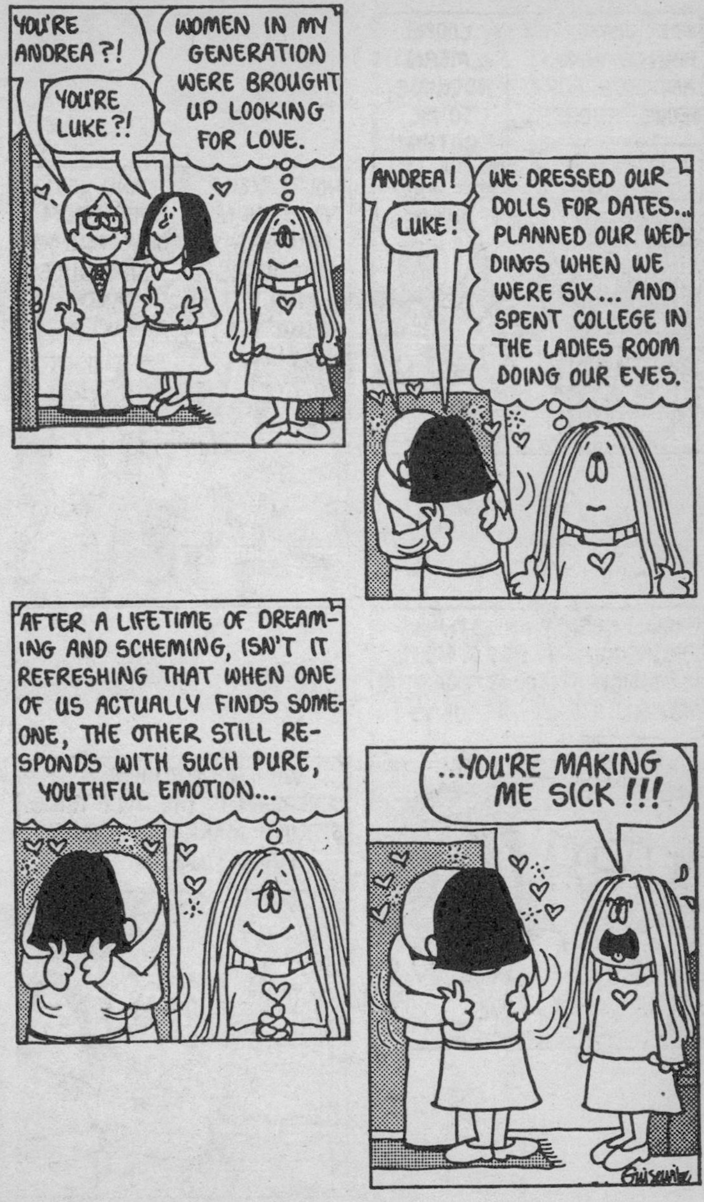
YOU'RE ANDREA?!
YOU'RE LUKE?!
WOMEN IN MY GENERATION WERE BROUGHT UP LOOKING FOR LOVE.
ANDREA!
LUKE!
WE DRESSED OUR DOLLS FOR DATES... PLANNED OUR WEDDINGS WHEN WE WERE SIX... AND SPENT COLLEGE IN THE LADIES ROOM DOING OUR EYES.
AFTER A LIFETIME OF DREAMING AND SCHEMING, ISN'T IT REFRESHING THAT WHEN ONE OF US ACTUALLY FINDS SOMEONE, THE OTHER STILL RESPONDS WITH SUCH PURE, YOUTHFUL EMOTION...
...YOU'RE MAKING ME SICK!!!
Guisewite

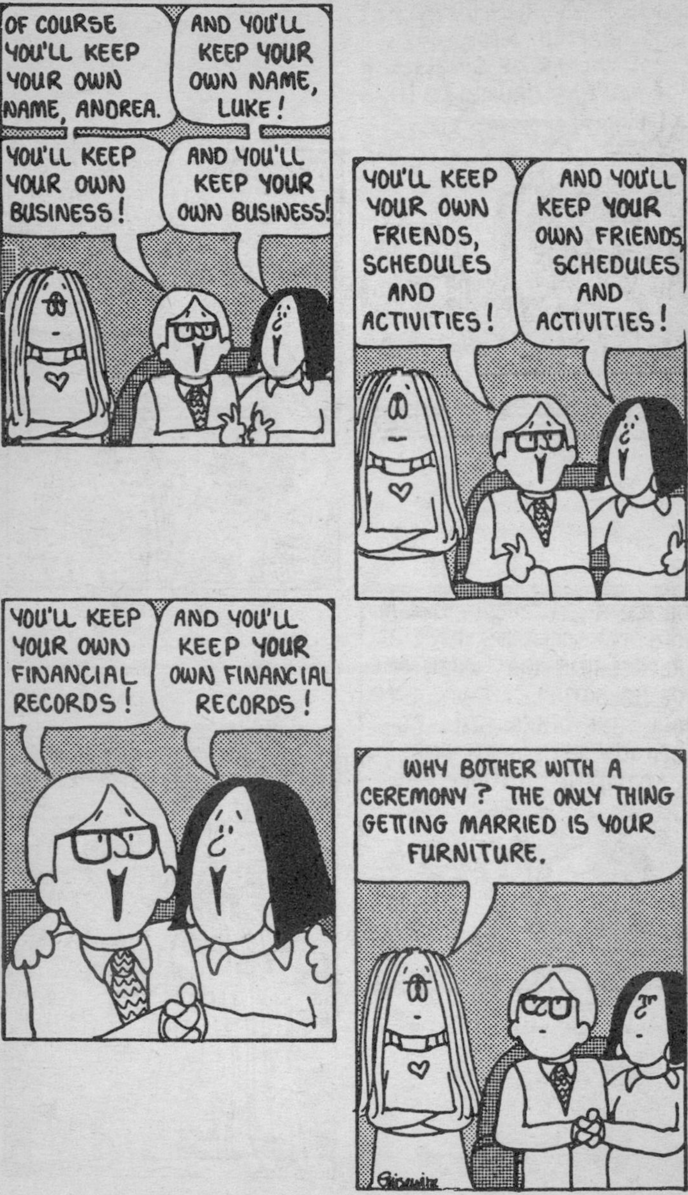
OF COURSE YOU'LL KEEP YOUR OWN NAME, ANDREA.
AND YOU'LL KEEP YOUR OWN NAME, LUKE!
YOU'LL KEEP YOUR OWN BUSINESS!
AND YOU'LL KEEP YOUR OWN BUSINESS!
YOU'LL KEEP YOUR OWN FRIENDS, SCHEDULES AND ACTIVITIES!
AND YOU'LL KEEP YOUR OWN FRIENDS, SCHEDULES AND ACTIVITIES!
YOU'LL KEEP YOUR OWN FINANCIAL RECORDS!
AND YOU'LL KEEP YOUR OWN FINANCIAL RECORDS!
WHY BOTHER WITH A CEREMONY? THE ONLY THING GETTING MARRIED IS YOUR FURNITURE.

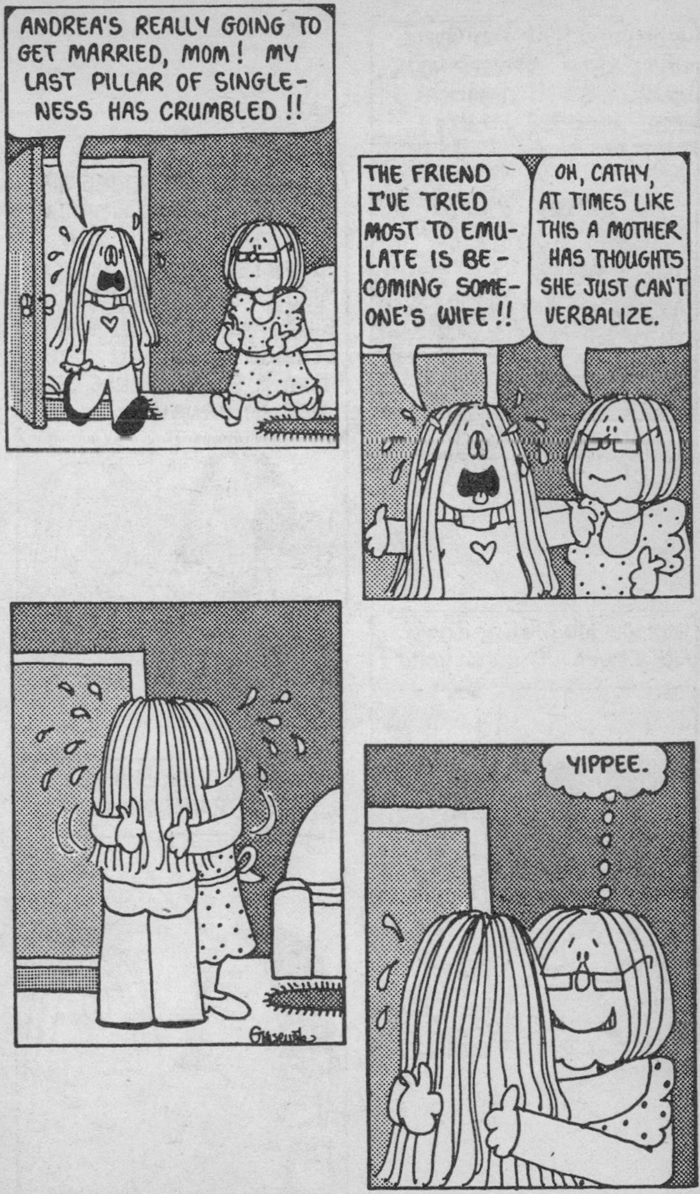
ANDREA'S REALLY GOING TO GET MARRIED, MOM! MY LAST PILLAR OF SINGLE-NESS HAS CRUMBLED!!
THE FRIEND I'VE TRIED MOST TO EMU-LATE IS BE-COMING SOME-ONE'S WIFE!!
OH, CATHY, AT TIMES LIKE THIS A MOTHER HAS THOUGHTS SHE JUST CAN'T VERBALIZE.
YIPPEE.

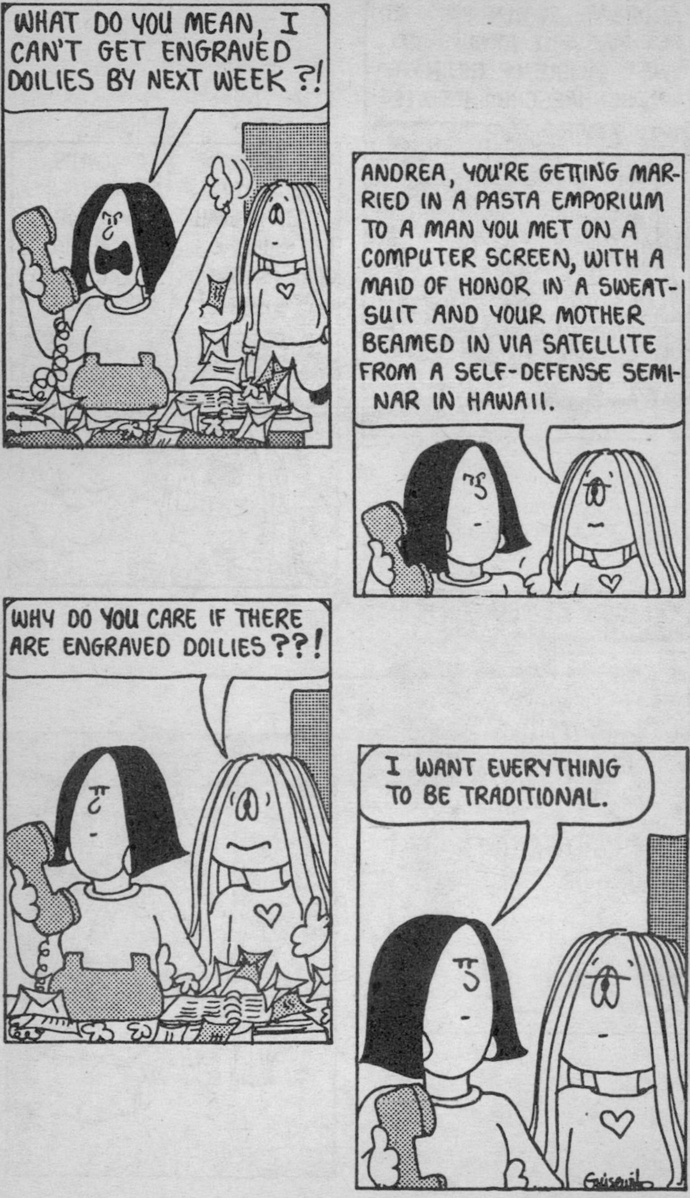
WHAT DO YOU MEAN, I CAN'T GET ENGRAVED DOILIES BY NEXT WEEK ?!
ANDREA, YOU'RE GETTING MARRIED IN A PASTA EMPORIUM TO A MAN YOU MET ON A COMPUTER SCREEN, WITH A MAID OF HONOR IN A SWEATSUIT AND YOUR MOTHER BEAMED IN VIA SATELLITE FROM A SELF-DEFENSE SEMINAR IN HAWAII.
WHY DO YOU CARE IF THERE ARE ENGRAVED DOILIES??!
I WANT EVERYTHING TO BE TRADITIONAL.

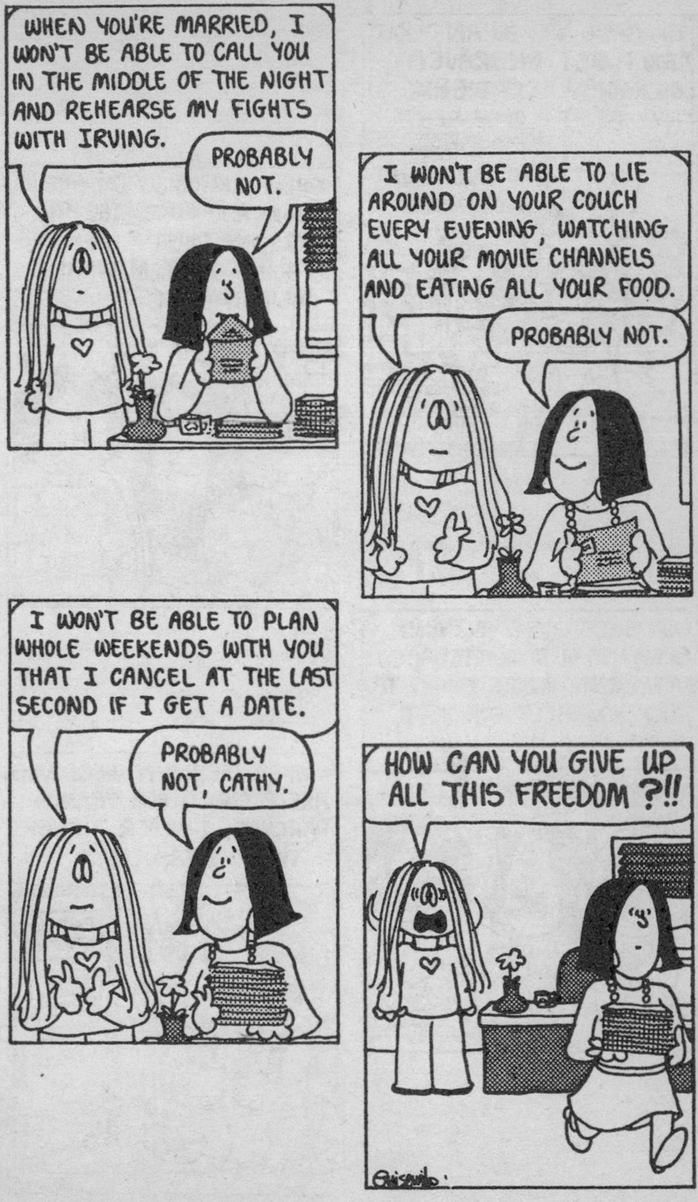
WHEN YOU'RE MARRIED, I WON'T BE ABLE TO CALL YOU IN THE MIDDLE OF THE NIGHT AND REHEARSE MY FIGHTS WITH IRVING.
PROBABLY NOT.
I WON'T BE ABLE TO LIE AROUND ON YOUR COUCH EVERY EVENING, WATCHING ALL YOUR MOVIE CHANNELS AND EATING ALL YOUR FOOD.
PROBABLY NOT.
I WON'T BE ABLE TO PLAN WHOLE WEEKENDS WITH YOU THAT I CANCEL AT THE LAST SECOND IF I GET A DATE.
PROBABLY NOT, CATHY.
HOW CAN YOU GIVE UP ALL THIS FREEDOM ?!!

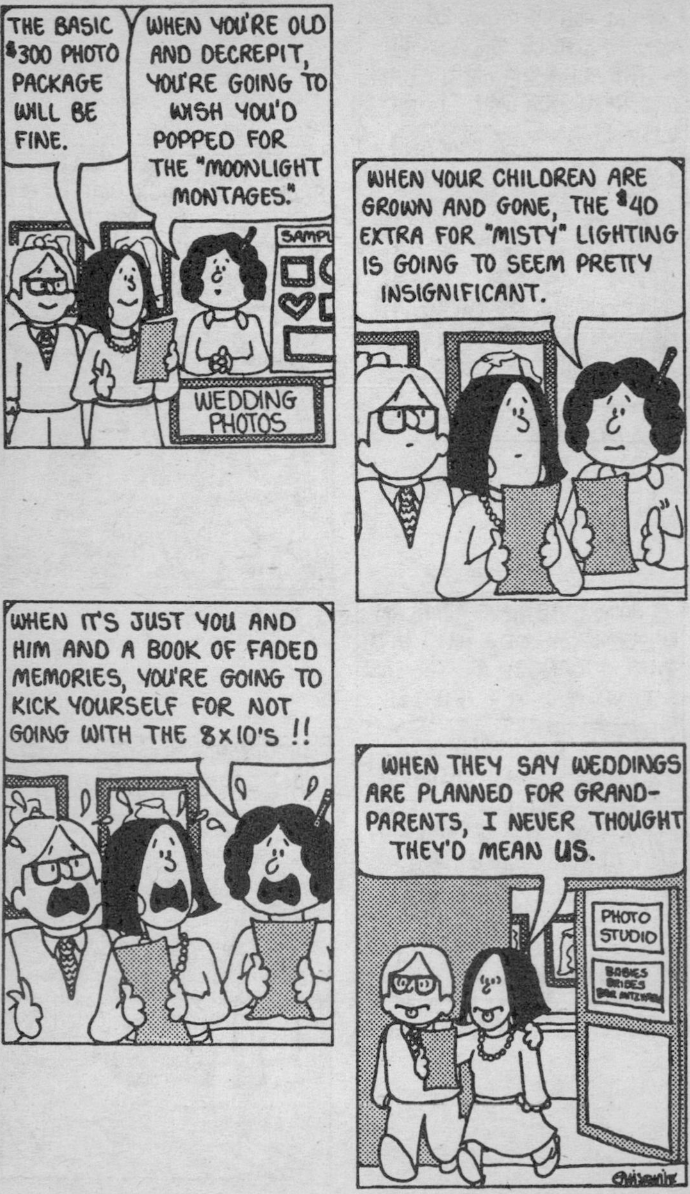
THE BASIC $300 PHOTO PACKAGE WILL BE FINE.
WHEN YOU'RE OLD AND DECREPIT, YOU'RE GOING TO WISH YOU'D POPPED FOR THE "MOONLIGHT MONTAGES."
WEDDING PHOTOS
WHEN YOUR CHILDREN ARE GROWN AND GONE, THE $40 EXTRA FOR "MISTY" LIGHTING IS GOING TO SEEM PRETTY INSIGNIFICANT.
WHEN IT'S JUST YOU AND HIM AND A BOOK OF FADED MEMORIES, YOU'RE GOING TO KICK YOURSELF FOR NOT GOING WITH THE 8x10'S !!
WHEN THEY SAY WEDDINGS ARE PLANNED FOR GRAND-PARENTS, I NEVER THOUGHT THEY'D MEAN US.
PHOTO STUDIO
BABIES
BRIDES

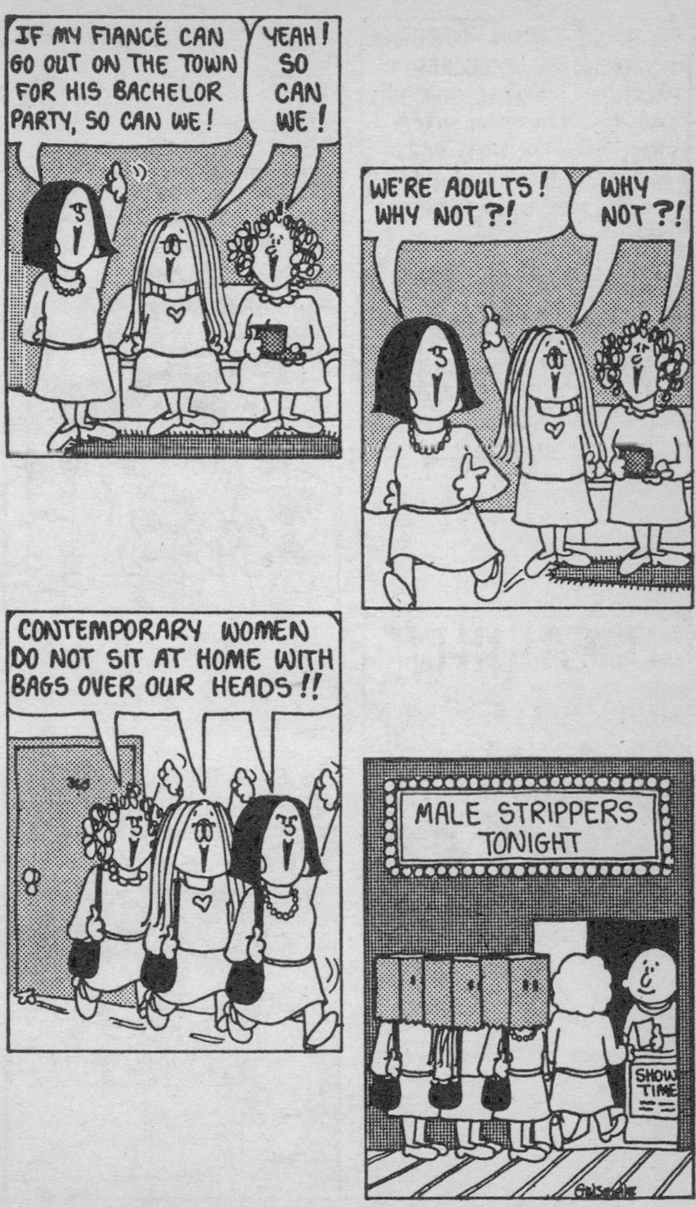
IF MY FIANCÉ CAN GO OUT ON THE TOWN FOR HIS BACHELOR PARTY, SO CAN WE!
YEAH! SO CAN WE!
WE'RE ADULTS! WHY NOT?!
WHY NOT?!
CONTEMPORARY WOMEN DO NOT SIT AT HOME WITH BAGS OVER OUR HEADS!!
MALE STRIPPERS TONIGHT
SHOW TIME

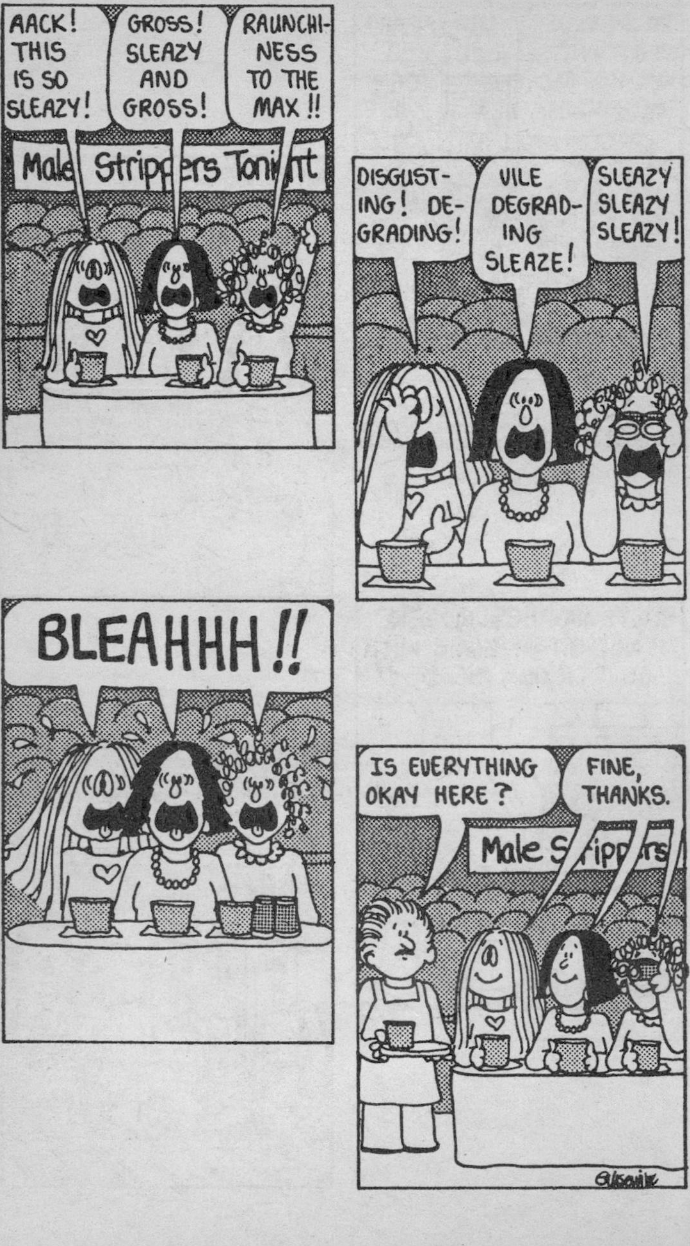
AACK! THIS IS SO SLEAZY!
GROSS! SLEAZY AND GROSS!
RAUNCHINESS TO THE MAX!!
Male Strippers Tonight
DISGUSTING! DEGRADING!
VILE DEGRADING SLEAZE!
SLEAZY SLEAZY SLEAZY!
BLEAHHH!!
IS EVERYTHING OKAY HERE?
FINE, THANKS.
Male Strippers
Guisewite

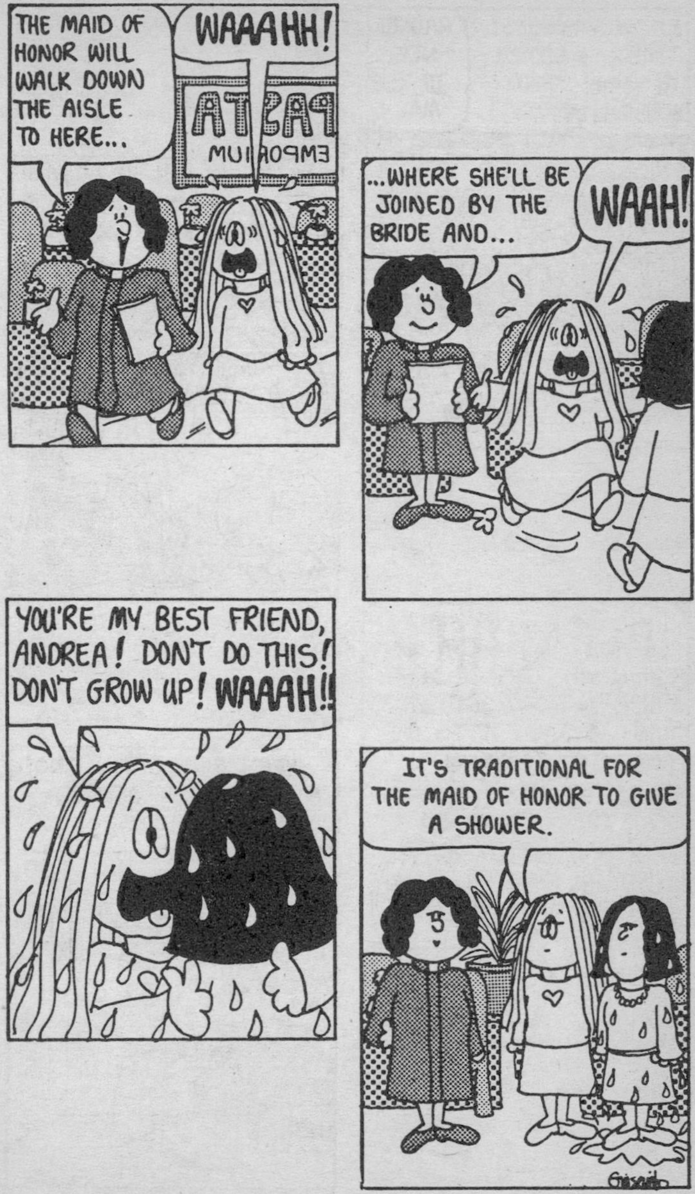
THE MAID OF HONOR WILL WALK DOWN THE AISLE TO HERE...
WAAAHH!
...WHERE SHE'LL BE JOINED BY THE BRIDE AND...
WAAH!
YOU'RE MY BEST FRIEND, ANDREA! DON'T DO THIS! DON'T GROW UP! WAAAH!!
IT'S TRADITIONAL FOR THE MAID OF HONOR TO GIVE A SHOWER.

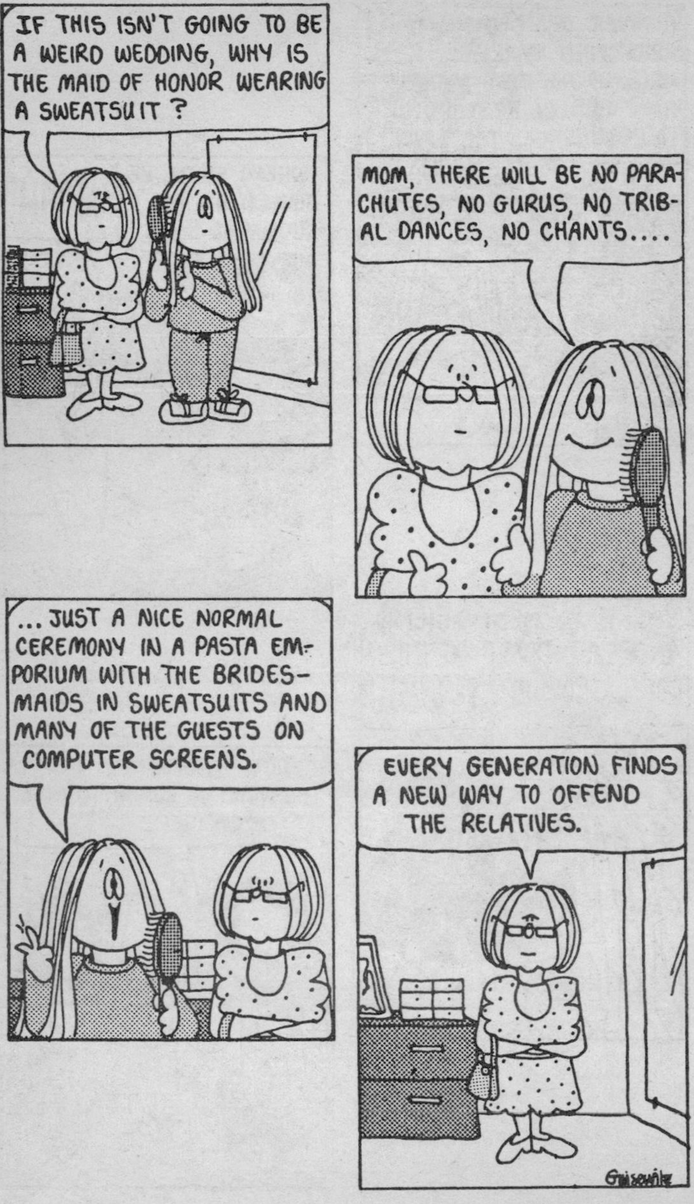
IF THIS ISN'T GOING TO BE A WEIRD WEDDING, WHY IS THE MAID OF HONOR WEARING A SWEATSUIT?
MOM, THERE WILL BE NO PARACHUTES, NO GURUS, NO TRIBAL DANCES, NO CHANTS....
...JUST A NICE NORMAL CEREMONY IN A PASTA EMPORIUM WITH THE BRIDESMAIDS IN SWEATSUITS AND MANY OF THE GUESTS ON COMPUTER SCREENS.
EVERY GENERATION FINDS A NEW WAY TO OFFEND THE RELATIVES.
Guisewite

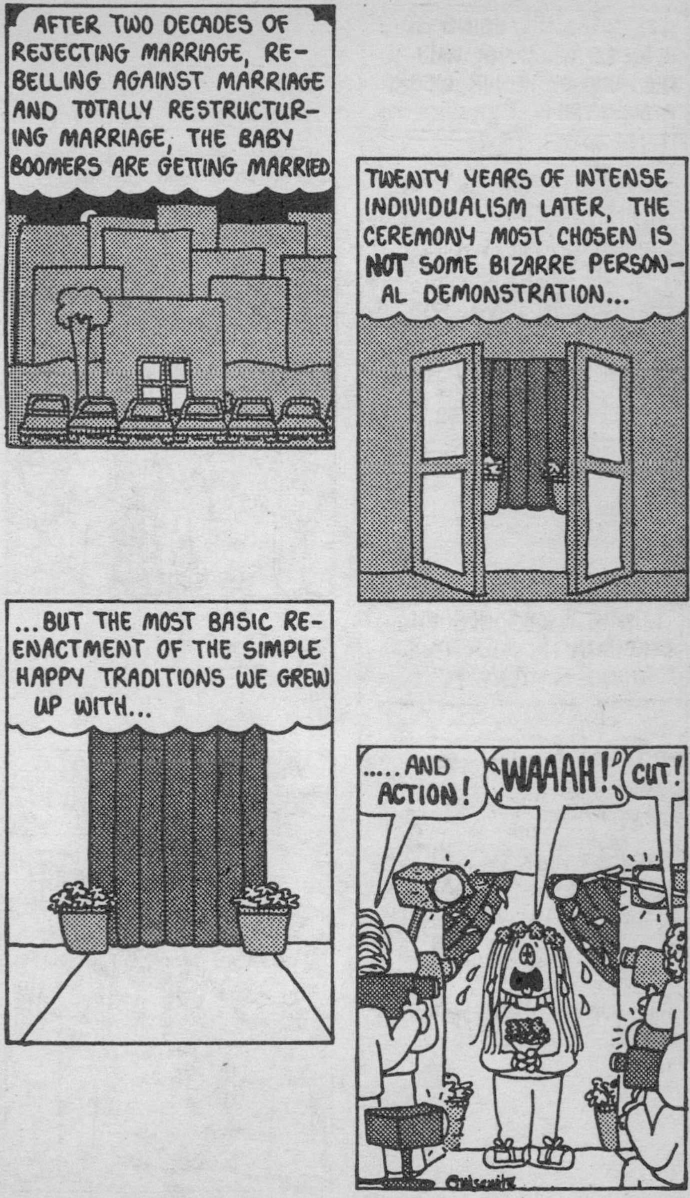
AFTER TWO DECADES OF REJECTING MARRIAGE, REBELLING AGAINST MARRIAGE AND TOTALLY RESTRUCTURING MARRIAGE, THE BABY BOOMERS ARE GETTING MARRIED
TWENTY YEARS OF INTENSE INDIVIDUALISM LATER, THE CEREMONY MOST CHOSEN IS NOT SOME BIZARRE PERSONAL DEMONSTRATION...
...BUT THE MOST BASIC REENACTMENT OF THE SIMPLE HAPPY TRADITIONS WE GREW UP WITH...
.....AND ACTION!
WAAAH!
CUT!

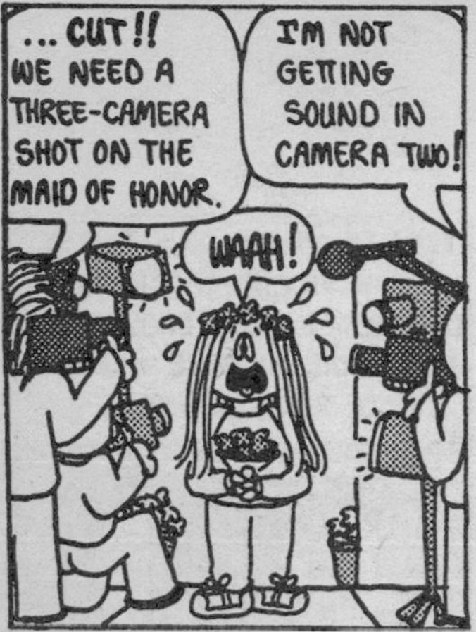
...CUT!! WE NEED A THREE-CAMERA SHOT ON THE MAID OF HONOR.
I'M NOT GETTING SOUND IN CAMERA TWO!
WAAH!

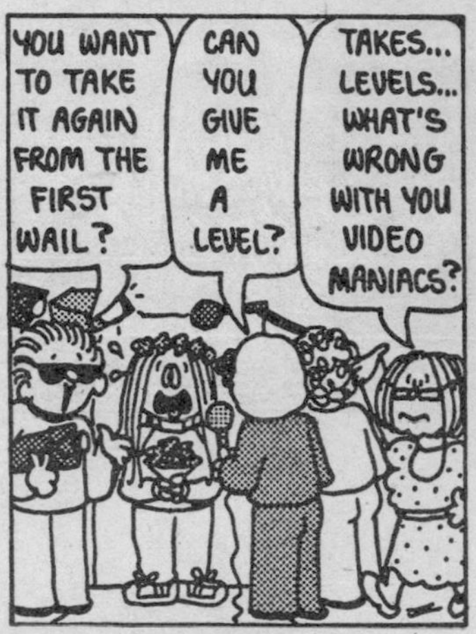
YOU WANT TO TAKE IT AGAIN FROM THE FIRST WAIL?
CAN YOU GIVE ME A LEVEL?
TAKES... LEVELS... WHAT'S WRONG WITH YOU VIDEO MANIACS?

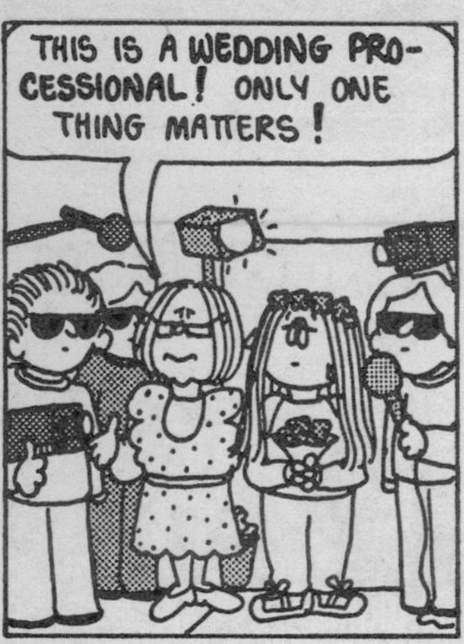
THIS IS A WEDDING PROCESSIONAL! ONLY ONE THING MATTERS!

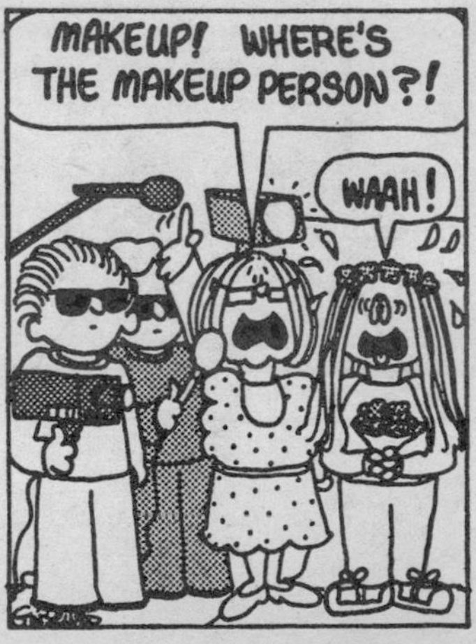
MAKEUP! WHERE'S THE MAKEUP PERSON?!
WAAH!

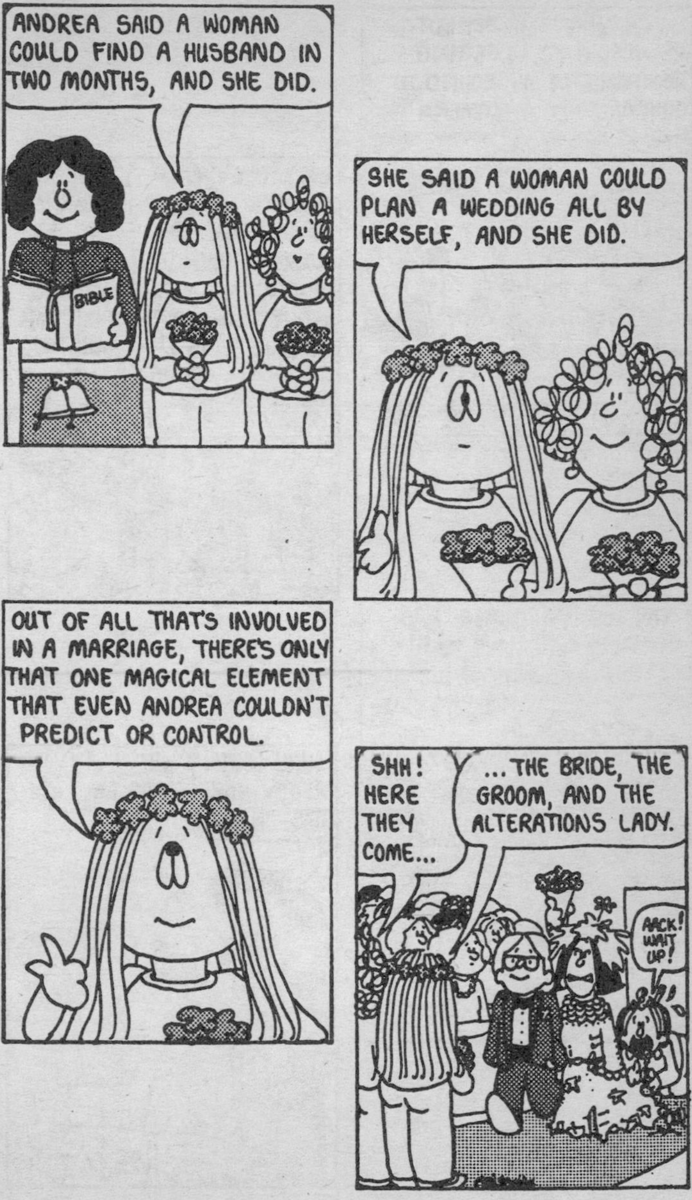
ANDREA SAID A WOMAN COULD FIND A HUSBAND IN TWO MONTHS, AND SHE DID.
BIBLE
SHE SAID A WOMAN COULD PLAN A WEDDING ALL BY HERSELF, AND SHE DID.
OUT OF ALL THAT'S INVOLVED IN A MARRIAGE, THERE'S ONLY THAT ONE MAGICAL ELEMENT THAT EVEN ANDREA COULDN'T PREDICT OR CONTROL.
SHH! HERE THEY COME...
... THE BRIDE, THE GROOM, AND THE ALTERATIONS LADY.
AACK! WAIT UP!

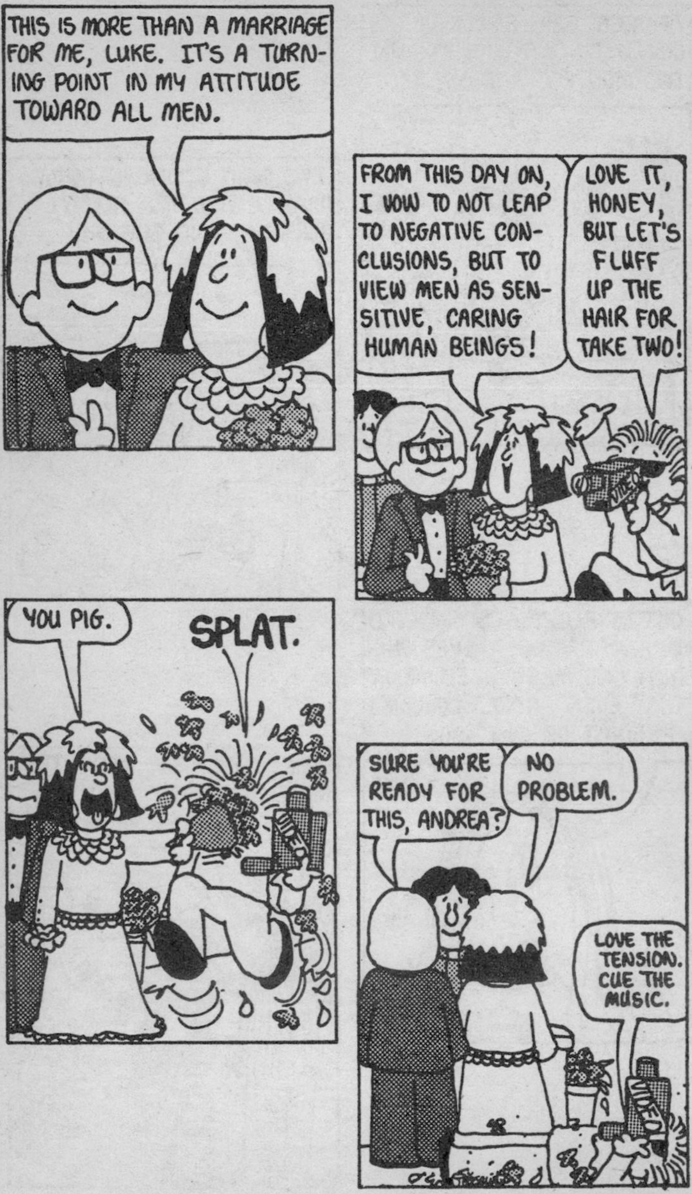
THIS IS MORE THAN A MARRIAGE FOR ME, LUKE. IT'S A TURNING POINT IN MY ATTITUDE TOWARD ALL MEN.
FROM THIS DAY ON, I VOW TO NOT LEAP TO NEGATIVE CONCLUSIONS, BUT TO VIEW MEN AS SENSITIVE, CARING HUMAN BEINGS!
LOVE IT, HONEY, BUT LET'S FLUFF UP THE HAIR FOR TAKE TWO!
YOU PIG.
SPLAT.
SURE YOU'RE READY FOR THIS, ANDREA?
NO PROBLEM.
LOVE THE TENSION. CUE THE MUSIC.

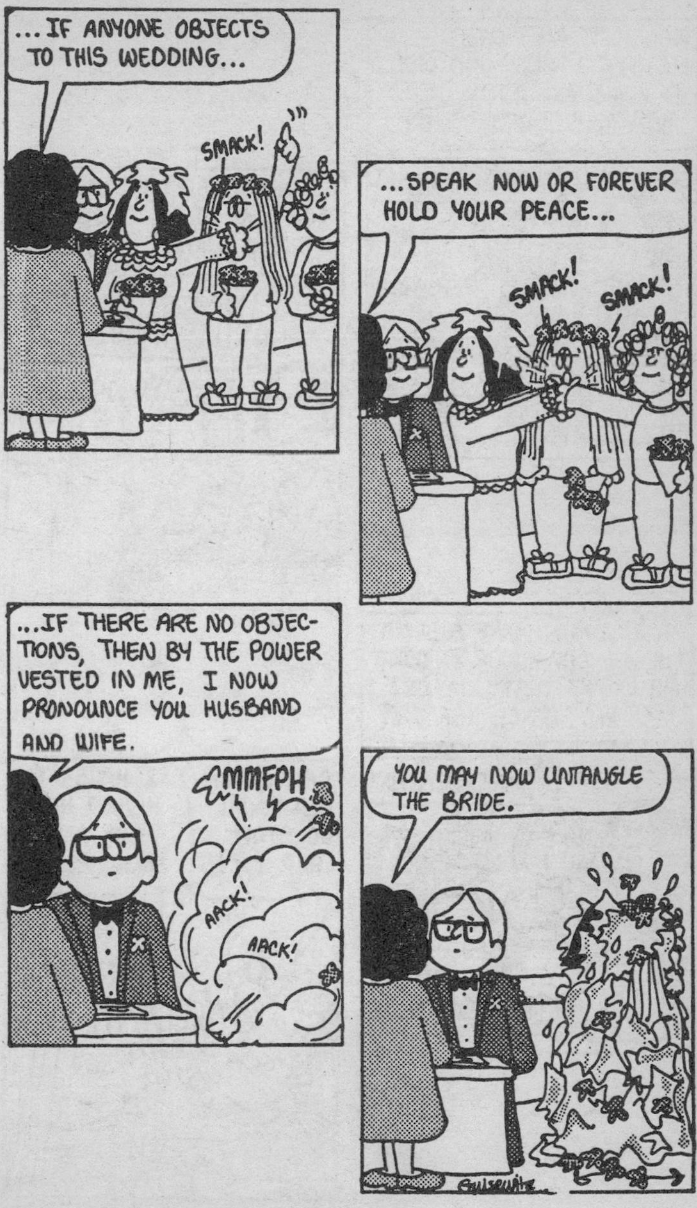
...IF ANYONE OBJECTS TO THIS WEDDING...
SMACK!
...SPEAK NOW OR FOREVER HOLD YOUR PEACE...
SMACK!
SMACK!
...IF THERE ARE NO OBJECTIONS, THEN BY THE POWER VESTED IN ME, I NOW PRONOUNCE YOU HUSBAND AND WIFE.
MMFPH
AACK!
AACK!
YOU MAY NOW UNTANGLE THE BRIDE.

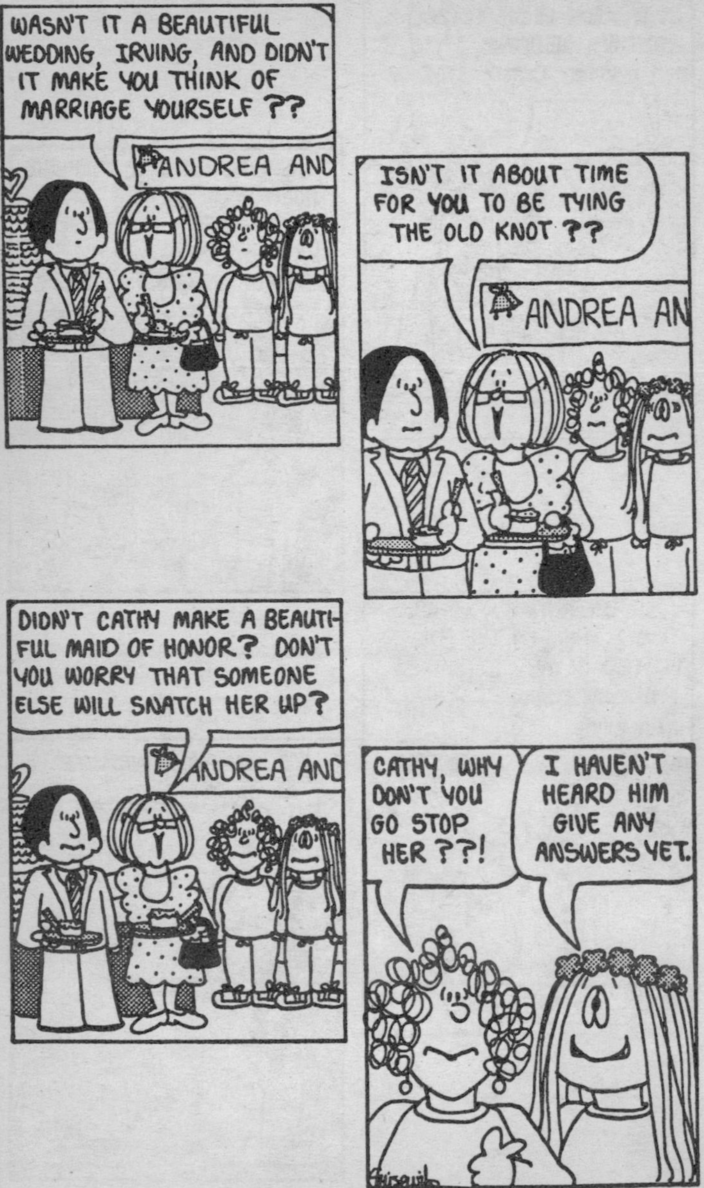
WASN'T IT A BEAUTIFUL WEDDING, IRVING, AND DIDN'T IT MAKE YOU THINK OF MARRIAGE YOURSELF ??
ANDREA AND
ISN'T IT ABOUT TIME FOR YOU TO BE TYING THE OLD KNOT ??
ANDREA AN
DIDN'T CATHY MAKE A BEAUTIFUL MAID OF HONOR? DON'T YOU WORRY THAT SOMEONE ELSE WILL SNATCH HER UP?
ANDREA AND
CATHY, WHY DON'T YOU GO STOP HER ??!
I HAVEN'T HEARD HIM GIVE ANY ANSWERS YET.

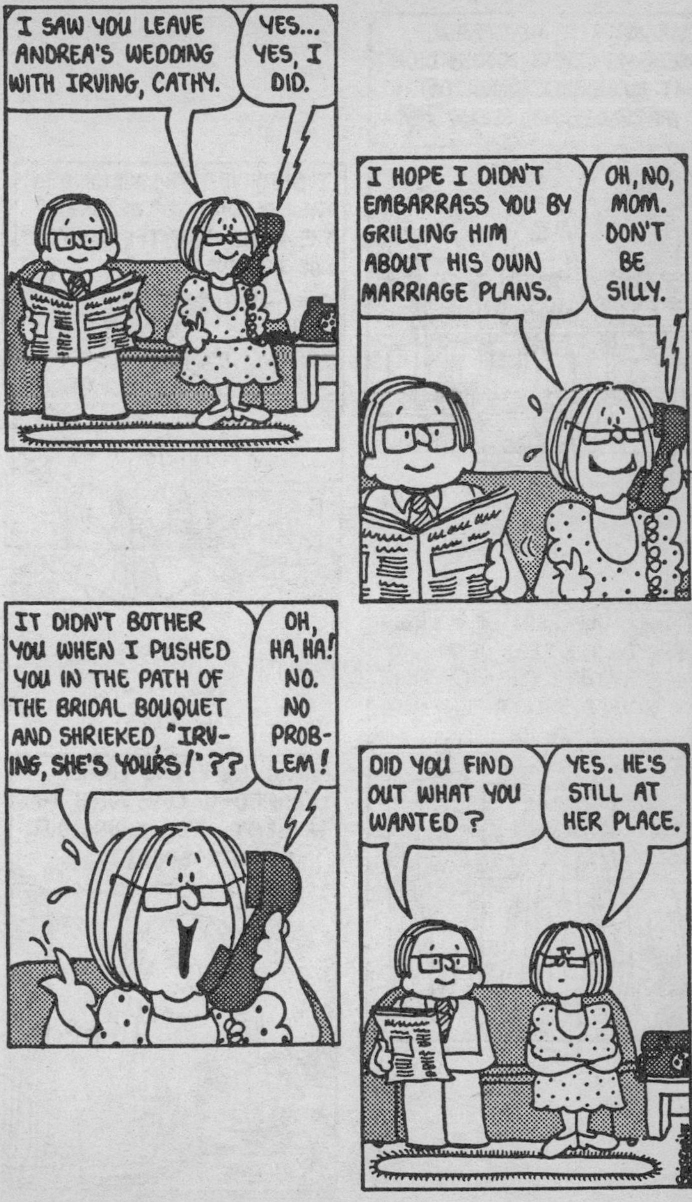
I SAW YOU LEAVE ANDREA'S WEDDING WITH IRVING, CATHY.
YES... YES, I DID.
I HOPE I DIDN'T EMBARRASS YOU BY GRILLING HIM ABOUT HIS OWN MARRIAGE PLANS.
OH, NO, MOM. DON'T BE SILLY.
IT DIDN'T BOTHER YOU WHEN I PUSHED YOU IN THE PATH OF THE BRIDAL BOUQUET AND SHRIEKED, "IRVING, SHE'S YOURS!"??
OH, HA, HA! NO. NO PROBLEM!
DID YOU FIND OUT WHAT YOU WANTED?
YES. HE'S STILL AT HER PLACE.

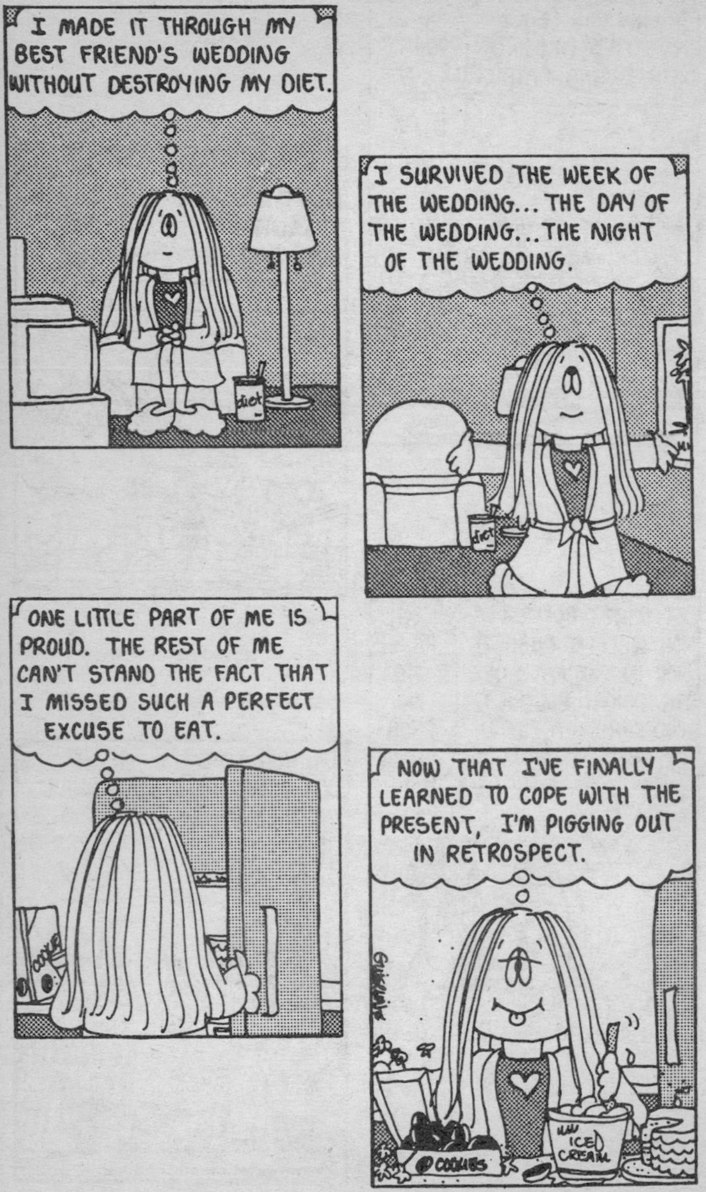
I MADE IT THROUGH MY BEST FRIEND'S WEDDING WITHOUT DESTROYING MY DIET.
diet
I SURVIVED THE WEEK OF THE WEDDING... THE DAY OF THE WEDDING... THE NIGHT OF THE WEDDING.
diet
ONE LITTLE PART OF ME IS PROUD. THE REST OF ME CAN'T STAND THE FACT THAT I MISSED SUCH A PERFECT EXCUSE TO EAT.
NOW THAT I'VE FINALLY LEARNED TO COPE WITH THE PRESENT, I'M PIGGING OUT IN RETROSPECT.
Guisewite
ICE CREAM
COOKIES

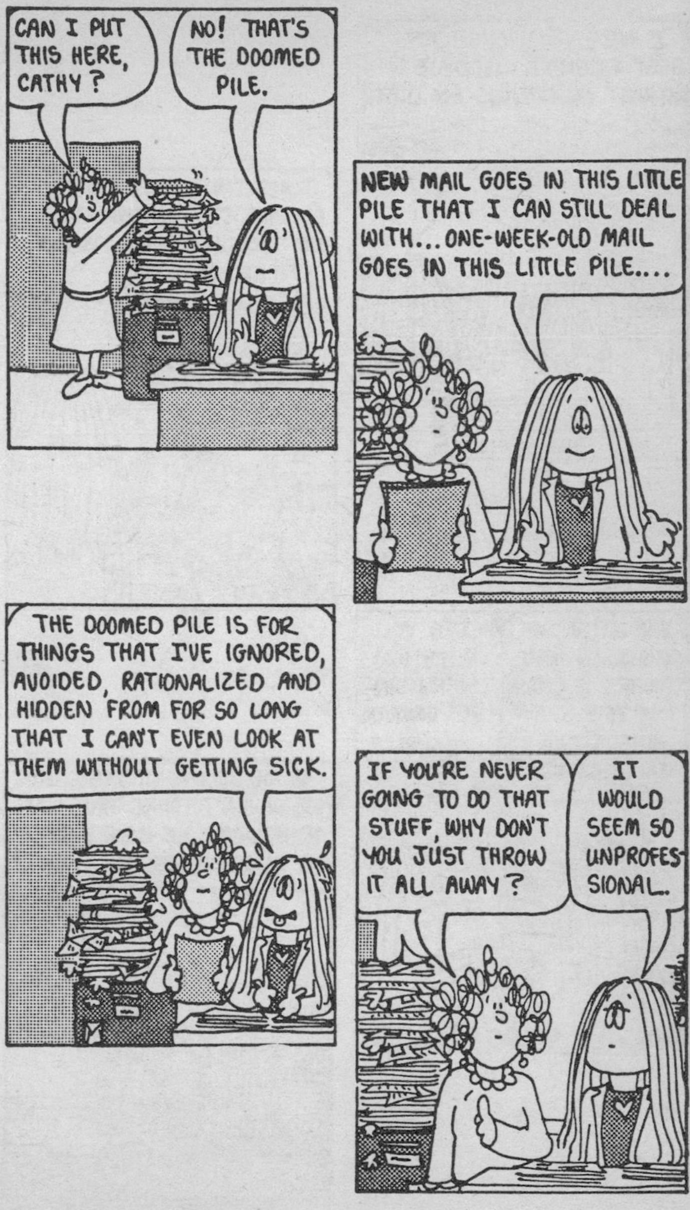
CAN I PUT THIS HERE, CATHY?
NO! THAT'S THE DOOMED PILE.
NEW MAIL GOES IN THIS LITTLE PILE THAT I CAN STILL DEAL WITH... ONE-WEEK-OLD MAIL GOES IN THIS LITTLE PILE....
THE DOOMED PILE IS FOR THINGS THAT I'VE IGNORED, AVOIDED, RATIONALIZED AND HIDDEN FROM FOR SO LONG THAT I CAN'T EVEN LOOK AT THEM WITHOUT GETTING SICK.
IF YOU'RE NEVER GOING TO DO THAT STUFF, WHY DON'T YOU JUST THROW IT ALL AWAY?
IT WOULD SEEM SO UNPROFESSIONAL.

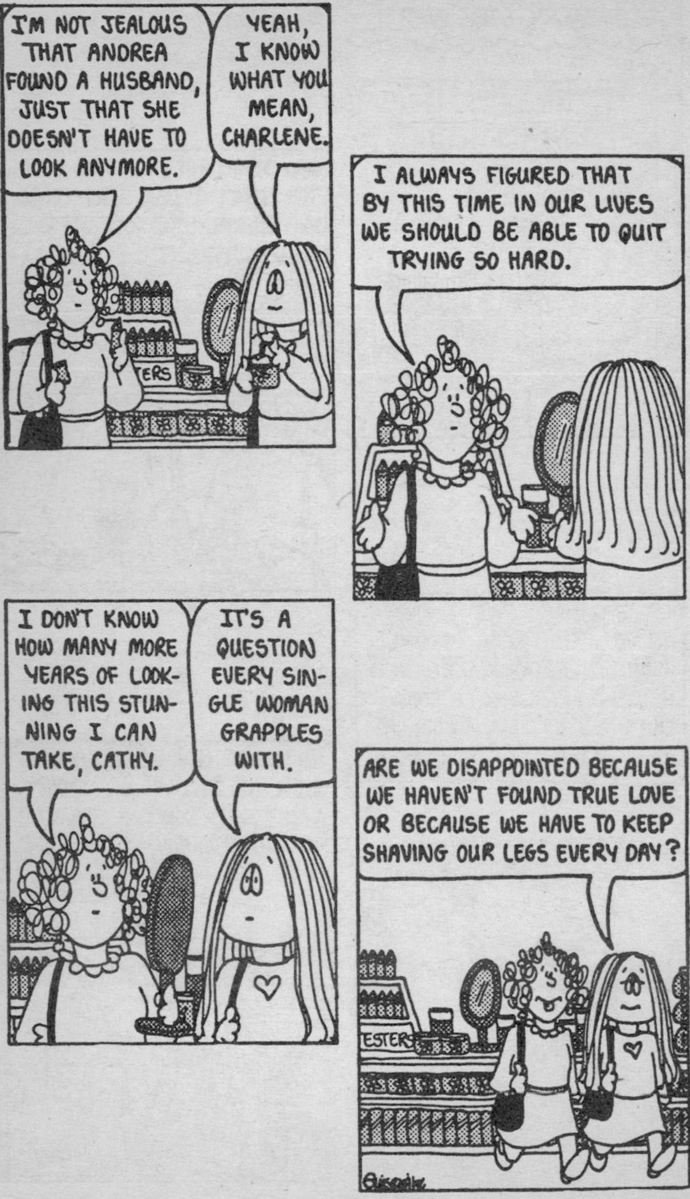
I'M NOT JEALOUS THAT ANDREA FOUND A HUSBAND, JUST THAT SHE DOESN'T HAVE TO LOOK ANYMORE.
YEAH, I KNOW WHAT YOU MEAN, CHARLENE.
I ALWAYS FIGURED THAT BY THIS TIME IN OUR LIVES WE SHOULD BE ABLE TO QUIT TRYING SO HARD.
I DON'T KNOW HOW MANY MORE YEARS OF LOOK-ING THIS STUN-NING I CAN TAKE, CATHY.
IT'S A QUESTION EVERY SIN-GLE WOMAN GRAPPLES WITH.
ARE WE DISAPPOINTED BECAUSE WE HAVEN'T FOUND TRUE LOVE OR BECAUSE WE HAVE TO KEEP SHAVING OUR LEGS EVERY DAY?

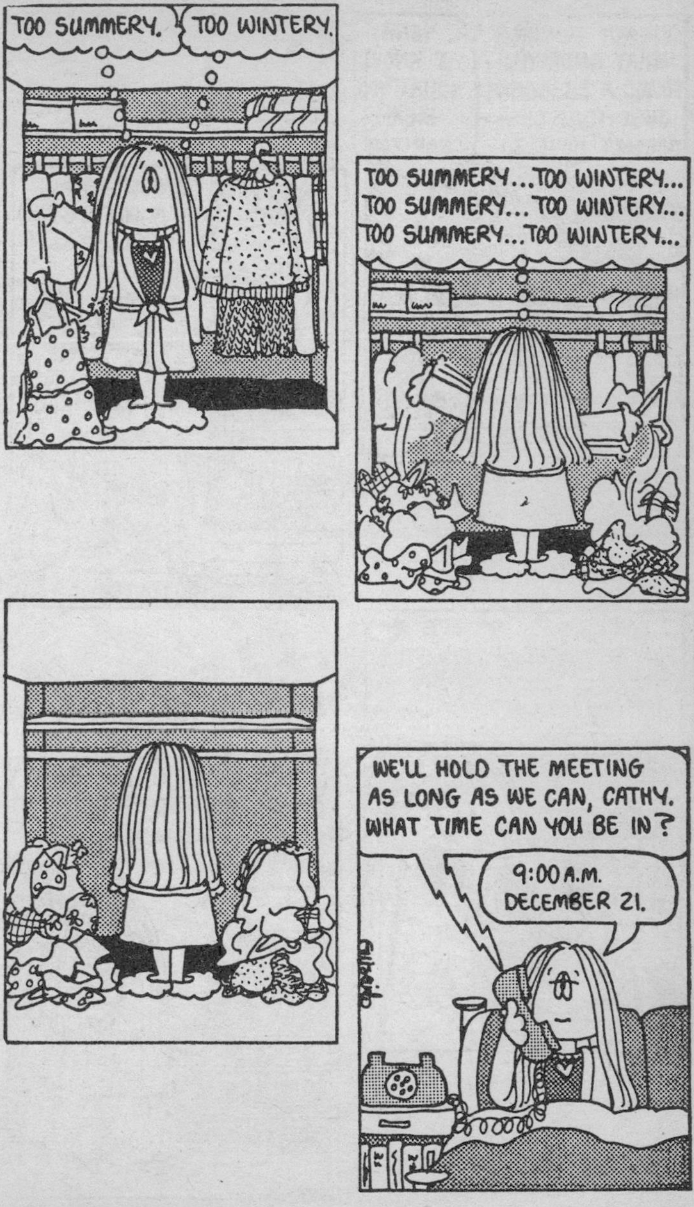
TOO SUMMERY.
TOO WINTERY.
TOO SUMMERY...TOO WINTERY...
TOO SUMMERY... TOO WINTERY...
TOO SUMMERY...TOO WINTERY...
WE'LL HOLD THE MEETING AS LONG AS WE CAN, CATHY. WHAT TIME CAN YOU BE IN?
9:00 A.M. DECEMBER 21.

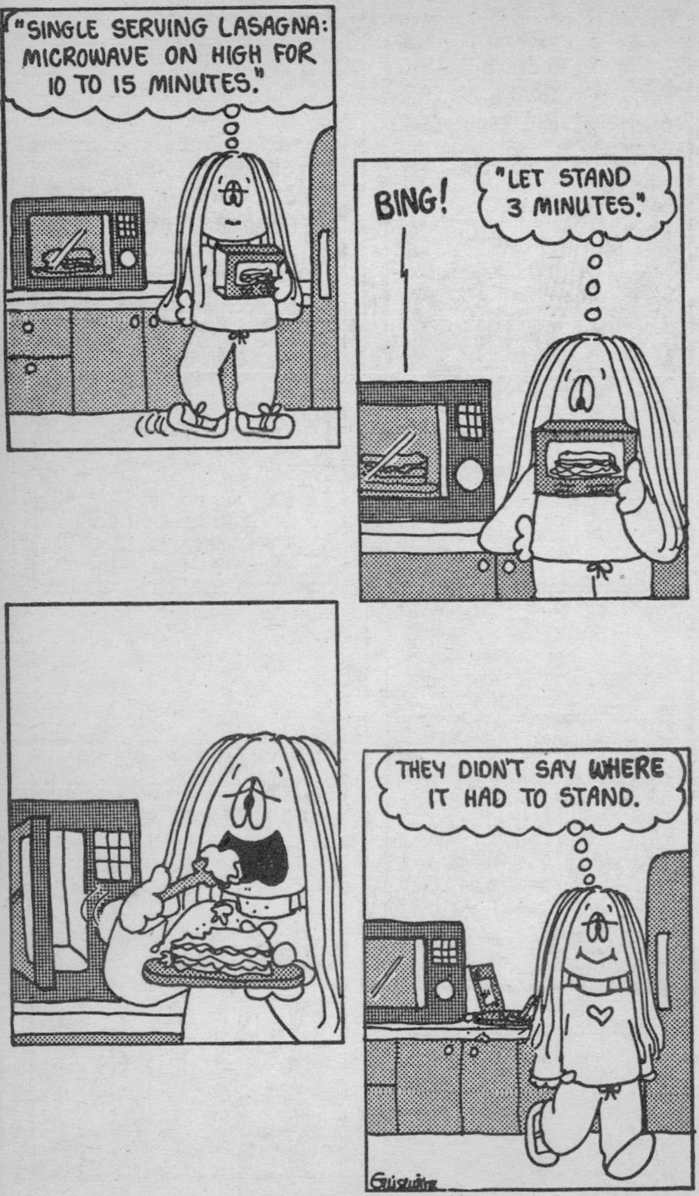
"SINGLE SERVING LASAGNA: MICROWAVE ON HIGH FOR 10 TO 15 MINUTES."
BING!
"LET STAND 3 MINUTES."
THEY DIDN'T SAY WHERE IT HAD TO STAND.
Guisewite

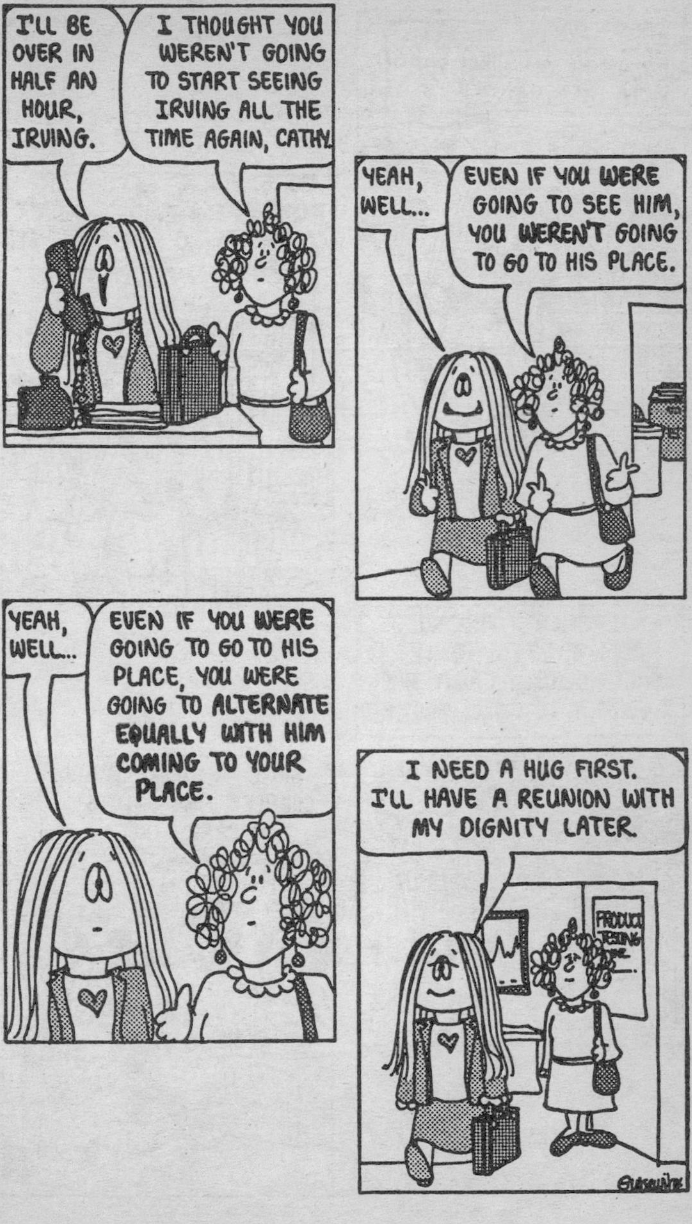
I'LL BE OVER IN HALF AN HOUR, IRVING.
I THOUGHT YOU WEREN'T GOING TO START SEEING IRVING ALL THE TIME AGAIN, CATHY.
YEAH, WELL...
EVEN IF YOU WERE GOING TO SEE HIM, YOU WEREN'T GOING TO GO TO HIS PLACE.
YEAH, WELL...
EVEN IF YOU WERE GOING TO GO TO HIS PLACE, YOU WERE GOING TO ALTERNATE EQUALLY WITH HIM COMING TO YOUR PLACE.
I NEED A HUG FIRST. I'LL HAVE A REUNION WITH MY DIGNITY LATER.

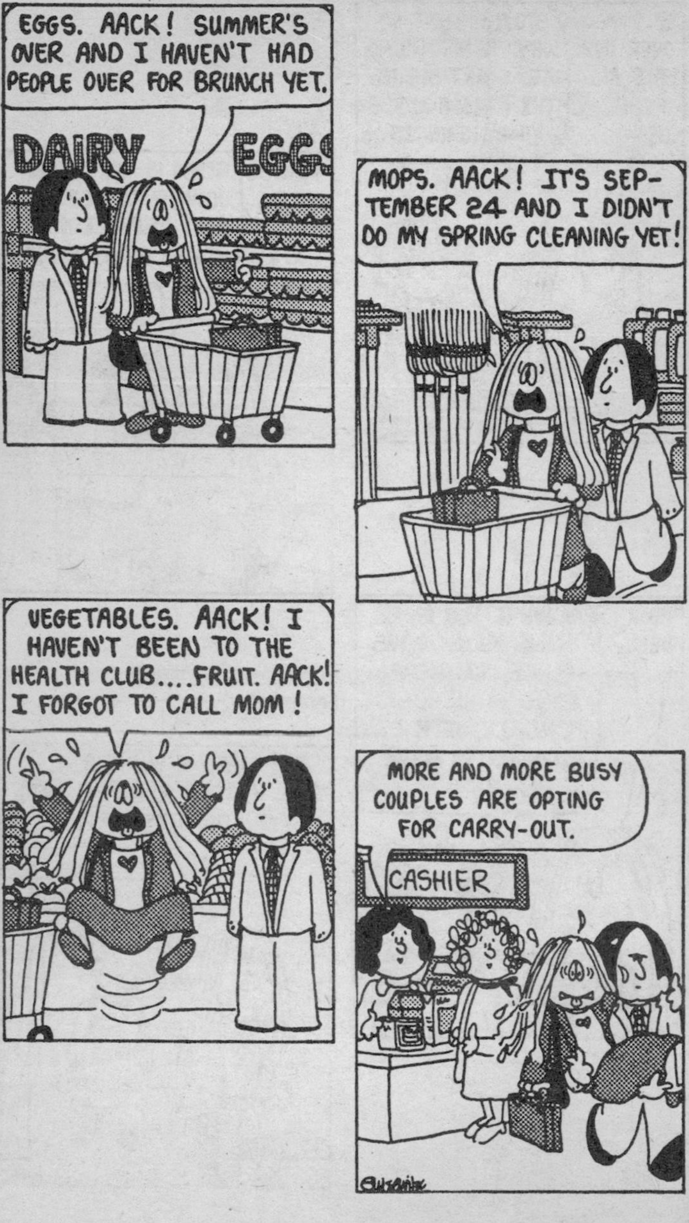
EGGS. AACK! SUMMER'S OVER AND I HAVEN'T HAD PEOPLE OVER FOR BRUNCH YET.
DAIRY
EGGS
MOPS. AACK! IT'S SEP-TEMBER 24 AND I DIDN'T DO MY SPRING CLEANING YET!
VEGETABLES. AACK! I HAVEN'T BEEN TO THE HEALTH CLUB.... FRUIT. AACK! I FORGOT TO CALL MOM!
MORE AND MORE BUSY COUPLES ARE OPTING FOR CARRY-OUT.
CASHIER

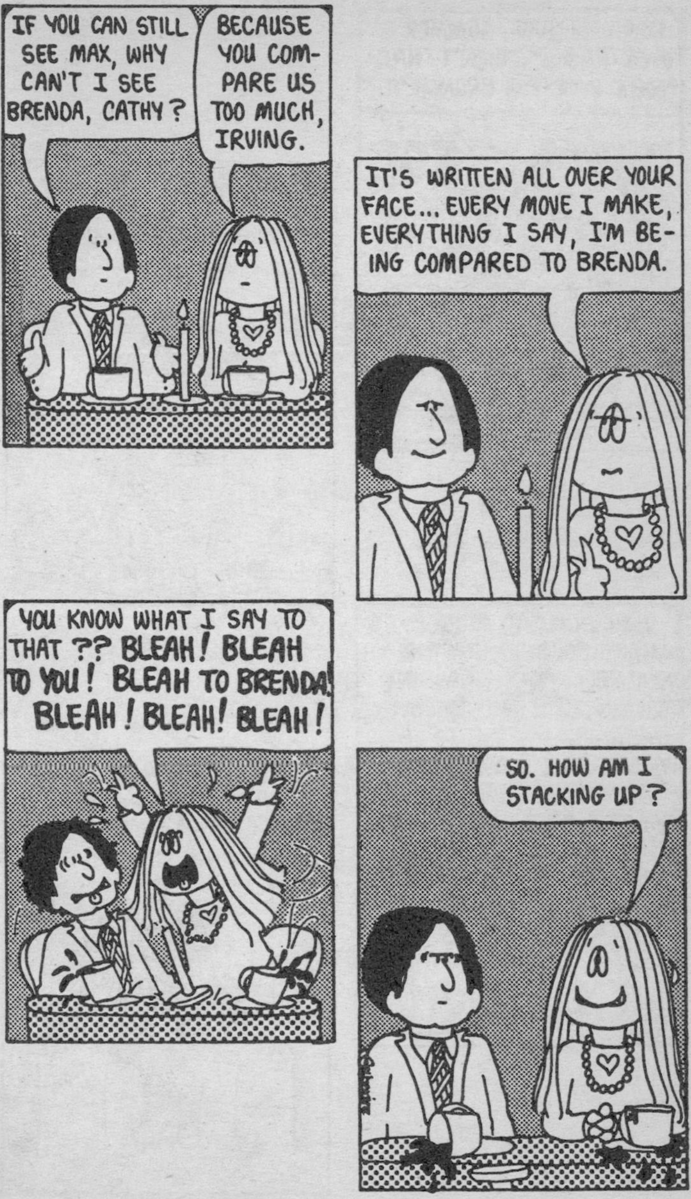
IF YOU CAN STILL SEE MAX, WHY CAN'T I SEE BRENDA, CATHY?
BECAUSE YOU COMPARE US TOO MUCH, IRVING.
IT'S WRITTEN ALL OVER YOUR FACE... EVERY MOVE I MAKE, EVERYTHING I SAY, I'M BEING COMPARED TO BRENDA.
YOU KNOW WHAT I SAY TO THAT?? BLEAH! BLEAH TO YOU! BLEAH TO BRENDA! BLEAH! BLEAH! BLEAH!
SO. HOW AM I STACKING UP?

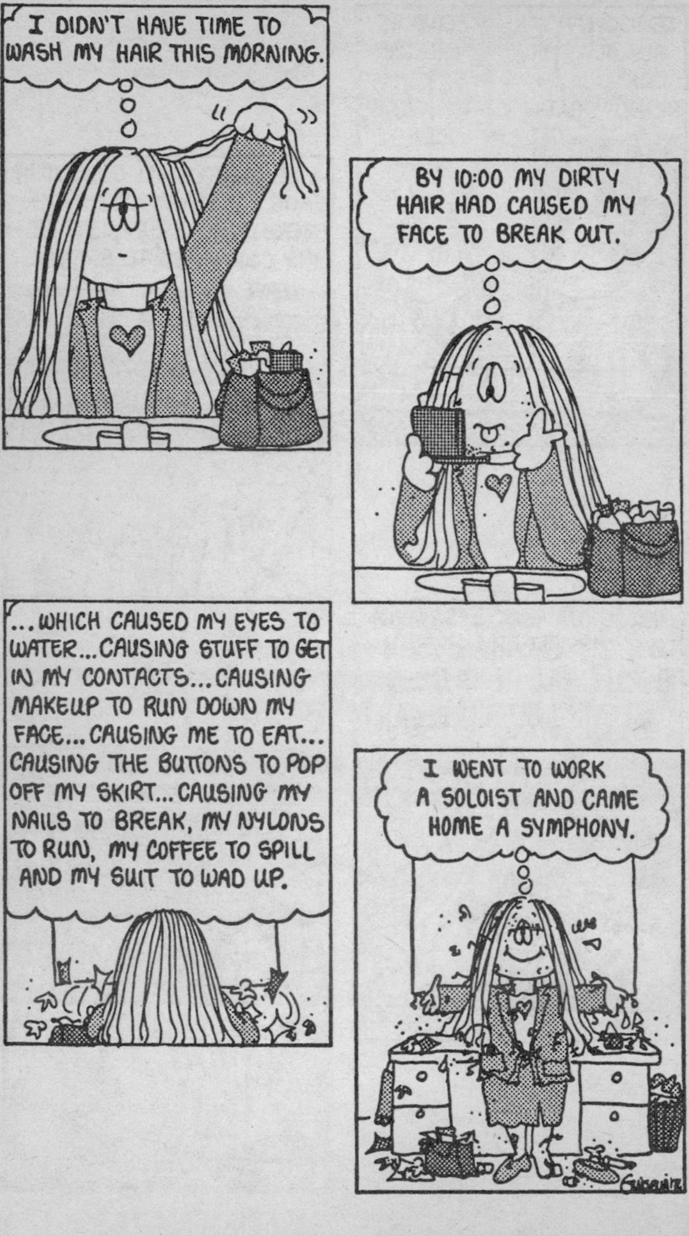
I DIDN'T HAVE TIME TO WASH MY HAIR THIS MORNING.
BY 10:00 MY DIRTY HAIR HAD CAUSED MY FACE TO BREAK OUT.
...WHICH CAUSED MY EYES TO WATER...CAUSING STUFF TO GET IN MY CONTACTS...CAUSING MAKEUP TO RUN DOWN MY FACE...CAUSING ME TO EAT...CAUSING THE BUTTONS TO POP OFF MY SKIRT...CAUSING MY NAILS TO BREAK, MY NYLONS TO RUN, MY COFFEE TO SPILL AND MY SUIT TO WAD UP.
I WENT TO WORK A SOLOIST AND CAME HOME A SYMPHONY.
GUISEWITE

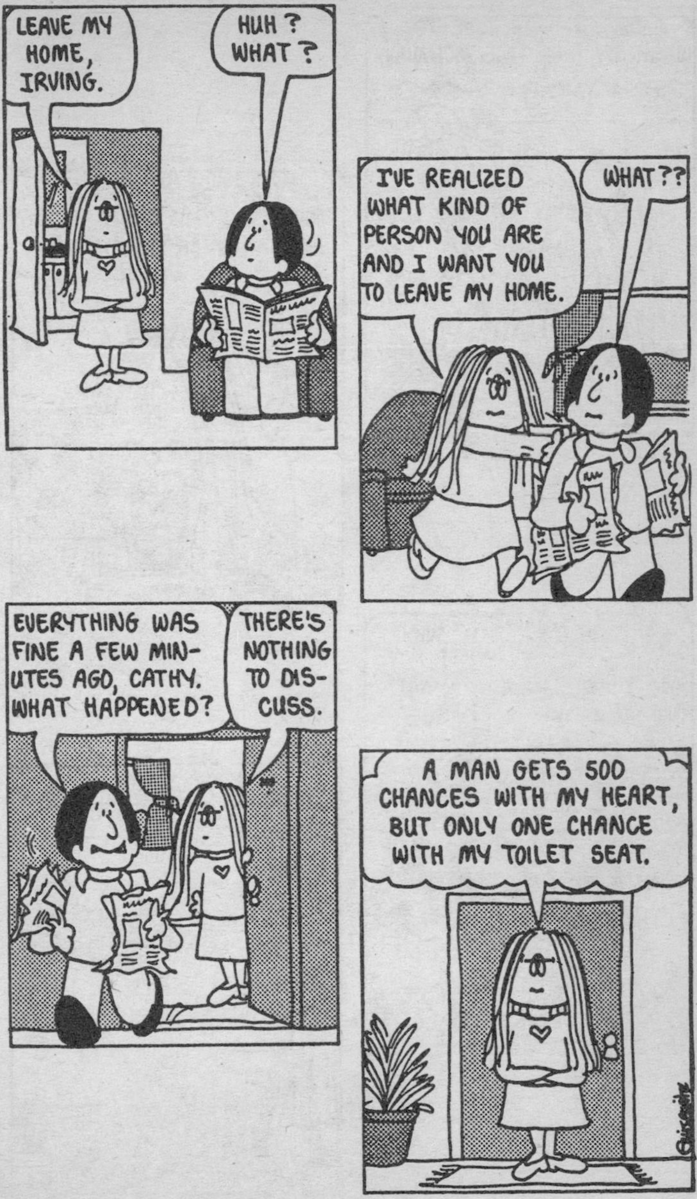
LEAVE MY HOME, IRVING.
HUH? WHAT?
I'VE REALIZED WHAT KIND OF PERSON YOU ARE AND I WANT YOU TO LEAVE MY HOME.
WHAT??
EVERYTHING WAS FINE A FEW MINUTES AGO, CATHY. WHAT HAPPENED?
THERE'S NOTHING TO DISCUSS.
A MAN GETS 500 CHANCES WITH MY HEART, BUT ONLY ONE CHANCE WITH MY TOILET SEAT.
Guisewite

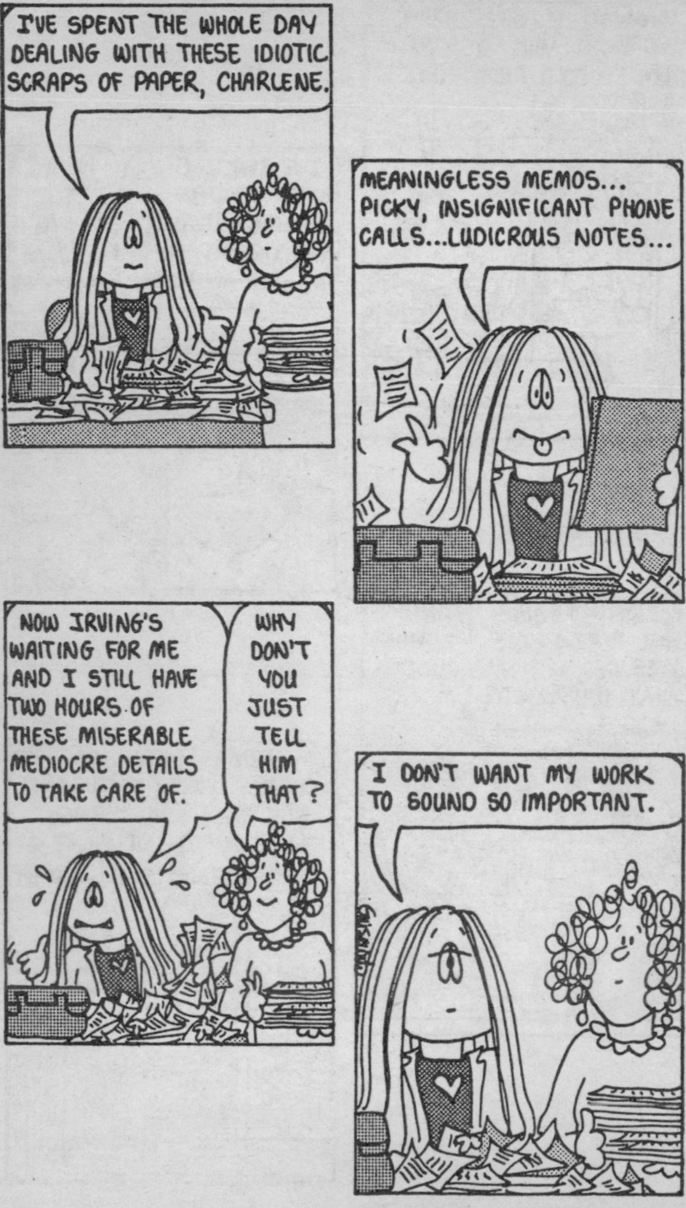
I'VE SPENT THE WHOLE DAY DEALING WITH THESE IDIOTIC SCRAPS OF PAPER, CHARLENE.
MEANINGLESS MEMOS... PICKY, INSIGNIFICANT PHONE CALLS...LUDICROUS NOTES...
NOW IRVING'S WAITING FOR ME AND I STILL HAVE TWO HOURS OF THESE MISERABLE MEDIOCRE DETAILS TO TAKE CARE OF.
WHY DON'T YOU JUST TELL HIM THAT?
I DON'T WANT MY WORK TO SOUND SO IMPORTANT.

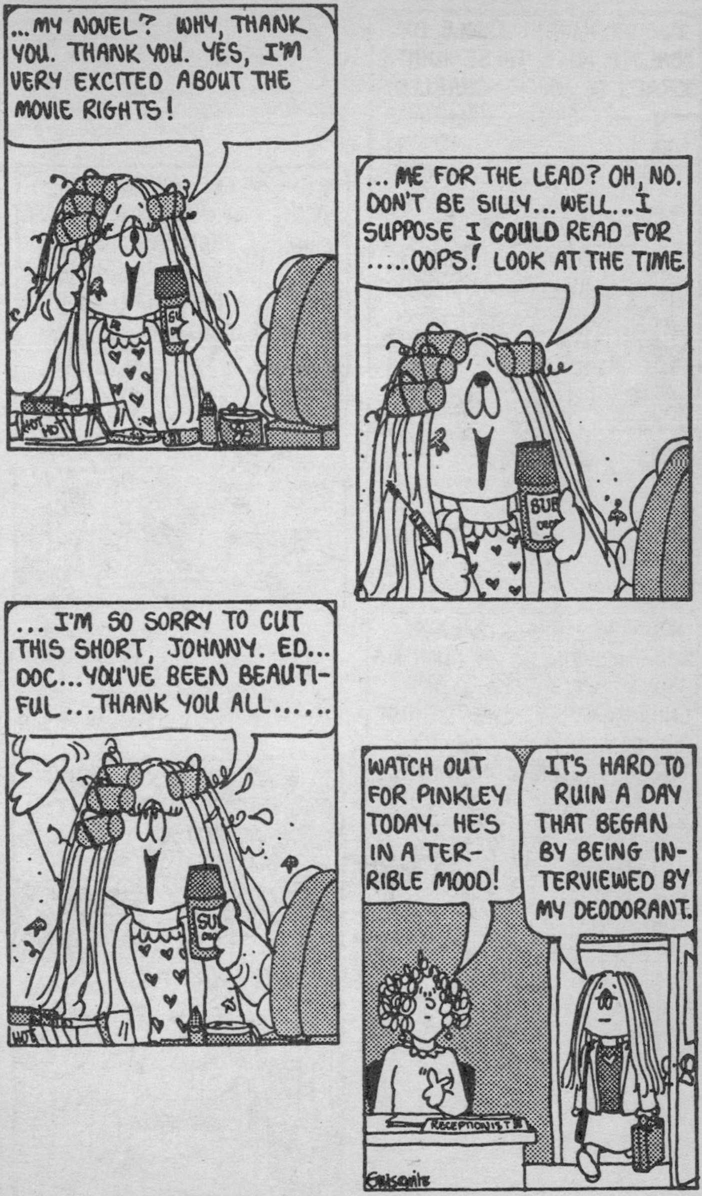
...MY NOVEL? WHY, THANK YOU. THANK YOU. YES, I'M VERY EXCITED ABOUT THE MOVIE RIGHTS!
... ME FOR THE LEAD? OH, NO. DON'T BE SILLY... WELL... I SUPPOSE I COULD READ FOR .....OOPS! LOOK AT THE TIME.
... I'M SO SORRY TO CUT THIS SHORT, JOHNNY. ED... DOC... YOU'VE BEEN BEAUTIFUL... THANK YOU ALL......
WATCH OUT FOR PINKLEY TODAY. HE'S IN A TERRIBLE MOOD!
IT'S HARD TO RUIN A DAY THAT BEGAN BY BEING INTERVIEWED BY MY DEODORANT.
RECEPTIONIST

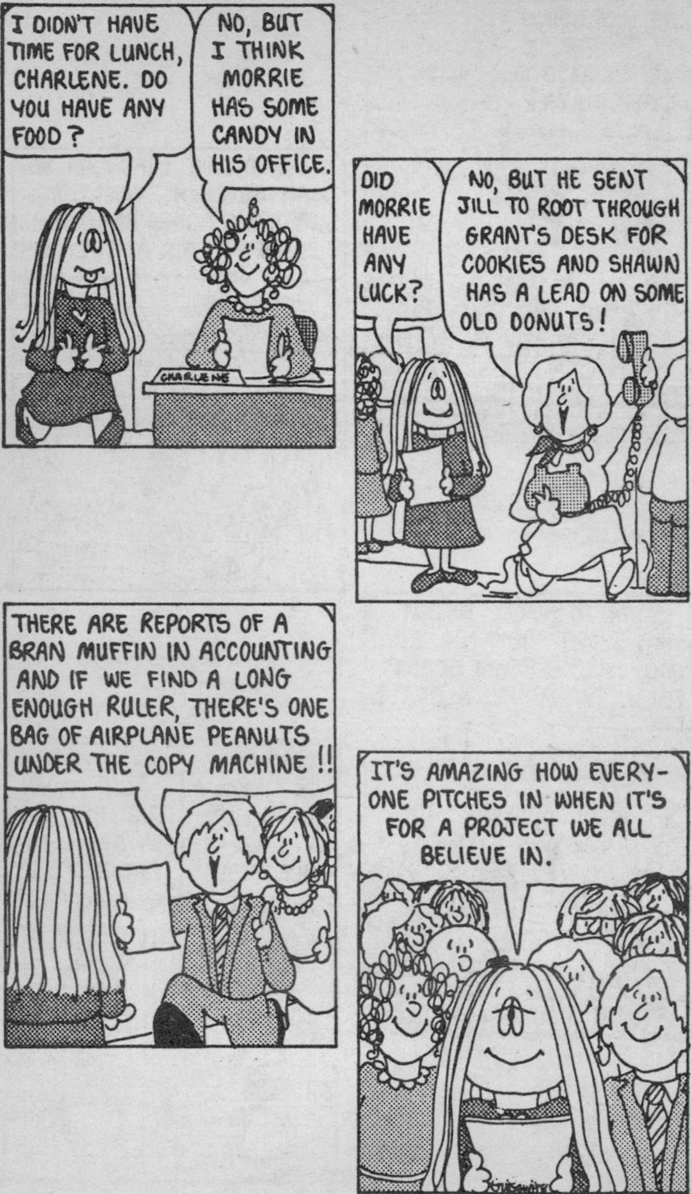
I DIDN'T HAVE TIME FOR LUNCH, CHARLENE. DO YOU HAVE ANY FOOD?
NO, BUT I THINK MORRIE HAS SOME CANDY IN HIS OFFICE.
CHARLENE
DID MORRIE HAVE ANY LUCK?
NO, BUT HE SENT JILL TO ROOT THROUGH GRANT'S DESK FOR COOKIES AND SHAWN HAS A LEAD ON SOME OLD DONUTS!
THERE ARE REPORTS OF A BRAN MUFFIN IN ACCOUNTING AND IF WE FIND A LONG ENOUGH RULER, THERE'S ONE BAG OF AIRPLANE PEANUTS UNDER THE COPY MACHINE!!
IT'S AMAZING HOW EVERYONE PITCHES IN WHEN IT'S FOR A PROJECT WE ALL BELIEVE IN.

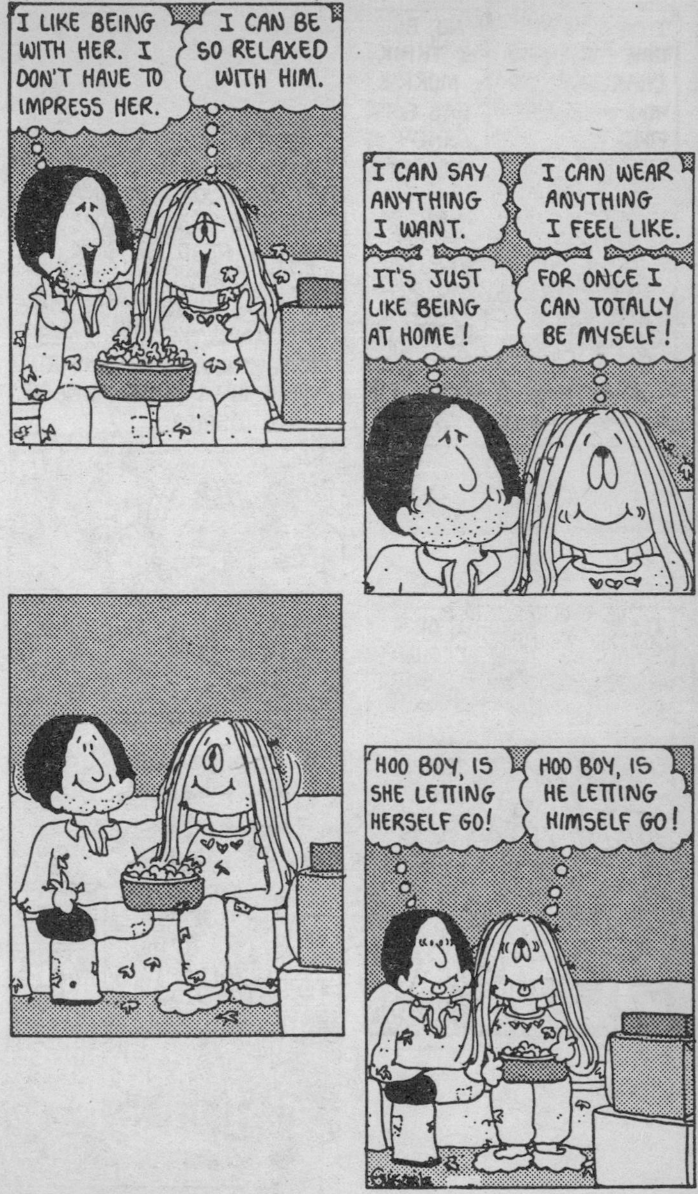
I LIKE BEING WITH HER. I DON'T HAVE TO IMPRESS HER.
I CAN BE SO RELAXED WITH HIM.
I CAN SAY ANYTHING I WANT.
I CAN WEAR ANYTHING I FEEL LIKE.
IT'S JUST LIKE BEING AT HOME!
FOR ONCE I CAN TOTALLY BE MYSELF!
HOO BOY, IS SHE LETTING HERSELF GO!
HOO BOY, IS HE LETTING HIMSELF GO!

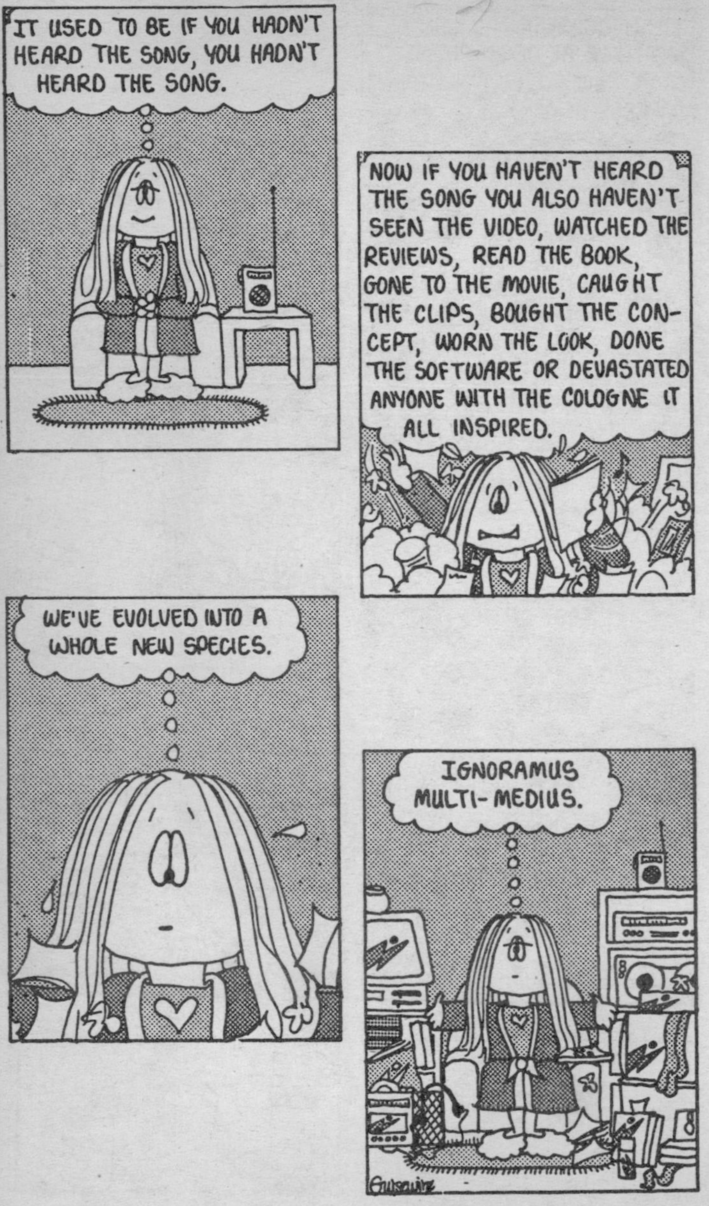
IT USED TO BE IF YOU HADN'T HEARD THE SONG, YOU HADN'T HEARD THE SONG.
NOW IF YOU HAVEN'T HEARD THE SONG YOU ALSO HAVEN'T SEEN THE VIDEO, WATCHED THE REVIEWS, READ THE BOOK, GONE TO THE MOVIE, CAUGHT THE CLIPS, BOUGHT THE CONCEPT, WORN THE LOOK, DONE THE SOFTWARE OR DEVASTATED ANYONE WITH THE COLOGNE IT ALL INSPIRED.
WE'VE EVOLVED INTO A WHOLE NEW SPECIES.
IGNORAMUS MULTI-MEDIUS.
GUISEWITE

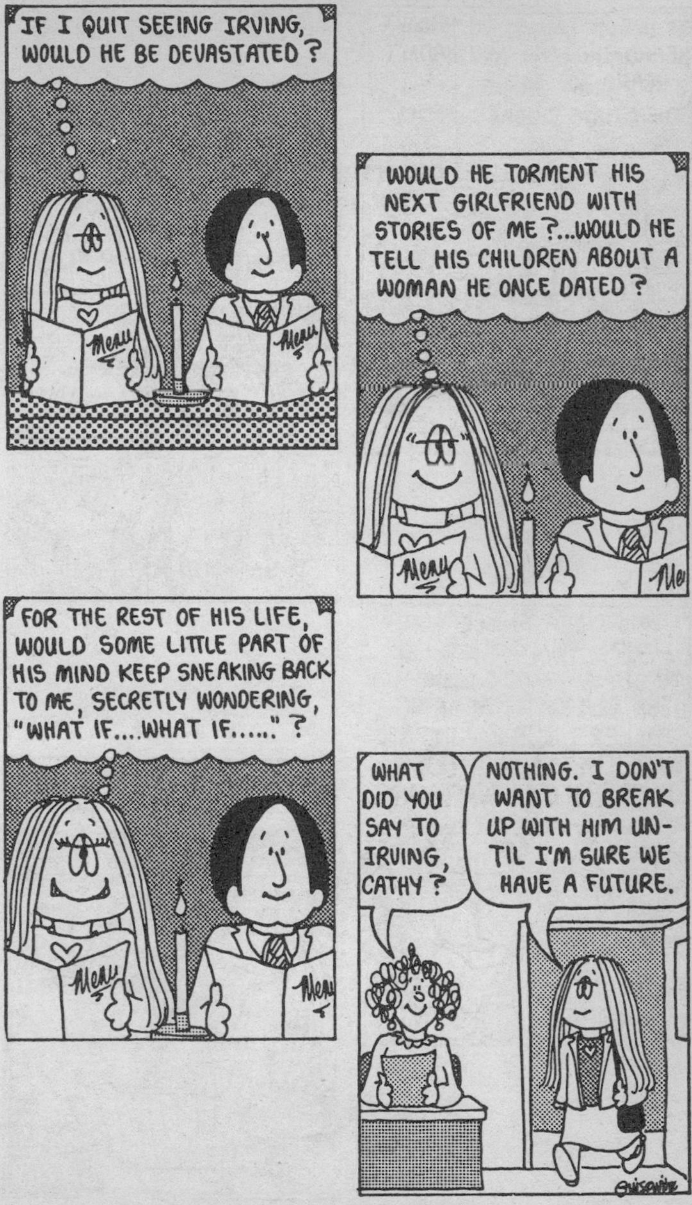
IF I QUIT SEEING IRVING, WOULD HE BE DEVASTATED?
Menu
Menu
WOULD HE TORMENT HIS NEXT GIRLFRIEND WITH STORIES OF ME?...WOULD HE TELL HIS CHILDREN ABOUT A WOMAN HE ONCE DATED?
Menu
FOR THE REST OF HIS LIFE, WOULD SOME LITTLE PART OF HIS MIND KEEP SNEAKING BACK TO ME, SECRETLY WONDERING, "WHAT IF....WHAT IF....."?
Menu
Menu
WHAT DID YOU SAY TO IRVING, CATHY?
NOTHING. I DON'T WANT TO BREAK UP WITH HIM UNTIL I'M SURE WE HAVE A FUTURE.
Guisewite

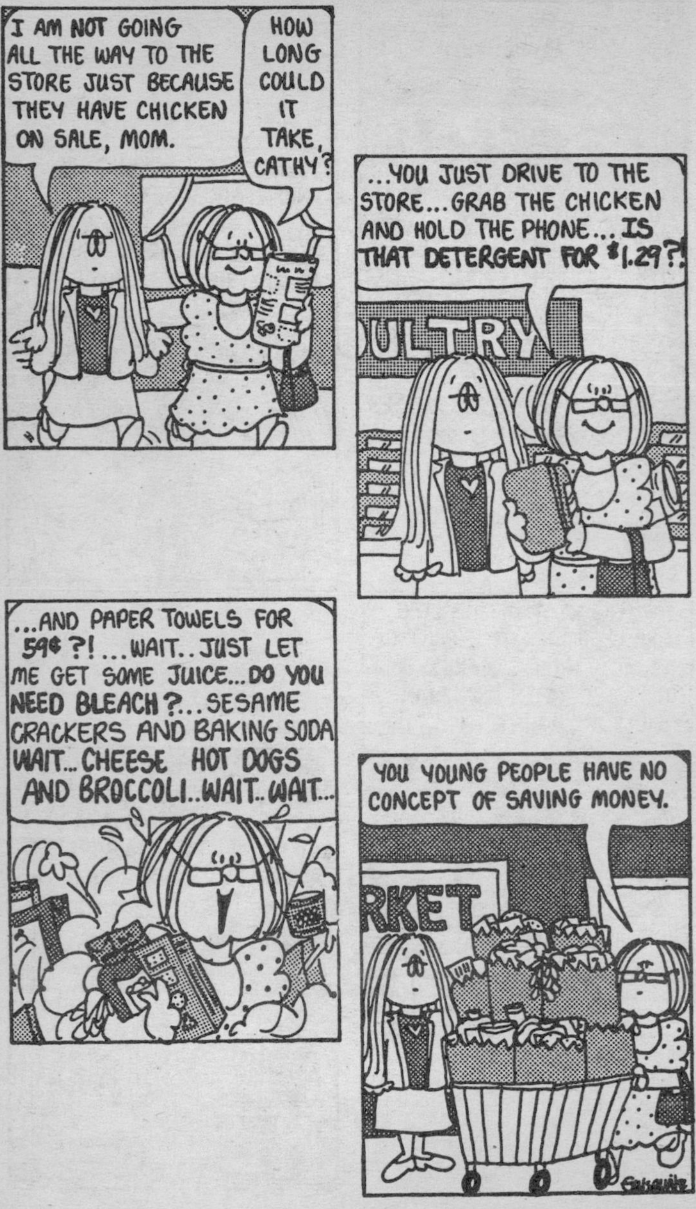
I AM NOT GOING ALL THE WAY TO THE STORE JUST BECAUSE THEY HAVE CHICKEN ON SALE, MOM.
HOW LONG COULD IT TAKE, CATHY?
...YOU JUST DRIVE TO THE STORE... GRAB THE CHICKEN AND HOLD THE PHONE... IS THAT DETERGENT FOR $1.29?!
ULTRY
...AND PAPER TOWELS FOR 59¢?! ...WAIT.. JUST LET ME GET SOME JUICE... DO YOU NEED BLEACH?... SESAME CRACKERS AND BAKING SODA WAIT... CHEESE HOT DOGS AND BROCCOLI.. WAIT.. WAIT...
YOU YOUNG PEOPLE HAVE NO CONCEPT OF SAVING MONEY.
RKET

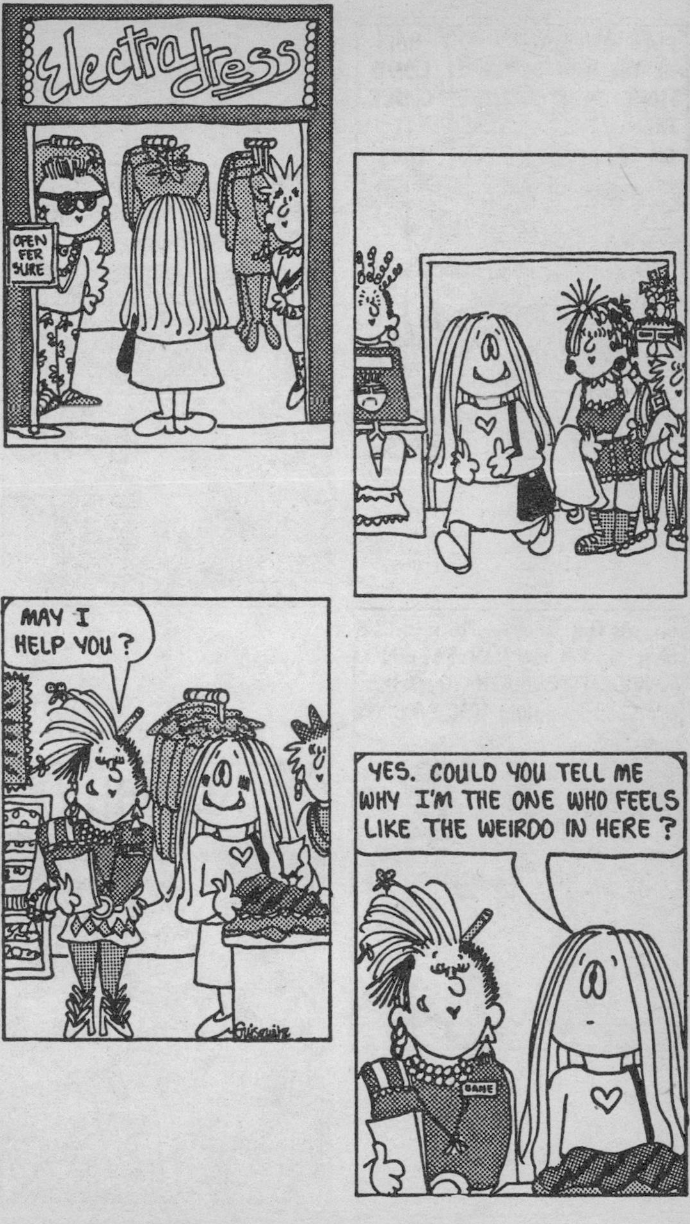
Electradress
OPEN FER SURE
MAY I HELP YOU?
YES. COULD YOU TELL ME WHY I'M THE ONE WHO FEELS LIKE THE WEIRDO IN HERE?

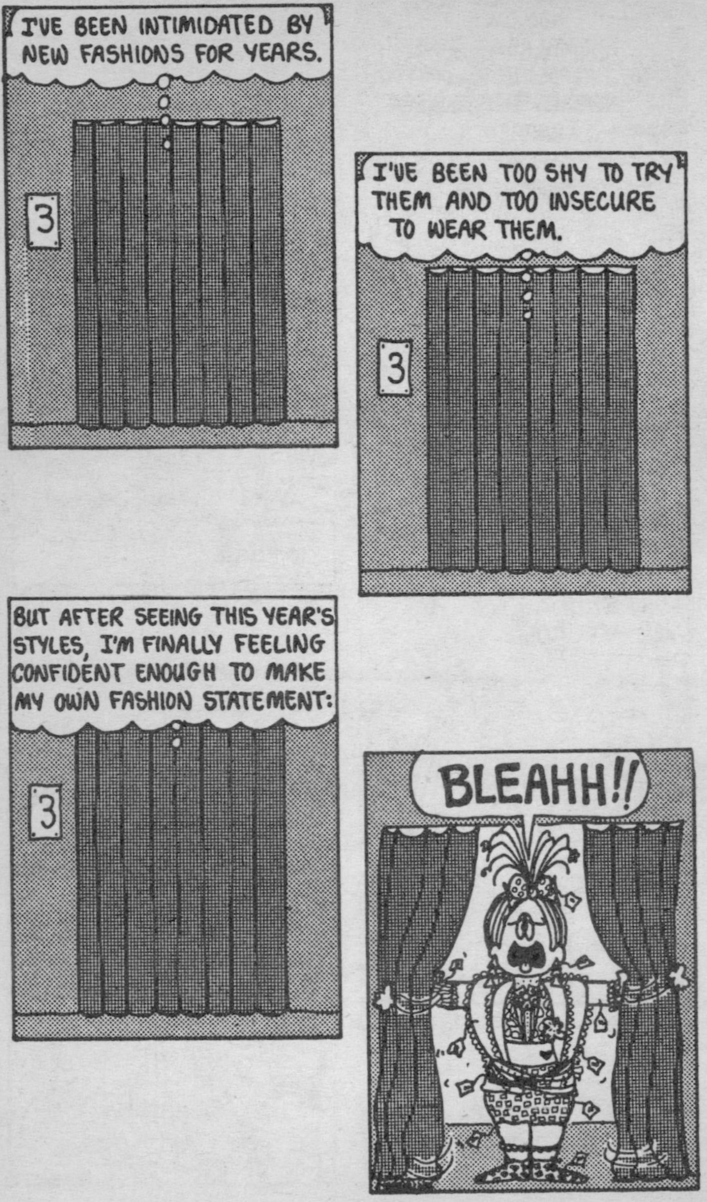
I'VE BEEN INTIMIDATED BY NEW FASHIONS FOR YEARS.
3
I'VE BEEN TOO SHY TO TRY THEM AND TOO INSECURE TO WEAR THEM.
3
BUT AFTER SEEING THIS YEAR'S STYLES, I'M FINALLY FEELING CONFIDENT ENOUGH TO MAKE MY OWN FASHION STATEMENT:
3
BLEAHH!!

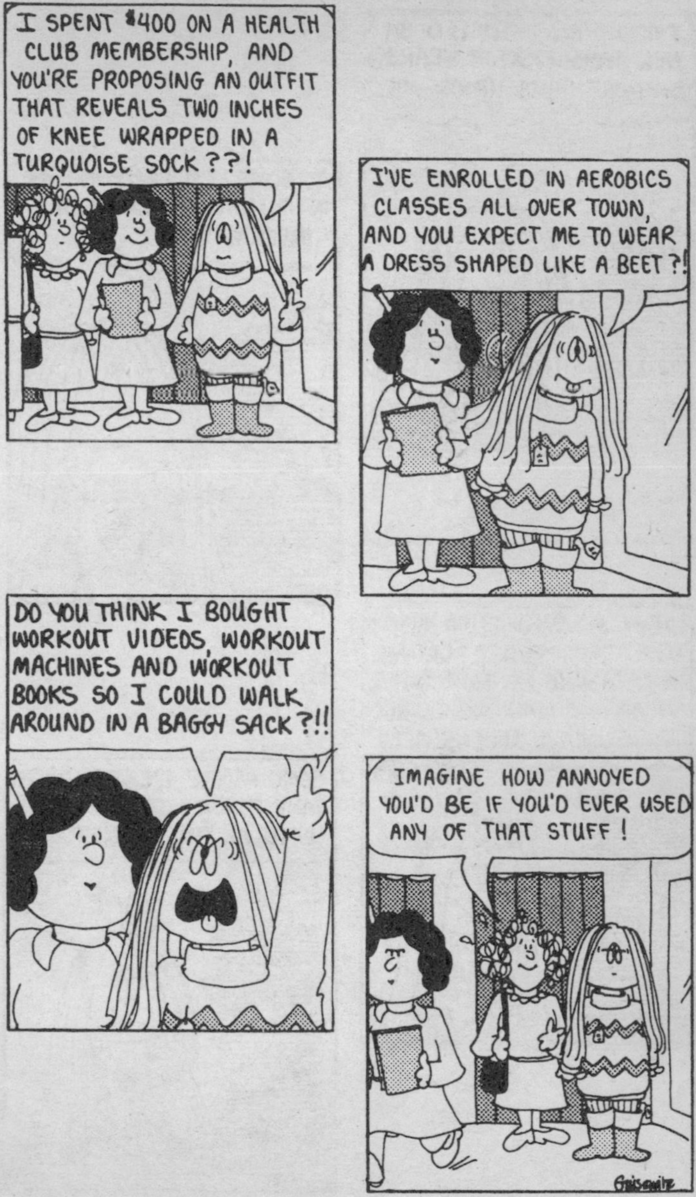
I SPENT $400 ON A HEALTH CLUB MEMBERSHIP, AND YOU'RE PROPOSING AN OUTFIT THAT REVEALS TWO INCHES OF KNEE WRAPPED IN A TURQUOISE SOCK ??!
I'VE ENROLLED IN AEROBICS CLASSES ALL OVER TOWN, AND YOU EXPECT ME TO WEAR A DRESS SHAPED LIKE A BEET ?!
DO YOU THINK I BOUGHT WORKOUT VIDEOS, WORKOUT MACHINES AND WORKOUT BOOKS SO I COULD WALK AROUND IN A BAGGY SACK ?!!
IMAGINE HOW ANNOYED YOU'D BE IF YOU'D EVER USED ANY OF THAT STUFF !
Guisewite

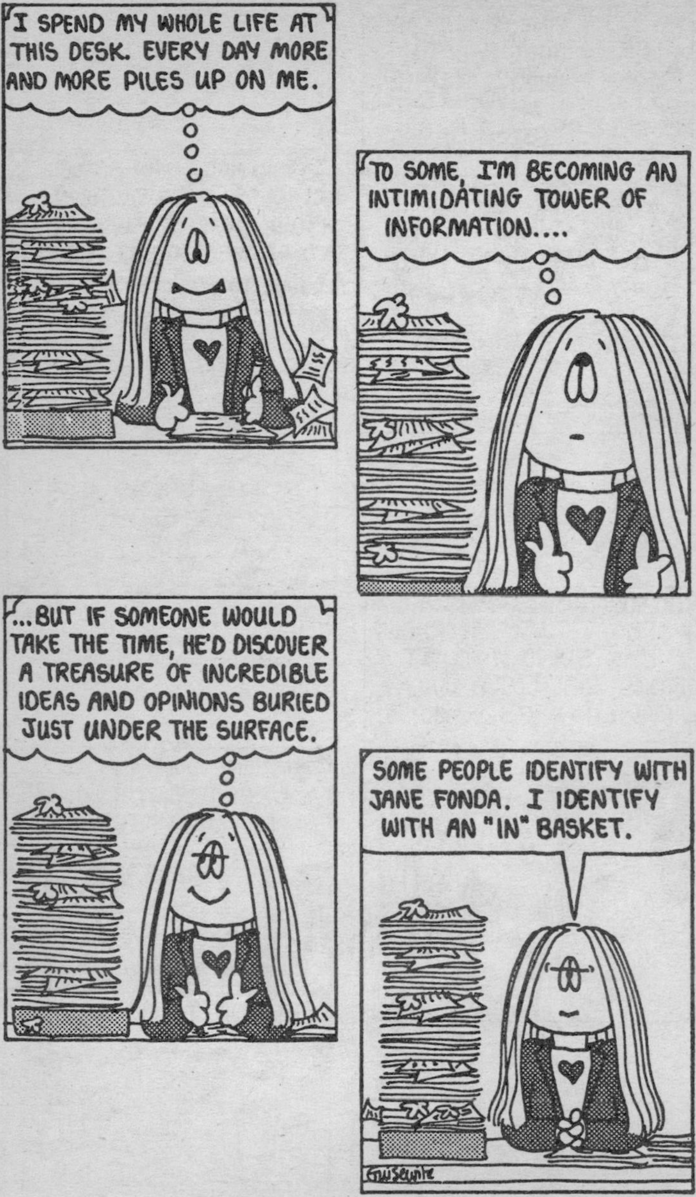
I SPEND MY WHOLE LIFE AT THIS DESK. EVERY DAY MORE AND MORE PILES UP ON ME.
TO SOME, I'M BECOMING AN INTIMIDATING TOWER OF INFORMATION....
...BUT IF SOMEONE WOULD TAKE THE TIME, HE'D DISCOVER A TREASURE OF INCREDIBLE IDEAS AND OPINIONS BURIED JUST UNDER THE SURFACE.
SOME PEOPLE IDENTIFY WITH JANE FONDA. I IDENTIFY WITH AN "IN" BASKET.
GUISEWITE

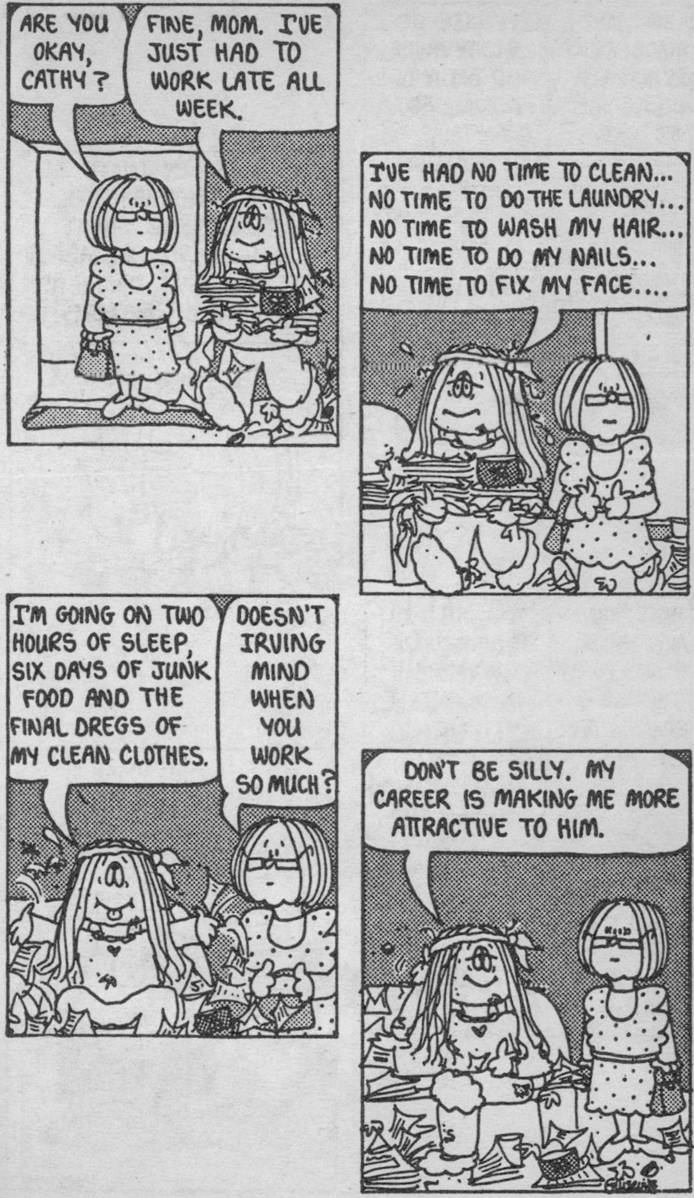
ARE YOU OKAY, CATHY?
FINE, MOM. I'VE JUST HAD TO WORK LATE ALL WEEK.
I'VE HAD NO TIME TO CLEAN... NO TIME TO DO THE LAUNDRY... NO TIME TO WASH MY HAIR... NO TIME TO DO MY NAILS... NO TIME TO FIX MY FACE....
I'M GOING ON TWO HOURS OF SLEEP, SIX DAYS OF JUNK FOOD AND THE FINAL DREGS OF MY CLEAN CLOTHES.
DOESN'T IRVING MIND WHEN YOU WORK SO MUCH?
DON'T BE SILLY. MY CAREER IS MAKING ME MORE ATTRACTIVE TO HIM.

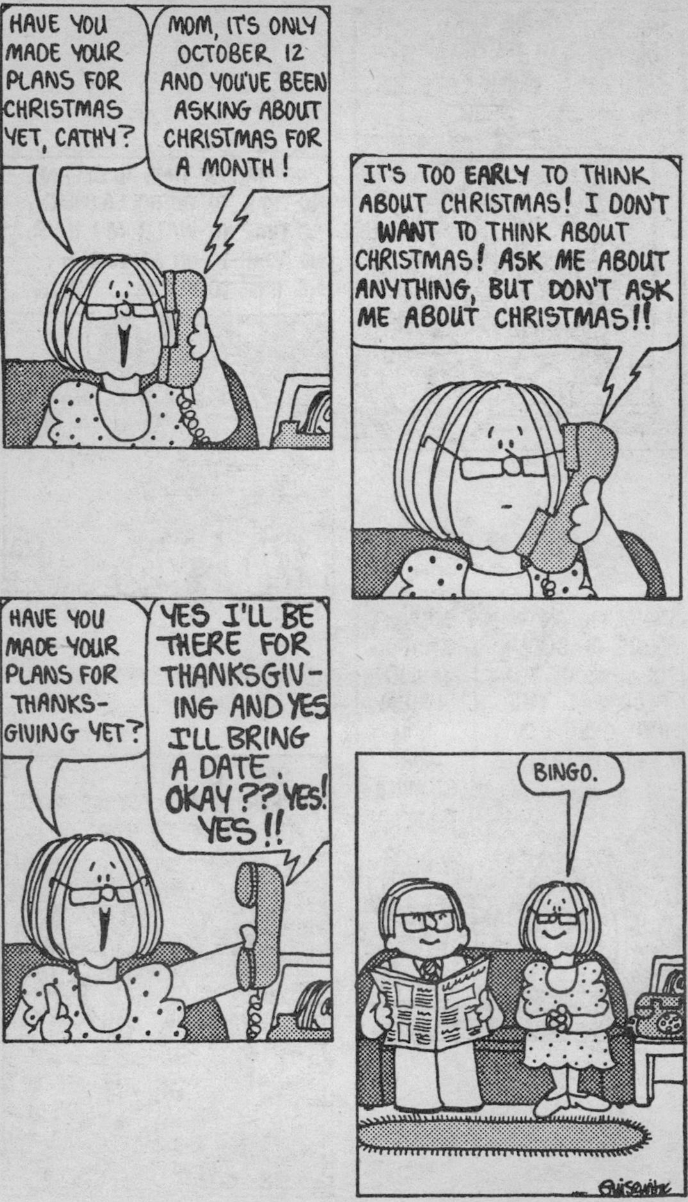
HAVE YOU MADE YOUR PLANS FOR CHRISTMAS YET, CATHY?
MOM, IT'S ONLY OCTOBER 12 AND YOU'VE BEEN ASKING ABOUT CHRISTMAS FOR A MONTH!
IT'S TOO EARLY TO THINK ABOUT CHRISTMAS! I DON'T WANT TO THINK ABOUT CHRISTMAS! ASK ME ABOUT ANYTHING, BUT DON'T ASK ME ABOUT CHRISTMAS!!
HAVE YOU MADE YOUR PLANS FOR THANKS-GIVING YET?
YES I'LL BE THERE FOR THANKSGIV-ING AND YES I'LL BRING A DATE. OKAY?? YES! YES!!
BINGO.

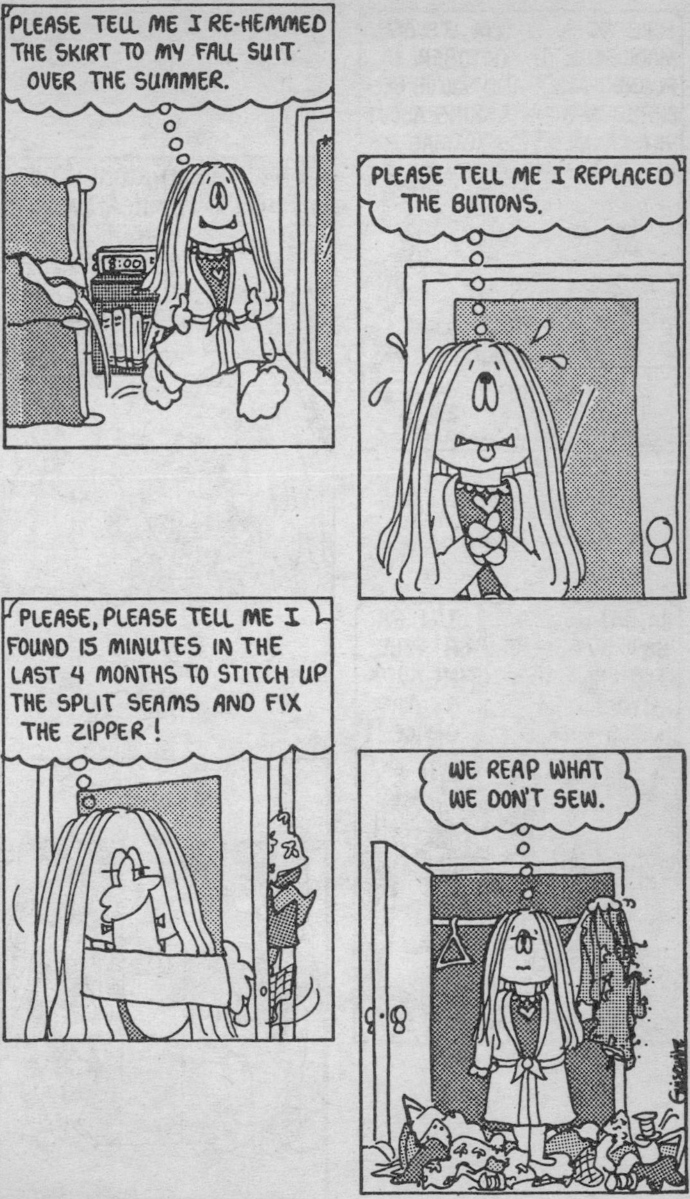
PLEASE TELL ME I RE-HEMMED THE SKIRT TO MY FALL SUIT OVER THE SUMMER.
8:00
PLEASE TELL ME I REPLACED THE BUTTONS.
PLEASE, PLEASE TELL ME I FOUND 15 MINUTES IN THE LAST 4 MONTHS TO STITCH UP THE SPLIT SEAMS AND FIX THE ZIPPER!
WE REAP WHAT WE DON'T SEW.

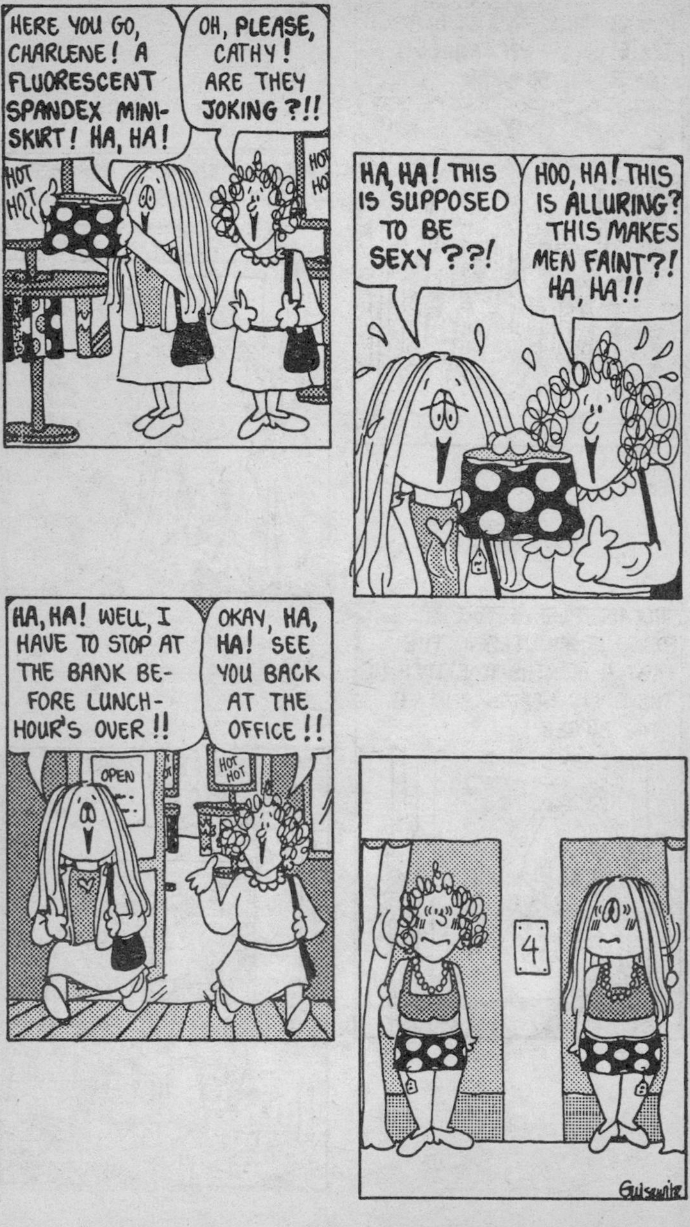
HERE YOU GO, CHARLENE! A FLUORESCENT SPANDEX MINI-SKIRT! HA, HA!
OH, PLEASE, CATHY! ARE THEY JOKING?!!
HA, HA! THIS IS SUPPOSED TO BE SEXY??!
HOO, HA! THIS IS ALLURING? THIS MAKES MEN FAINT?! HA, HA!!
HA, HA! WELL, I HAVE TO STOP AT THE BANK BEFORE LUNCH-HOUR'S OVER!!
OKAY, HA, HA! SEE YOU BACK AT THE OFFICE!!
OPEN
HOT HOT
4
Guisewite

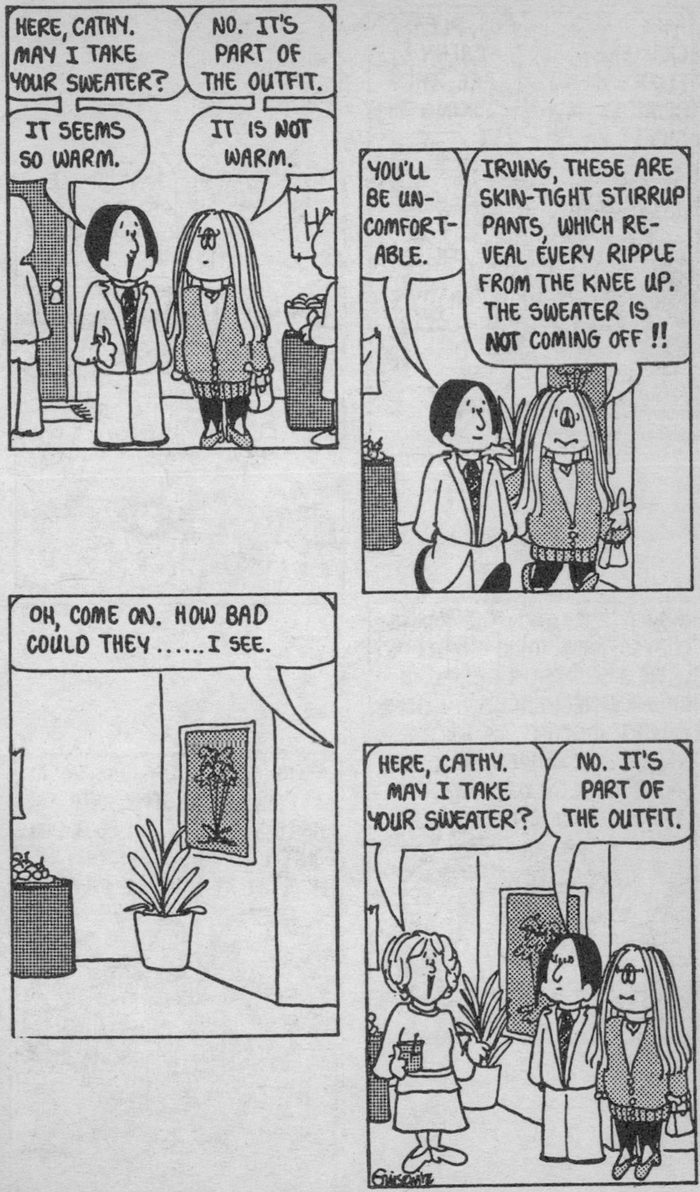

HERE, CATHY. MAY I TAKE YOUR SWEATER?
NO. IT'S PART OF THE OUTFIT.
IT SEEMS SO WARM.
IT IS NOT WARM.
YOU'LL BE UN-COMFORT-ABLE.
IRVING, THESE ARE SKIN-TIGHT STIRRUP PANTS, WHICH RE-VEAL EVERY RIPPLE FROM THE KNEE UP. THE SWEATER IS NOT COMING OFF !!
OH, COME ON. HOW BAD COULD THEY ......I SEE.
HERE, CATHY. MAY I TAKE YOUR SWEATER?
NO. IT'S PART OF THE OUTFIT.

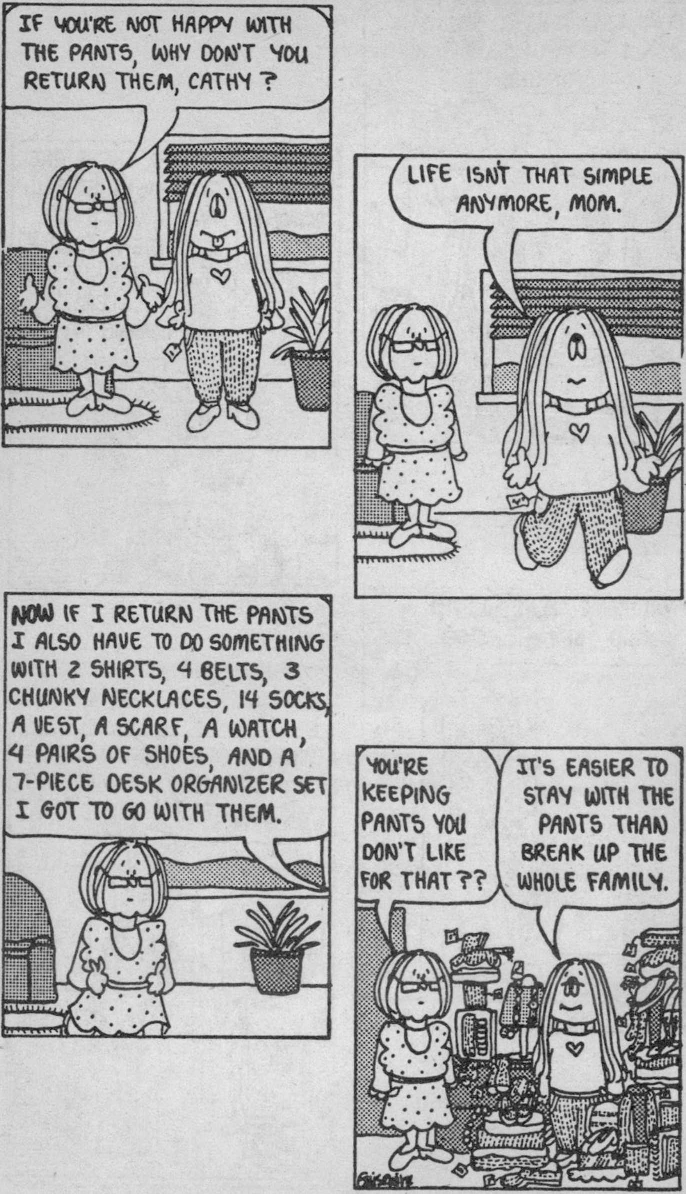
IF YOU'RE NOT HAPPY WITH THE PANTS, WHY DON'T YOU RETURN THEM, CATHY ?
LIFE ISN'T THAT SIMPLE ANYMORE, MOM.
NOW IF I RETURN THE PANTS I ALSO HAVE TO DO SOMETHING WITH 2 SHIRTS, 4 BELTS, 3 CHUNKY NECKLACES, 14 SOCKS, A VEST, A SCARF, A WATCH, 4 PAIRS OF SHOES, AND A 7-PIECE DESK ORGANIZER SET I GOT TO GO WITH THEM.
YOU'RE KEEPING PANTS YOU DON'T LIKE FOR THAT ??
IT'S EASIER TO STAY WITH THE PANTS THAN BREAK UP THE WHOLE FAMILY.

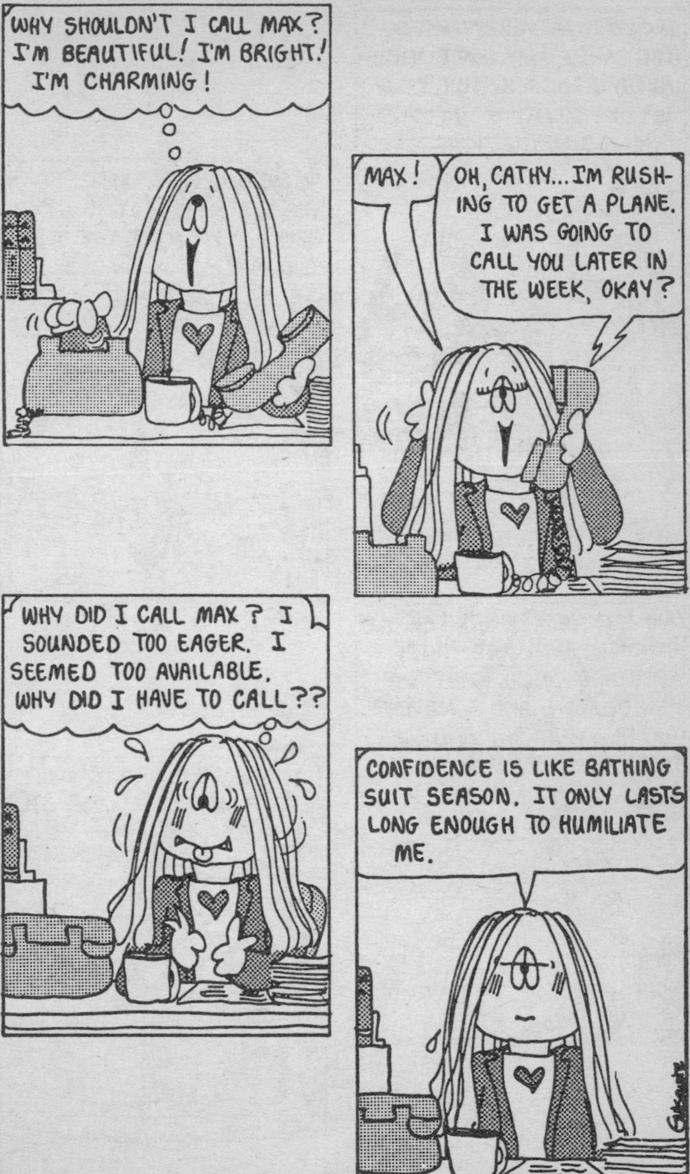
WHY SHOULDN'T I CALL MAX? I'M BEAUTIFUL! I'M BRIGHT! I'M CHARMING!
MAX!
OH, CATHY... I'M RUSHING TO GET A PLANE. I WAS GOING TO CALL YOU LATER IN THE WEEK, OKAY?
WHY DID I CALL MAX? I SOUNDED TOO EAGER. I SEEMED TOO AVAILABLE. WHY DID I HAVE TO CALL??
CONFIDENCE IS LIKE BATHING SUIT SEASON. IT ONLY LASTS LONG ENOUGH TO HUMILIATE ME.
Guisewite

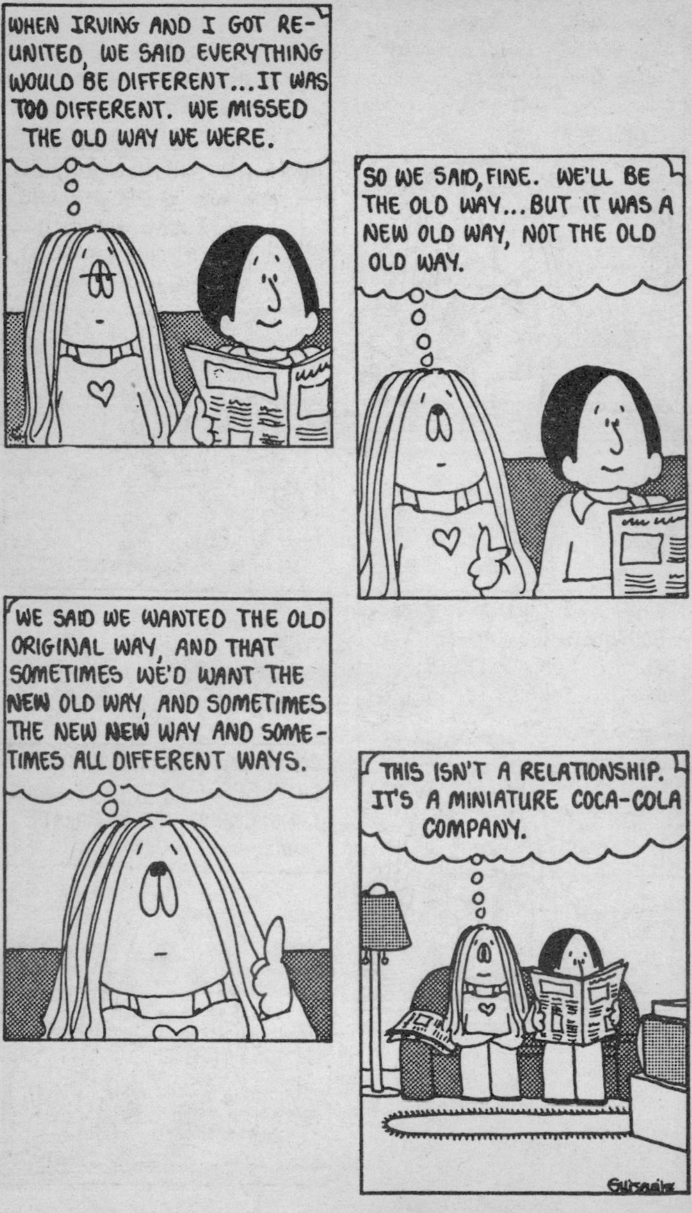
WHEN IRVING AND I GOT RE-UNITED, WE SAID EVERYTHING WOULD BE DIFFERENT... IT WAS TOO DIFFERENT. WE MISSED THE OLD WAY WE WERE.
SO WE SAID, FINE. WE'LL BE THE OLD WAY... BUT IT WAS A NEW OLD WAY, NOT THE OLD OLD WAY.
WE SAID WE WANTED THE OLD ORIGINAL WAY, AND THAT SOMETIMES WE'D WANT THE NEW OLD WAY, AND SOMETIMES THE NEW NEW WAY AND SOME-TIMES ALL DIFFERENT WAYS.
THIS ISN'T A RELATIONSHIP. IT'S A MINIATURE COCA-COLA COMPANY.

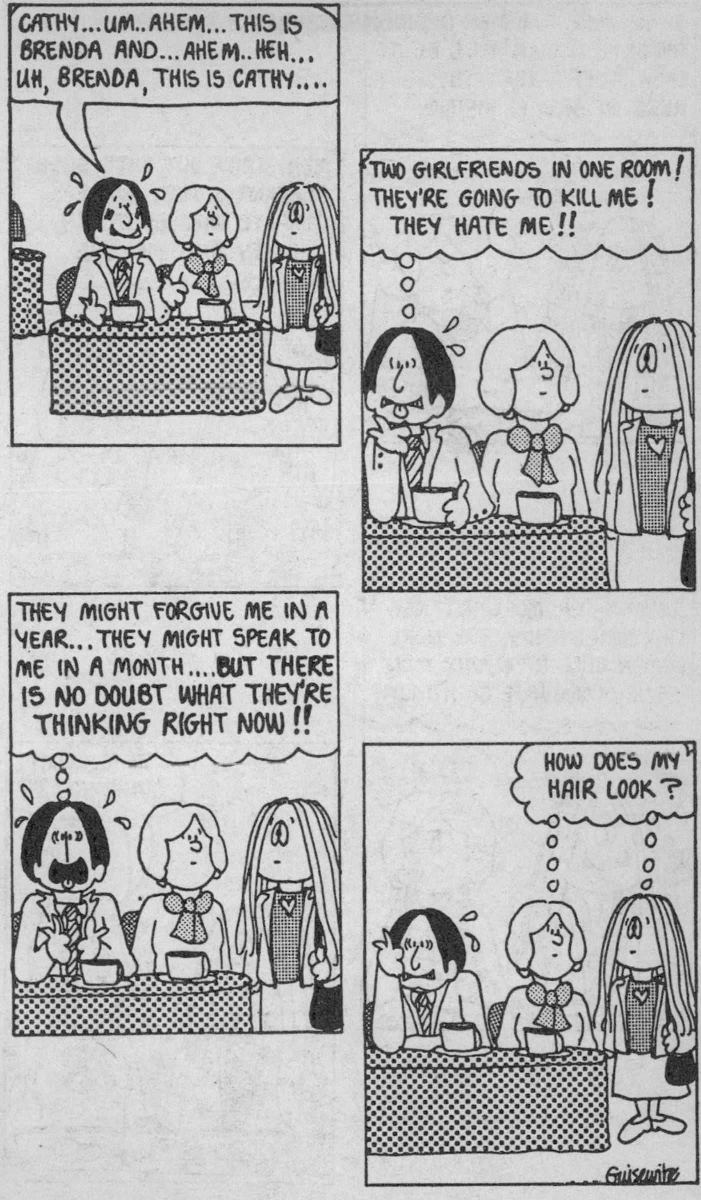
CATHY...UM..AHEM... THIS IS BRENDA AND...AHEM..HEH... UH, BRENDA, THIS IS CATHY....
TWO GIRLFRIENDS IN ONE ROOM! THEY'RE GOING TO KILL ME! THEY HATE ME!!
THEY MIGHT FORGIVE ME IN A YEAR... THEY MIGHT SPEAK TO ME IN A MONTH....BUT THERE IS NO DOUBT WHAT THEY'RE THINKING RIGHT NOW!!
HOW DOES MY HAIR LOOK?
Guisewite

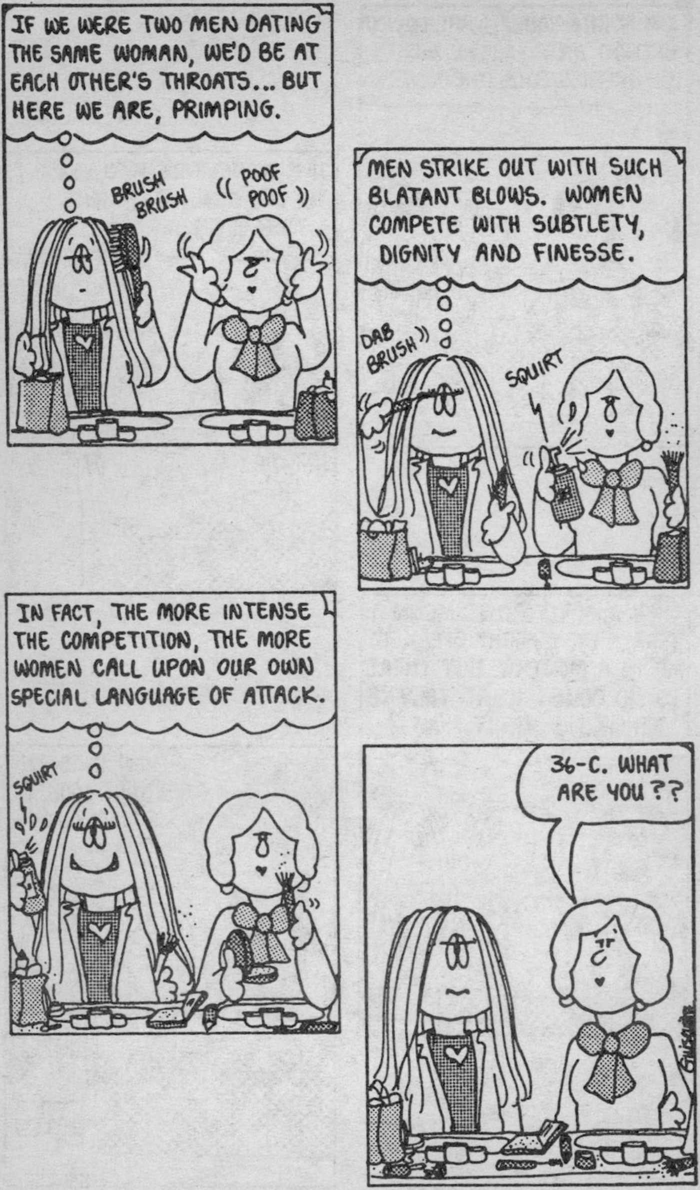
IF WE WERE TWO MEN DATING THE SAME WOMAN, WE'D BE AT EACH OTHER'S THROATS... BUT HERE WE ARE, PRIMPING.
BRUSH BRUSH
POOF POOF
MEN STRIKE OUT WITH SUCH BLATANT BLOWS. WOMEN COMPETE WITH SUBTLETY, DIGNITY AND FINESSE.
DAB BRUSH
SQUIRT
IN FACT, THE MORE INTENSE THE COMPETITION, THE MORE WOMEN CALL UPON OUR OWN SPECIAL LANGUAGE OF ATTACK.
SQUIRT
36-C. WHAT ARE YOU??

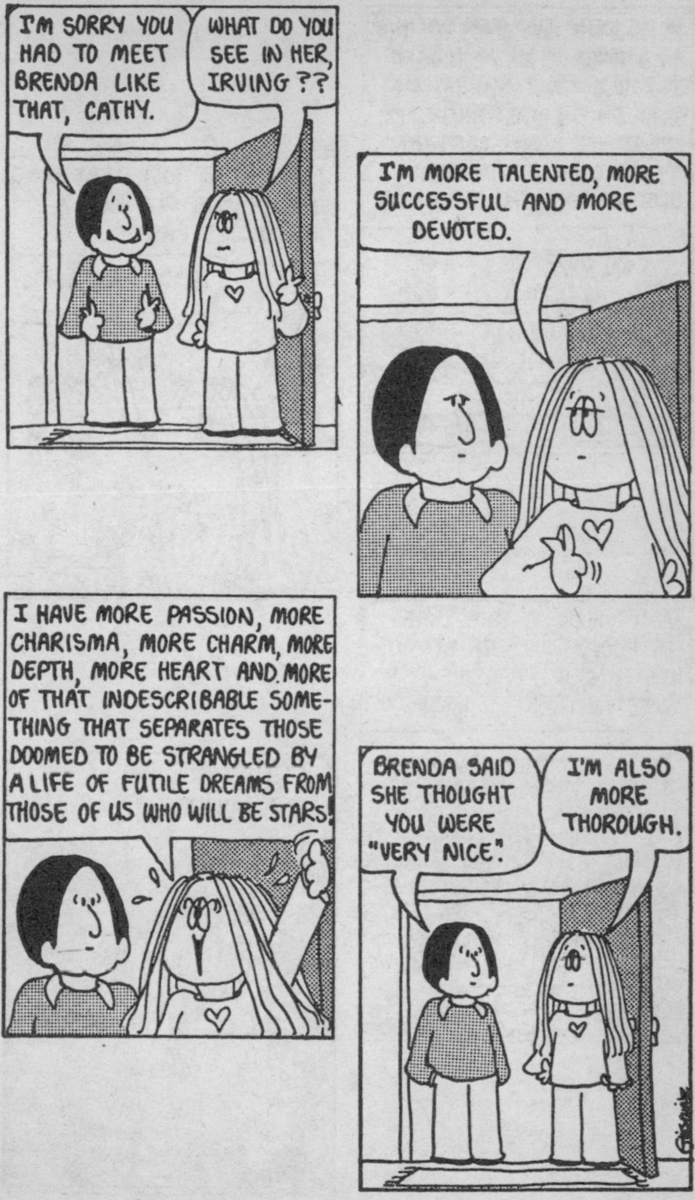
I'M SORRY YOU HAD TO MEET BRENDA LIKE THAT, CATHY.
WHAT DO YOU SEE IN HER, IRVING??
I'M MORE TALENTED, MORE SUCCESSFUL AND MORE DEVOTED.
I HAVE MORE PASSION, MORE CHARISMA, MORE CHARM, MORE DEPTH, MORE HEART AND MORE OF THAT INDESCRIBABLE SOMETHING THAT SEPARATES THOSE DOOMED TO BE STRANGLED BY A LIFE OF FUTILE DREAMS FROM THOSE OF US WHO WILL BE STARS!
BRENDA SAID SHE THOUGHT YOU WERE "VERY NICE."
I'M ALSO MORE THOROUGH.

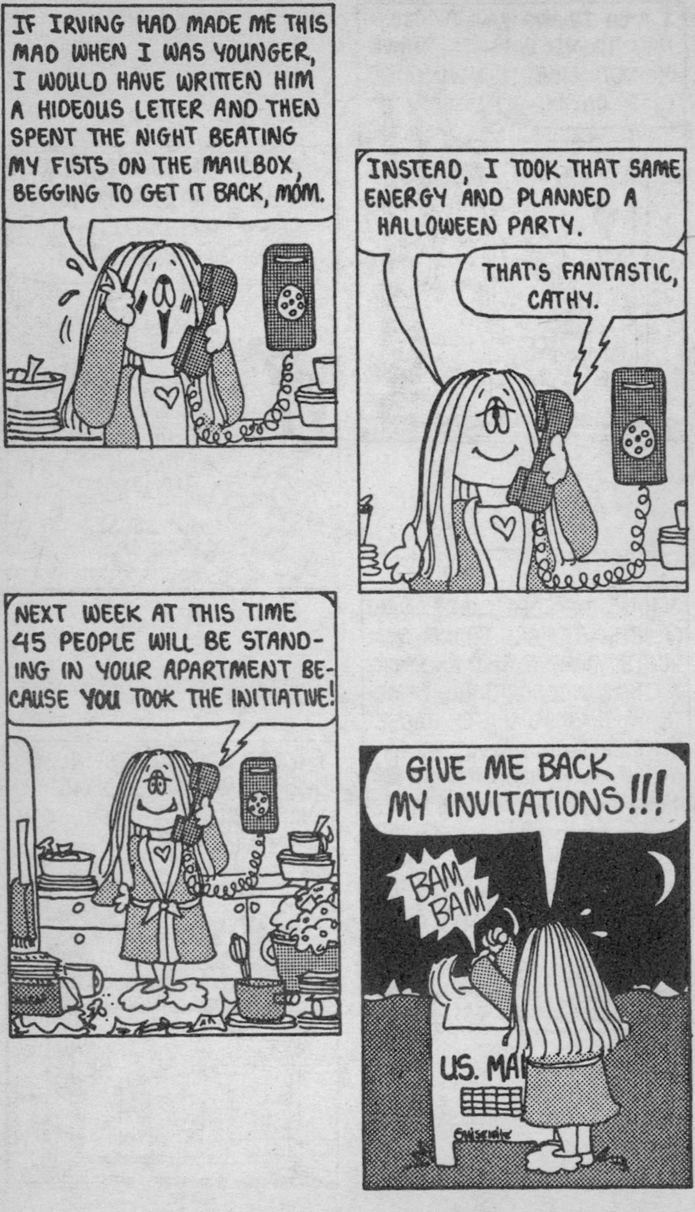
IF IRVING HAD MADE ME THIS MAD WHEN I WAS YOUNGER, I WOULD HAVE WRITTEN HIM A HIDEOUS LETTER AND THEN SPENT THE NIGHT BEATING MY FISTS ON THE MAILBOX, BEGGING TO GET IT BACK, MOM.
INSTEAD, I TOOK THAT SAME ENERGY AND PLANNED A HALLOWEEN PARTY.
THAT'S FANTASTIC, CATHY.
NEXT WEEK AT THIS TIME 45 PEOPLE WILL BE STANDING IN YOUR APARTMENT BECAUSE YOU TOOK THE INITIATIVE!
GIVE ME BACK MY INVITATIONS!!!
BAM BAM
US. MA

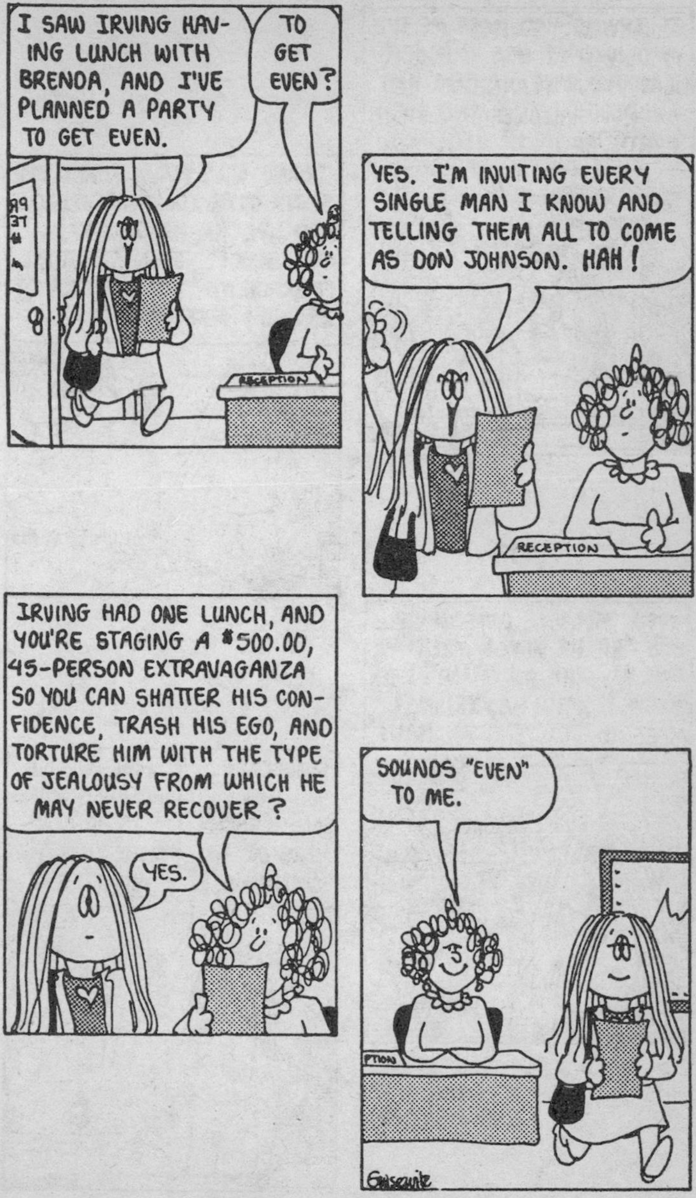
I SAW IRVING HAVING LUNCH WITH BRENDA, AND I'VE PLANNED A PARTY TO GET EVEN.
TO GET EVEN?
YES. I'M INVITING EVERY SINGLE MAN I KNOW AND TELLING THEM ALL TO COME AS DON JOHNSON. HAH!
RECEPTION
IRVING HAD ONE LUNCH, AND YOU'RE STAGING A $500.00, 45-PERSON EXTRAVAGANZA SO YOU CAN SHATTER HIS CONFIDENCE, TRASH HIS EGO, AND TORTURE HIM WITH THE TYPE OF JEALOUSY FROM WHICH HE MAY NEVER RECOVER?
YES.
SOUNDS "EVEN" TO ME.
Guisewite

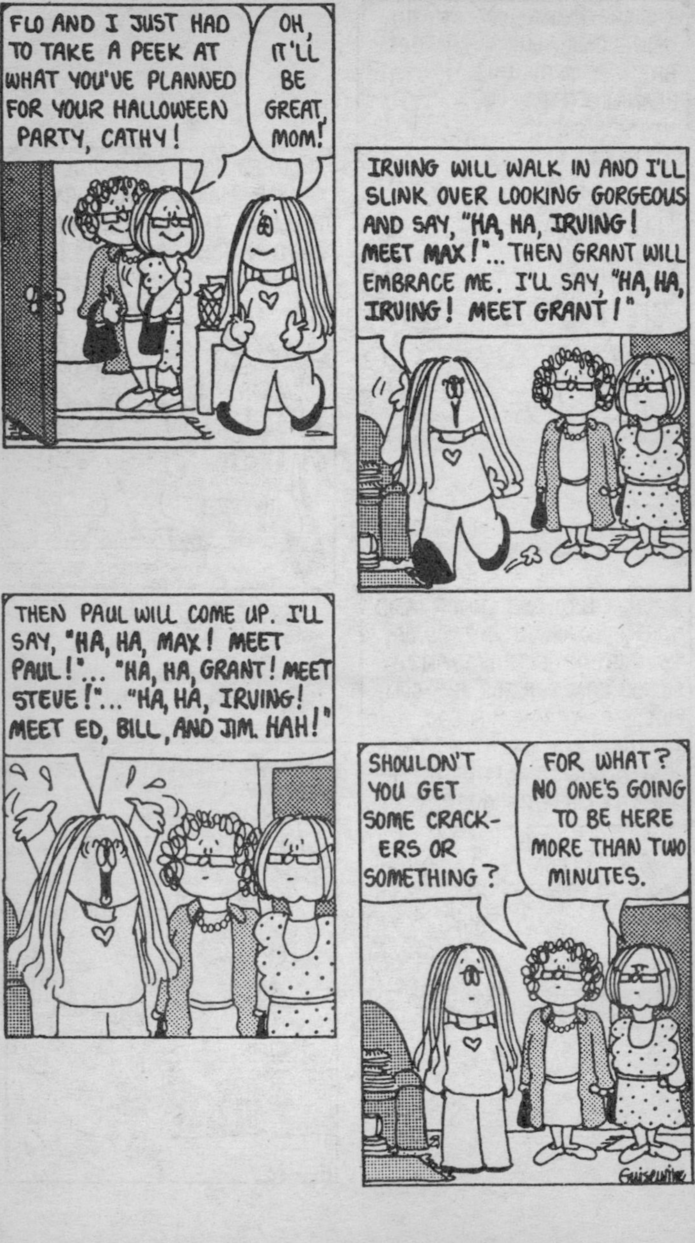
FLO AND I JUST HAD TO TAKE A PEEK AT WHAT YOU'VE PLANNED FOR YOUR HALLOWEEN PARTY, CATHY!
OH, IT'LL BE GREAT, MOM!
IRVING WILL WALK IN AND I'LL SLINK OVER LOOKING GORGEOUS AND SAY, "HA, HA, IRVING! MEET MAX!"... THEN GRANT WILL EMBRACE ME. I'LL SAY, "HA, HA, IRVING! MEET GRANT!"
THEN PAUL WILL COME UP. I'LL SAY, "HA, HA, MAX! MEET PAUL!"... "HA, HA, GRANT! MEET STEVE!"... "HA, HA, IRVING! MEET ED, BILL, AND JIM. HAH!"
SHOULDN'T YOU GET SOME CRACKERS OR SOMETHING?
FOR WHAT? NO ONE'S GOING TO BE HERE MORE THAN TWO MINUTES.
Guisewite

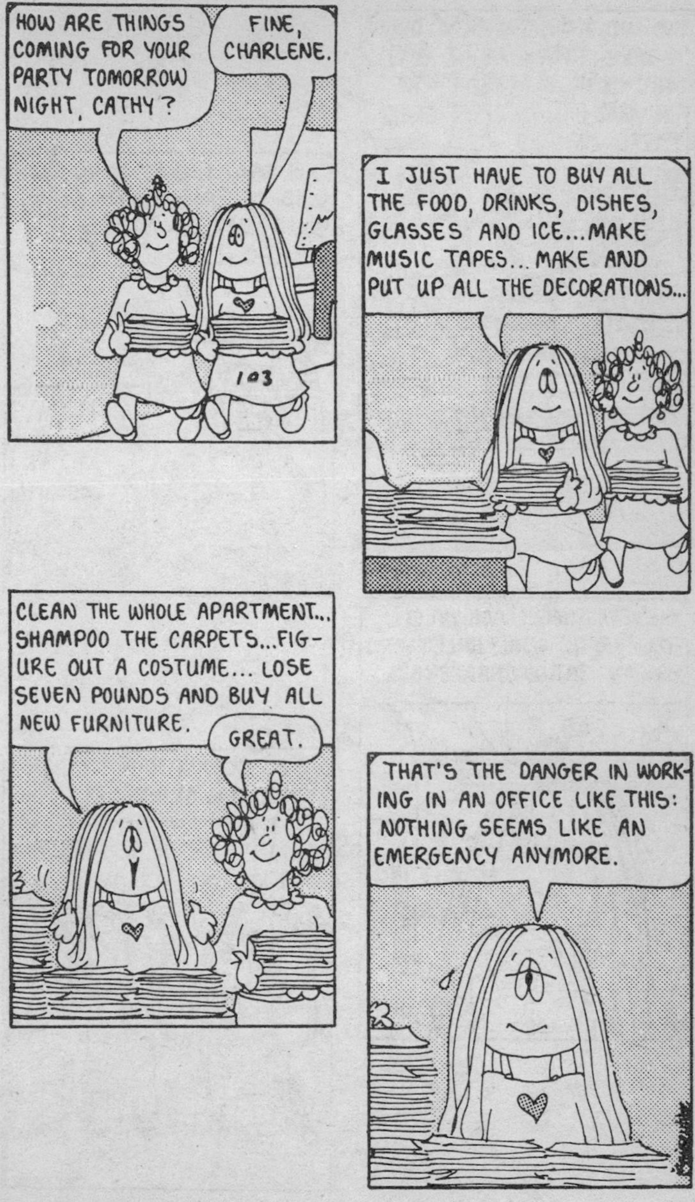
HOW ARE THINGS COMING FOR YOUR PARTY TOMORROW NIGHT, CATHY?
FINE, CHARLENE.
I JUST HAVE TO BUY ALL THE FOOD, DRINKS, DISHES, GLASSES AND ICE...MAKE MUSIC TAPES... MAKE AND PUT UP ALL THE DECORATIONS...
CLEAN THE WHOLE APARTMENT... SHAMPOO THE CARPETS...FIG-URE OUT A COSTUME... LOSE SEVEN POUNDS AND BUY ALL NEW FURNITURE.
GREAT.
THAT'S THE DANGER IN WORK-ING IN AN OFFICE LIKE THIS: NOTHING SEEMS LIKE AN EMERGENCY ANYMORE.

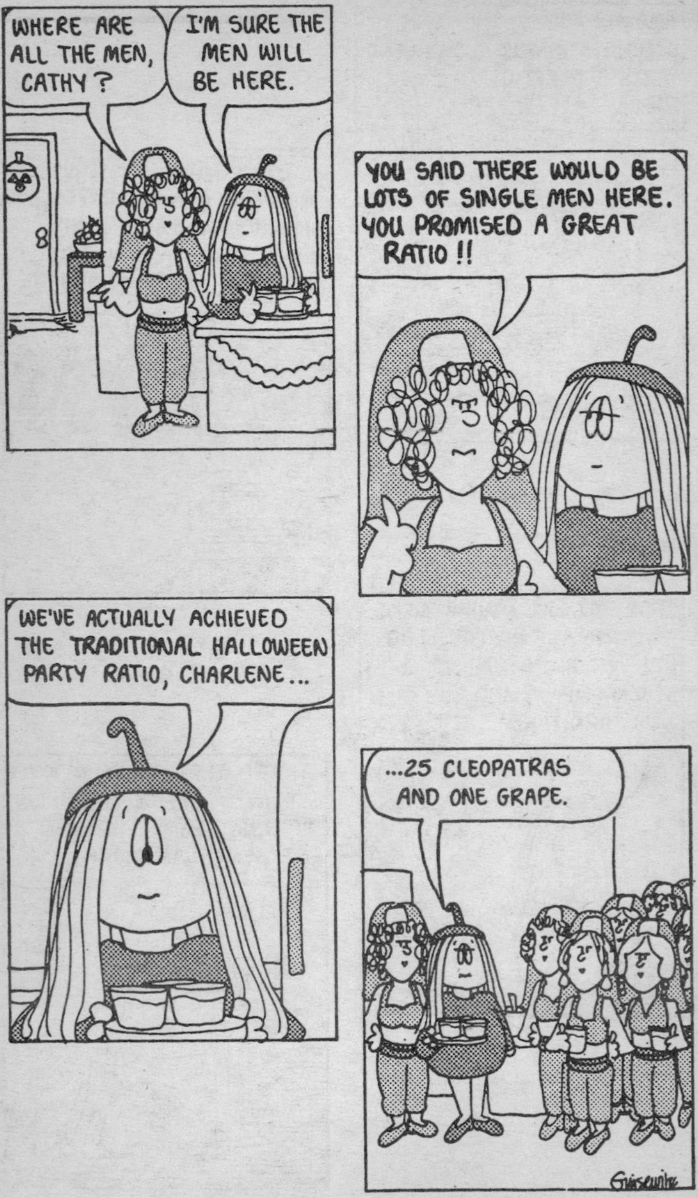
WHERE ARE ALL THE MEN, CATHY?
I'M SURE THE MEN WILL BE HERE.
8
YOU SAID THERE WOULD BE LOTS OF SINGLE MEN HERE. YOU PROMISED A GREAT RATIO!!
WE'VE ACTUALLY ACHIEVED THE TRADITIONAL HALLOWEEN PARTY RATIO, CHARLENE...
...25 CLEOPATRAS AND ONE GRAPE.
Guisewite

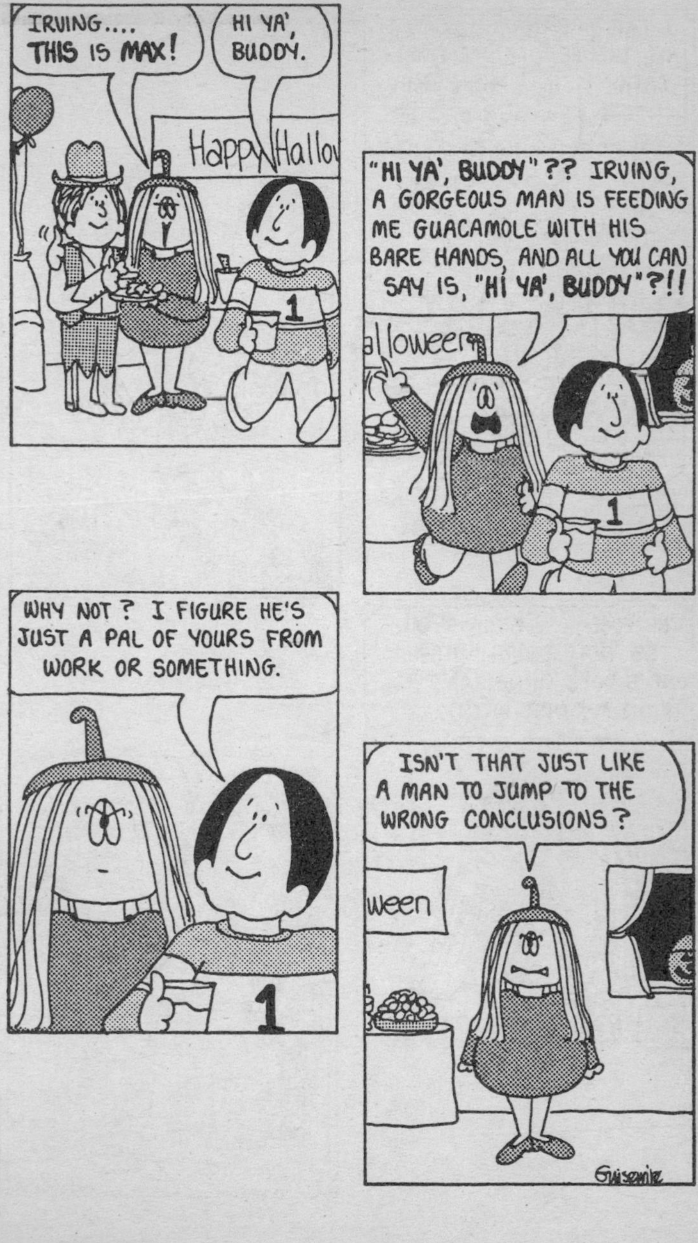
IRVING.... THIS IS MAX!
HI YA', BUDDY.
Happy Hallo
"HI YA', BUDDY"?? IRVING, A GORGEOUS MAN IS FEEDING ME GUACAMOLE WITH HIS BARE HANDS, AND ALL YOU CAN SAY IS, "HI YA', BUDDY"?!!
alloween
WHY NOT? I FIGURE HE'S JUST A PAL OF YOURS FROM WORK OR SOMETHING.
ISN'T THAT JUST LIKE A MAN TO JUMP TO THE WRONG CONCLUSIONS?
ween
Guisewite

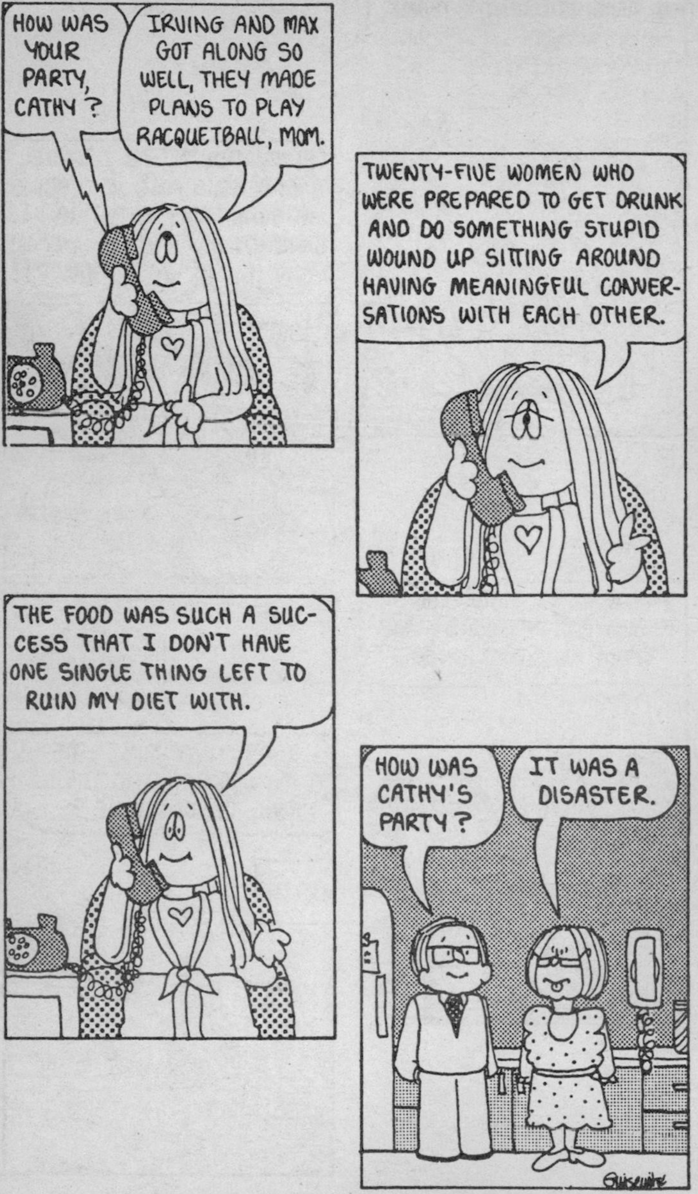
HOW WAS YOUR PARTY, CATHY?
IRVING AND MAX GOT ALONG SO WELL, THEY MADE PLANS TO PLAY RACQUETBALL, MOM.
TWENTY-FIVE WOMEN WHO WERE PREPARED TO GET DRUNK AND DO SOMETHING STUPID WOUND UP SITTING AROUND HAVING MEANINGFUL CONVER-SATIONS WITH EACH OTHER.
THE FOOD WAS SUCH A SUC-CESS THAT I DON'T HAVE ONE SINGLE THING LEFT TO RUIN MY DIET WITH.
HOW WAS CATHY'S PARTY?
IT WAS A DISASTER.

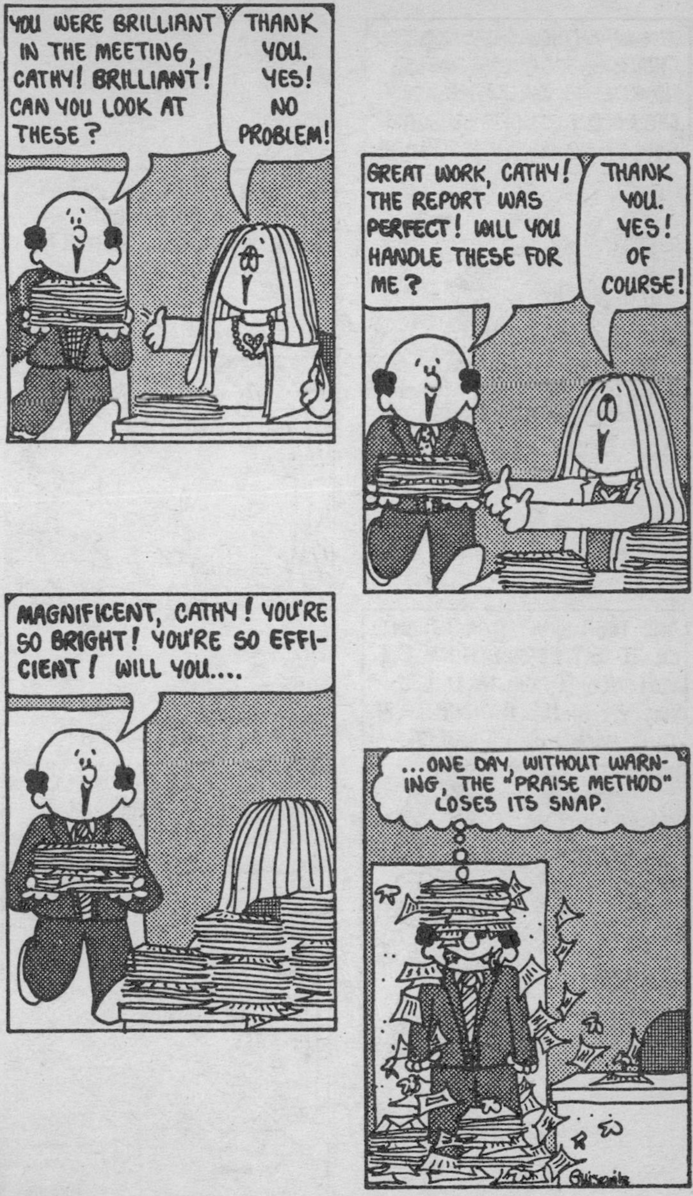
YOU WERE BRILLIANT IN THE MEETING, CATHY! BRILLIANT! CAN YOU LOOK AT THESE?
THANK YOU. YES! NO PROBLEM!
GREAT WORK, CATHY! THE REPORT WAS PERFECT! WILL YOU HANDLE THESE FOR ME?
THANK YOU. YES! OF COURSE!
MAGNIFICENT, CATHY! YOU'RE SO BRIGHT! YOU'RE SO EFFICIENT! WILL YOU....
...ONE DAY, WITHOUT WARNING, THE "PRAISE METHOD" LOSES ITS SNAP.
Guisewite

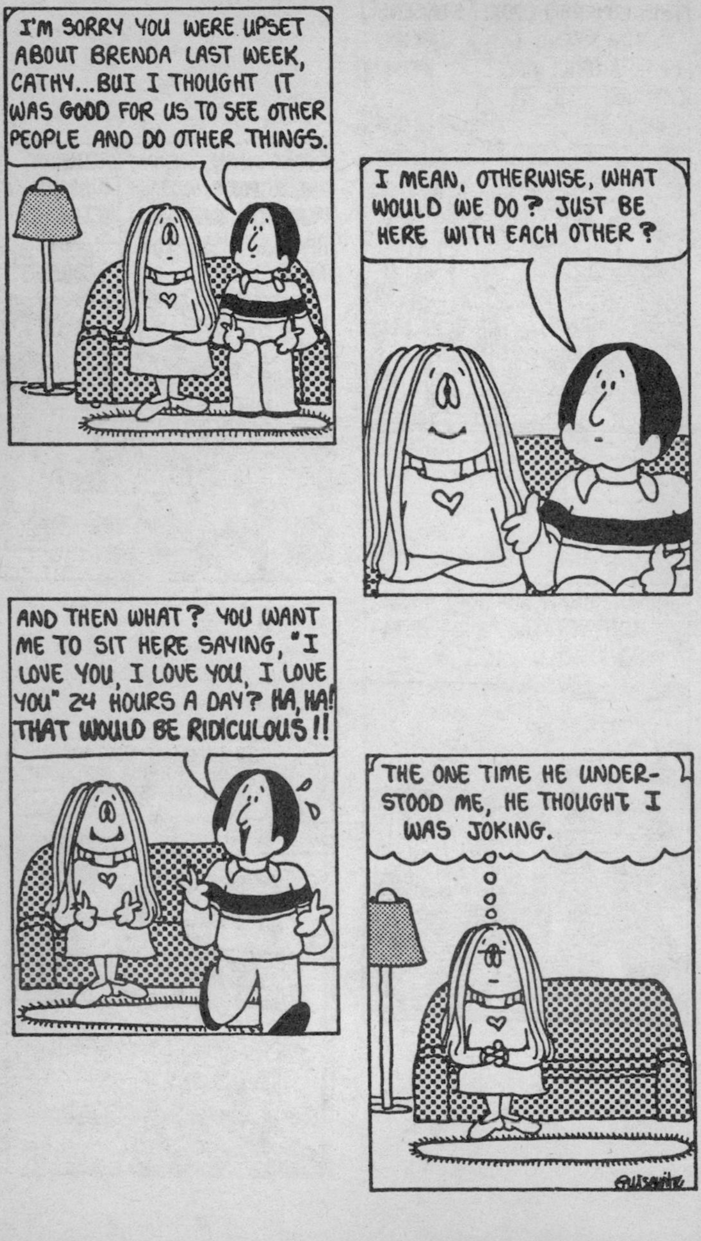
I'M SORRY YOU WERE UPSET ABOUT BRENDA LAST WEEK, CATHY...BUT I THOUGHT IT WAS GOOD FOR US TO SEE OTHER PEOPLE AND DO OTHER THINGS.
I MEAN, OTHERWISE, WHAT WOULD WE DO? JUST BE HERE WITH EACH OTHER?
AND THEN WHAT? YOU WANT ME TO SIT HERE SAYING, "I LOVE YOU, I LOVE YOU, I LOVE YOU" 24 HOURS A DAY? HA, HA! THAT WOULD BE RIDICULOUS!!
THE ONE TIME HE UNDER-STOOD ME, HE THOUGHT I WAS JOKING.

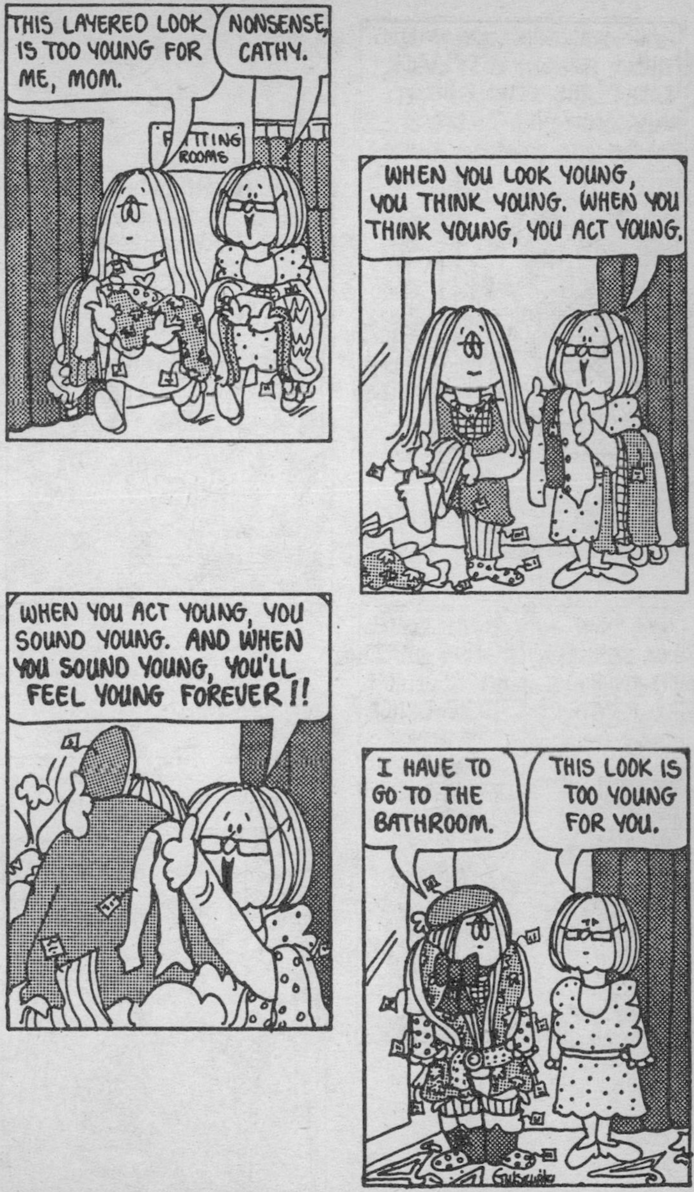
THIS LAYERED LOOK IS TOO YOUNG FOR ME, MOM.
NONSENSE, CATHY.
FITTING ROOMS
WHEN YOU LOOK YOUNG, YOU THINK YOUNG. WHEN YOU THINK YOUNG, YOU ACT YOUNG.
WHEN YOU ACT YOUNG, YOU SOUND YOUNG. AND WHEN YOU SOUND YOUNG, YOU'LL FEEL YOUNG FOREVER!!
I HAVE TO GO TO THE BATHROOM.
THIS LOOK IS TOO YOUNG FOR YOU.

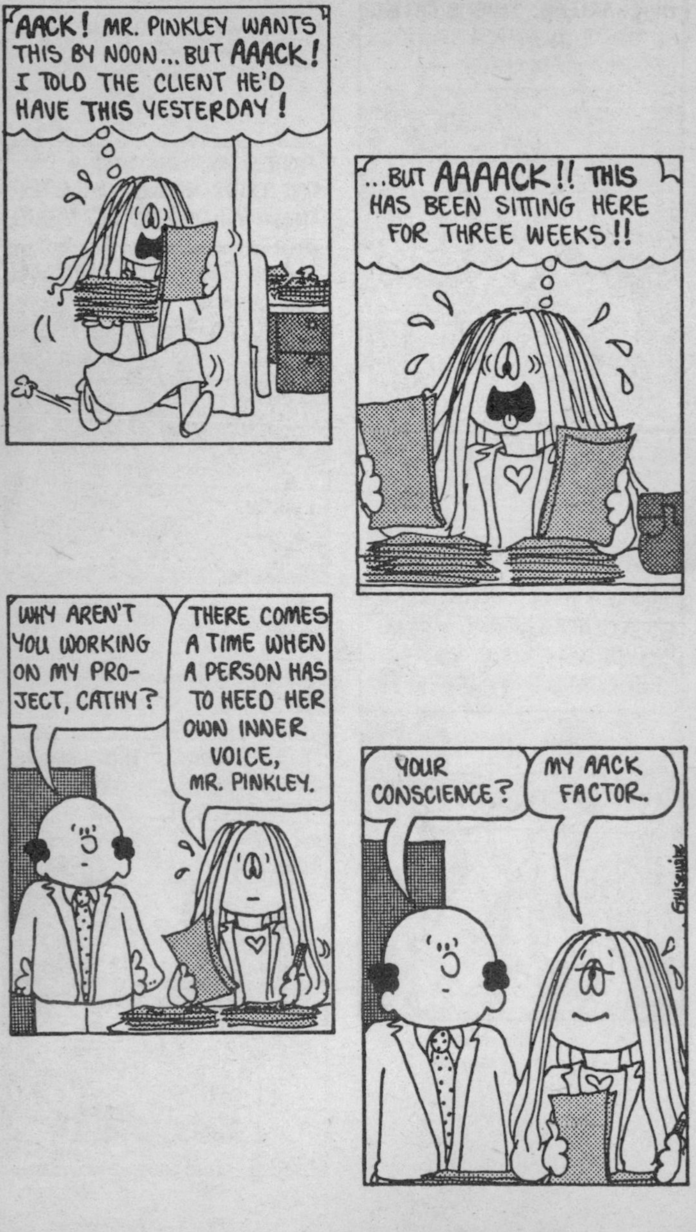
AACK! MR. PINKLEY WANTS THIS BY NOON... BUT AAACK! I TOLD THE CLIENT HE'D HAVE THIS YESTERDAY!
...BUT AAAACK!! THIS HAS BEEN SITTING HERE FOR THREE WEEKS!!
WHY AREN'T YOU WORKING ON MY PROJECT, CATHY?
THERE COMES A TIME WHEN A PERSON HAS TO HEED HER OWN INNER VOICE, MR. PINKLEY.
YOUR CONSCIENCE?
MY AACK FACTOR.

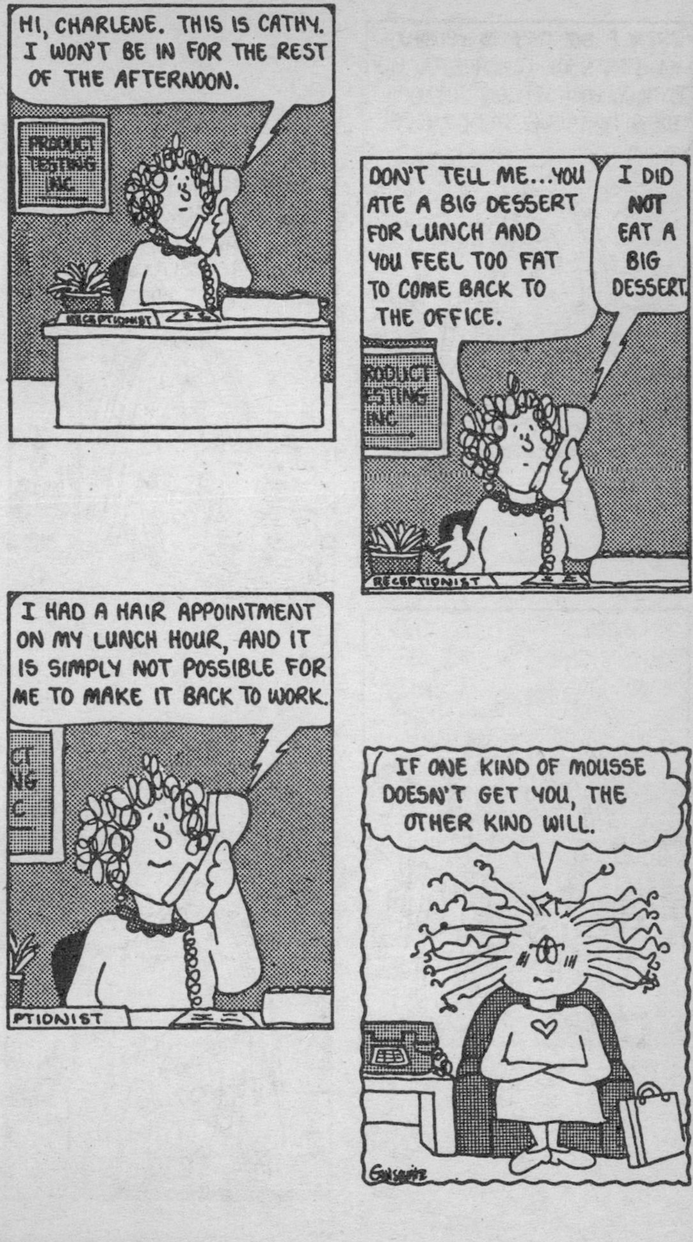
HI, CHARLENE. THIS IS CATHY. I WON'T BE IN FOR THE REST OF THE AFTERNOON.
PRODUCT TESTING INC.
RECEPTIONIST
DON'T TELL ME...YOU ATE A BIG DESSERT FOR LUNCH AND YOU FEEL TOO FAT TO COME BACK TO THE OFFICE.
I DID NOT EAT A BIG DESSERT.
I HAD A HAIR APPOINTMENT ON MY LUNCH HOUR, AND IT IS SIMPLY NOT POSSIBLE FOR ME TO MAKE IT BACK TO WORK.
IF ONE KIND OF MOUSSE DOESN'T GET YOU, THE OTHER KIND WILL.
Guisewite

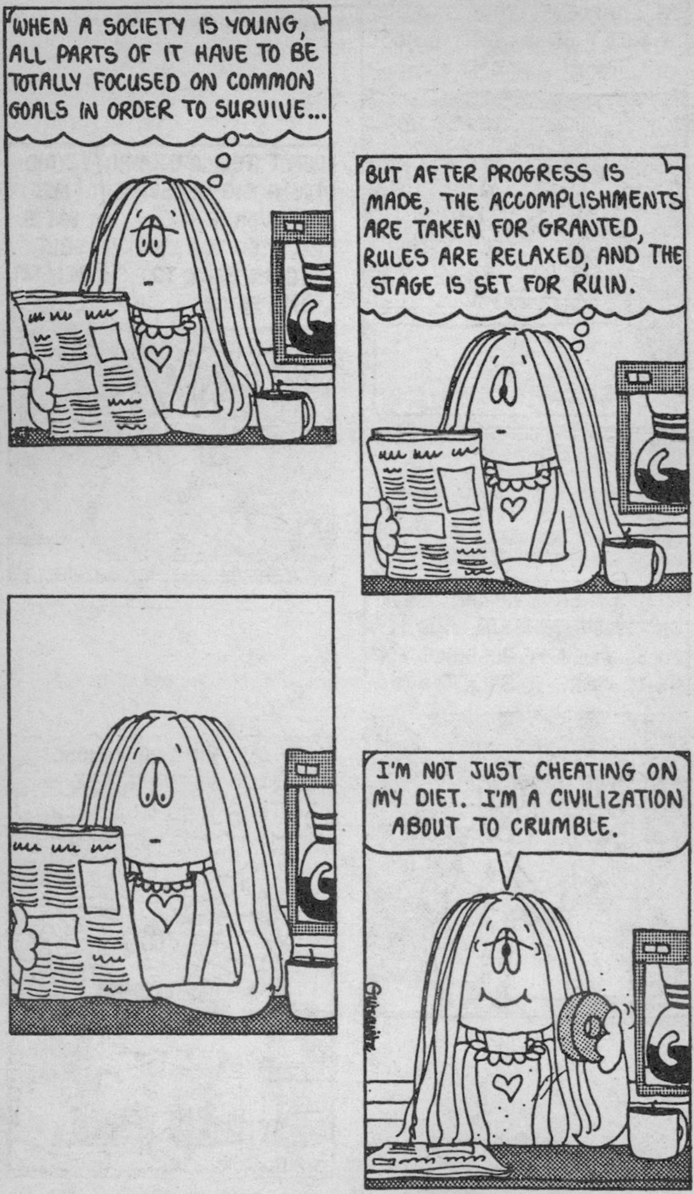
WHEN A SOCIETY IS YOUNG, ALL PARTS OF IT HAVE TO BE TOTALLY FOCUSED ON COMMON GOALS IN ORDER TO SURVIVE...
BUT AFTER PROGRESS IS MADE, THE ACCOMPLISHMENTS ARE TAKEN FOR GRANTED, RULES ARE RELAXED, AND THE STAGE IS SET FOR RUIN.
I'M NOT JUST CHEATING ON MY DIET. I'M A CIVILIZATION ABOUT TO CRUMBLE.
Guisewite

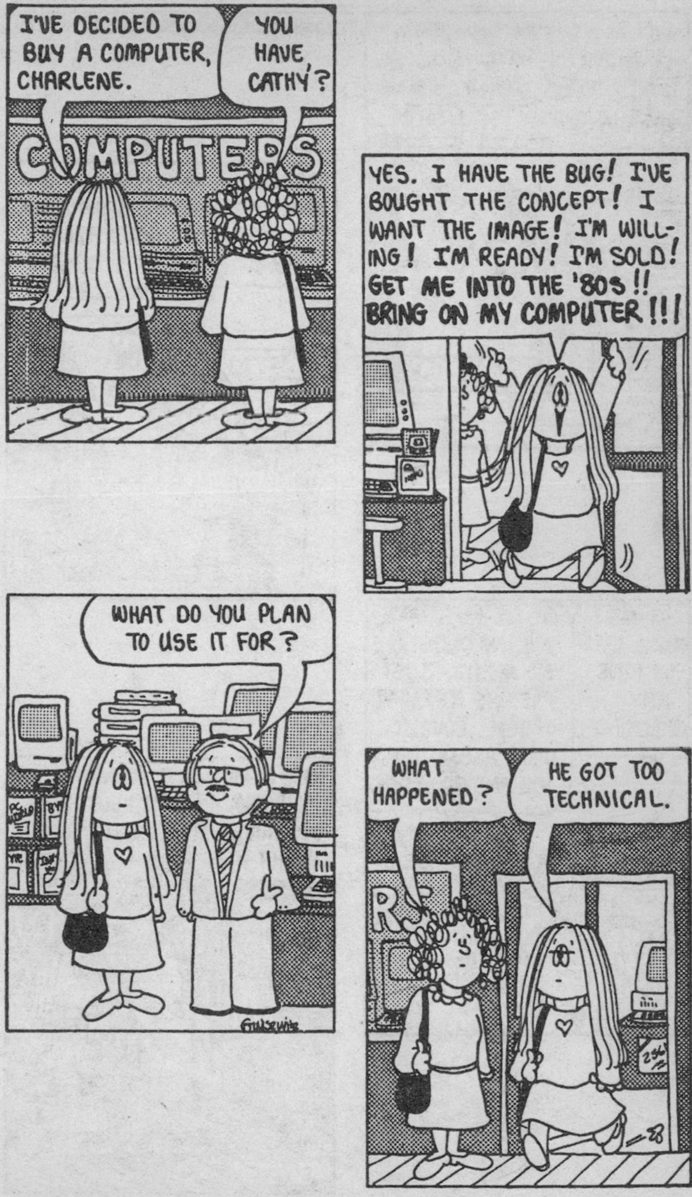
I'VE DECIDED TO BUY A COMPUTER, CHARLENE.
YOU HAVE, CATHY?
COMPUTERS
YES. I HAVE THE BUG! I'VE BOUGHT THE CONCEPT! I WANT THE IMAGE! I'M WILLING! I'M READY! I'M SOLD! GET ME INTO THE '80s!! BRING ON MY COMPUTER!!!
WHAT DO YOU PLAN TO USE IT FOR?
WHAT HAPPENED?
HE GOT TOO TECHNICAL.

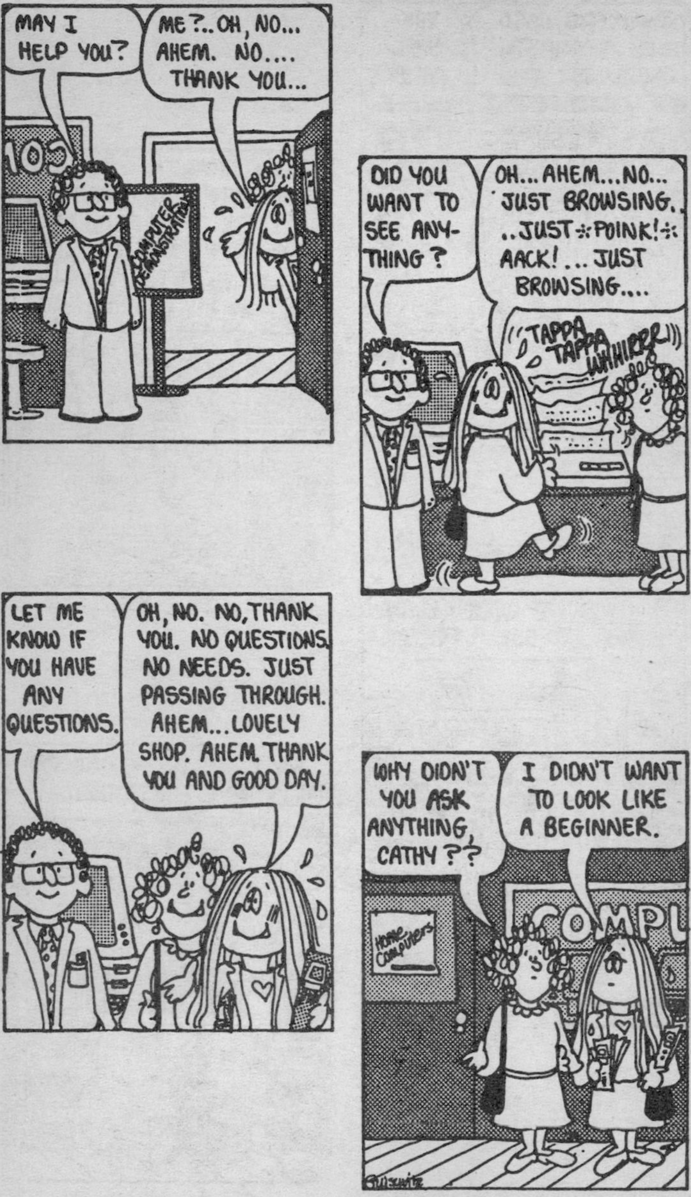
MAY I HELP YOU?
ME?.. OH, NO... AHEM. NO.... THANK YOU...
COMPUTER DEMONSTRATION
DID YOU WANT TO SEE ANY-THING?
OH... AHEM... NO... JUST BROWSING... JUST ✲POINK!✲ AACK! ... JUST BROWSING....
TAPPA TAPPA
LET ME KNOW IF YOU HAVE ANY QUESTIONS.
OH, NO. NO, THANK YOU. NO QUESTIONS. NO NEEDS. JUST PASSING THROUGH. AHEM... LOVELY SHOP. AHEM. THANK YOU AND GOOD DAY.
WHY DIDN'T YOU ASK ANYTHING, CATHY??
I DIDN'T WANT TO LOOK LIKE A BEGINNER.
Home Computers
COMPU

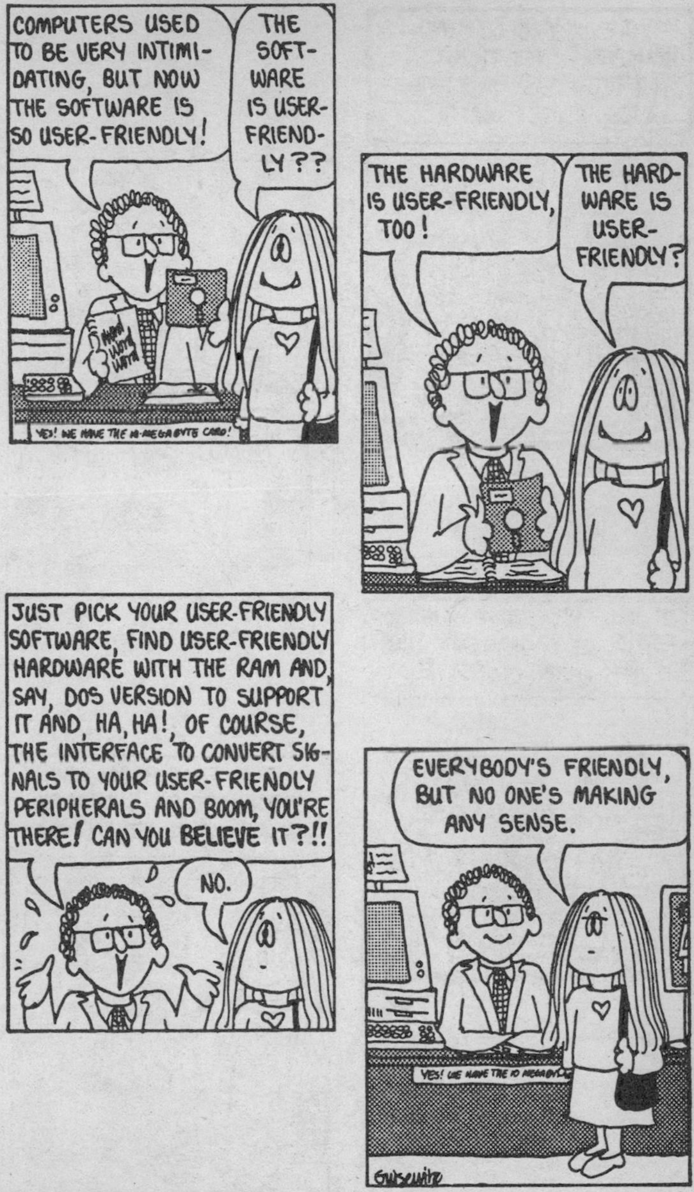
COMPUTERS USED TO BE VERY INTIMIDATING, BUT NOW THE SOFTWARE IS SO USER-FRIENDLY!
THE SOFTWARE IS USER-FRIENDLY??
YES! WE HAVE THE 10-MEGABYTE CARD!
THE HARDWARE IS USER-FRIENDLY, TOO!
THE HARDWARE IS USER-FRIENDLY?
JUST PICK YOUR USER-FRIENDLY SOFTWARE, FIND USER-FRIENDLY HARDWARE WITH THE RAM AND, SAY, DOS VERSION TO SUPPORT IT AND, HA, HA!, OF COURSE, THE INTERFACE TO CONVERT SIGNALS TO YOUR USER-FRIENDLY PERIPHERALS AND BOOM, YOU'RE THERE! CAN YOU BELIEVE IT?!!
NO.
EVERYBODY'S FRIENDLY, BUT NO ONE'S MAKING ANY SENSE.
GUISEWITE

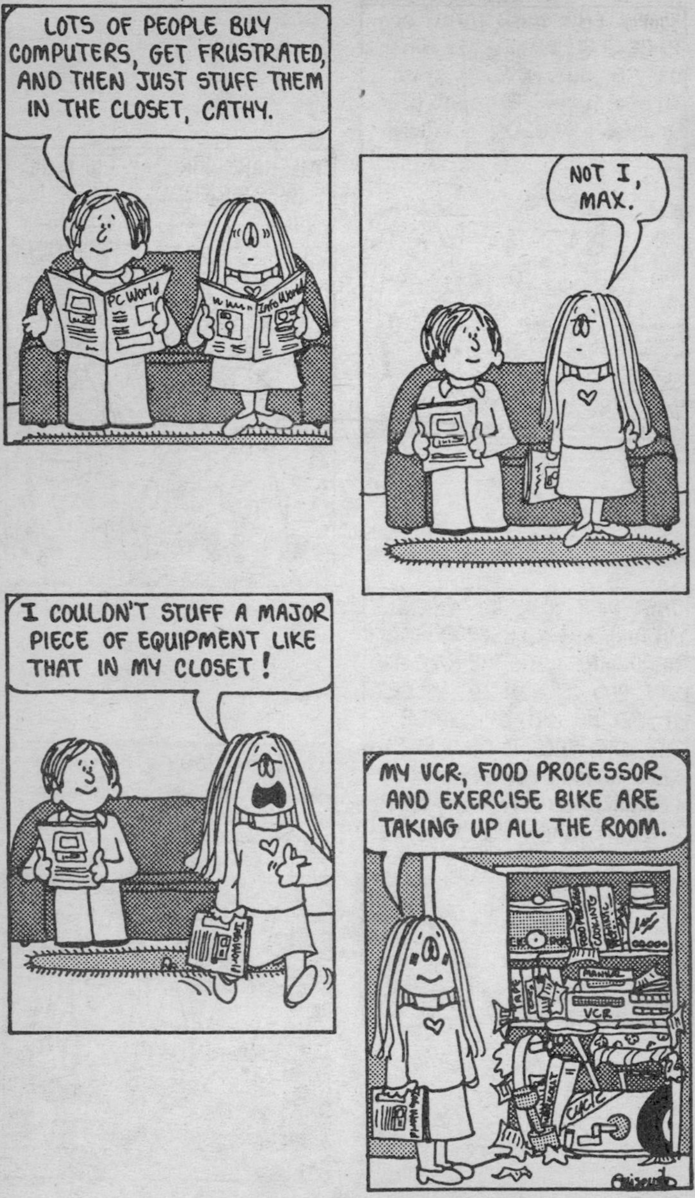
LOTS OF PEOPLE BUY COMPUTERS, GET FRUSTRATED, AND THEN JUST STUFF THEM IN THE CLOSET, CATHY.
PC World
Info World
NOT I, MAX.
I COULDN'T STUFF A MAJOR PIECE OF EQUIPMENT LIKE THAT IN MY CLOSET!
MY VCR, FOOD PROCESSOR AND EXERCISE BIKE ARE TAKING UP ALL THE ROOM.
MANUAL
VCR

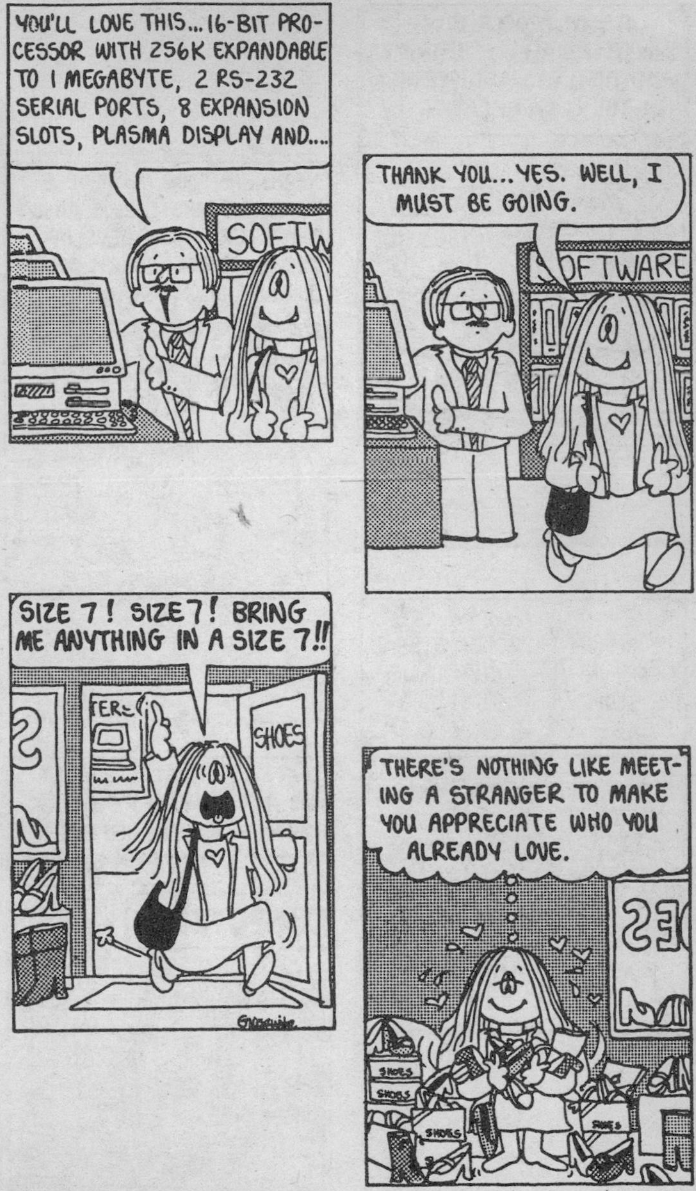
YOU'LL LOVE THIS... 16-BIT PROCESSOR WITH 256K EXPANDABLE TO 1 MEGABYTE, 2 RS-232 SERIAL PORTS, 8 EXPANSION SLOTS, PLASMA DISPLAY AND....
SOFTW
THANK YOU... YES. WELL, I MUST BE GOING.
SOFTWARE
SIZE 7! SIZE 7! BRING ME ANYTHING IN A SIZE 7!!
SHOES
THERE'S NOTHING LIKE MEETING A STRANGER TO MAKE YOU APPRECIATE WHO YOU ALREADY LOVE.
SHOES
SHOES
SHOES

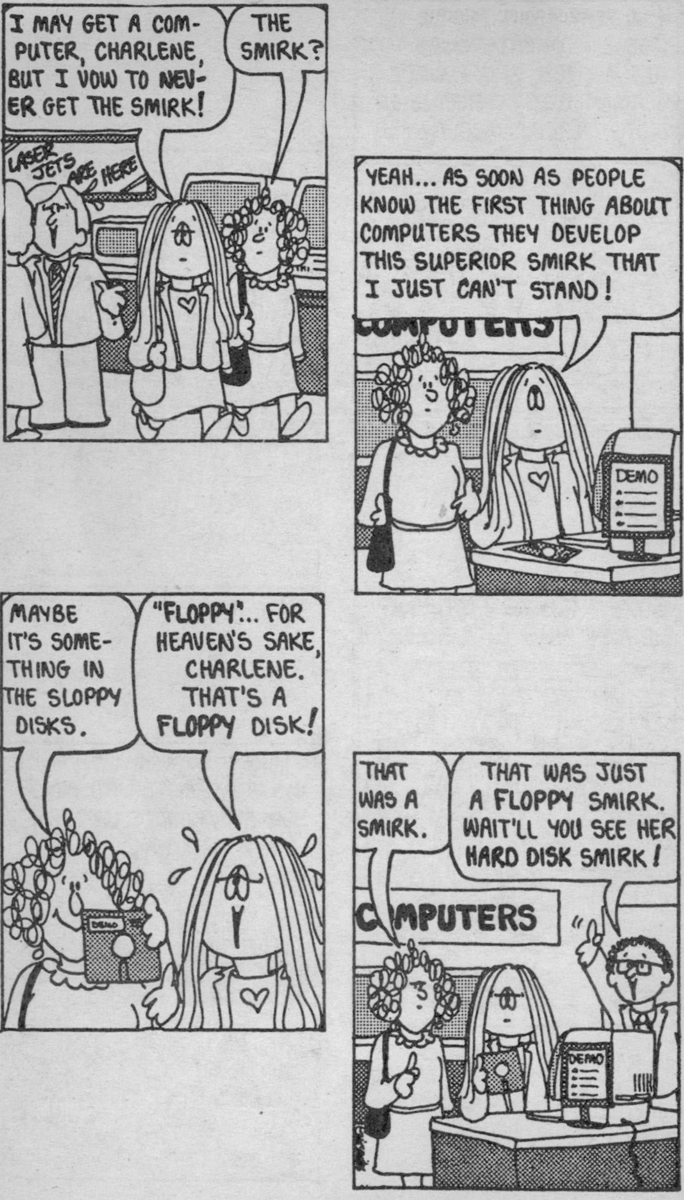
I MAY GET A COMPUTER, CHARLENE, BUT I VOW TO NEVER GET THE SMIRK!
THE SMIRK?
LASER JETS ARE HERE
YEAH... AS SOON AS PEOPLE KNOW THE FIRST THING ABOUT COMPUTERS THEY DEVELOP THIS SUPERIOR SMIRK THAT I JUST CAN'T STAND!
DEMO
MAYBE IT'S SOMETHING IN THE SLOPPY DISKS.
"FLOPPY"... FOR HEAVEN'S SAKE, CHARLENE. THAT'S A FLOPPY DISK!
DEMO
THAT WAS A SMIRK.
THAT WAS JUST A FLOPPY SMIRK. WAIT'LL YOU SEE HER HARD DISK SMIRK!
DEMO

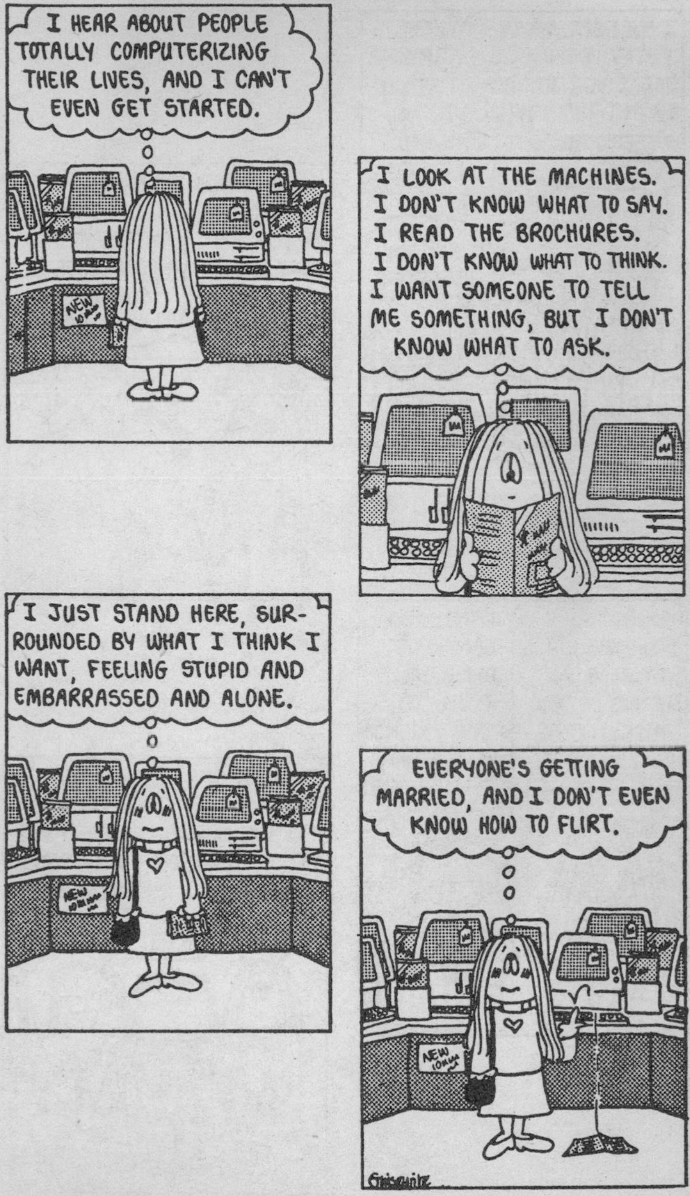
I HEAR ABOUT PEOPLE TOTALLY COMPUTERIZING THEIR LIVES, AND I CAN'T EVEN GET STARTED.
I LOOK AT THE MACHINES. I DON'T KNOW WHAT TO SAY. I READ THE BROCHURES. I DON'T KNOW WHAT TO THINK. I WANT SOMEONE TO TELL ME SOMETHING, BUT I DON'T KNOW WHAT TO ASK.
I JUST STAND HERE, SURROUNDED BY WHAT I THINK I WANT, FEELING STUPID AND EMBARRASSED AND ALONE.
EVERYONE'S GETTING MARRIED, AND I DON'T EVEN KNOW HOW TO FLIRT.

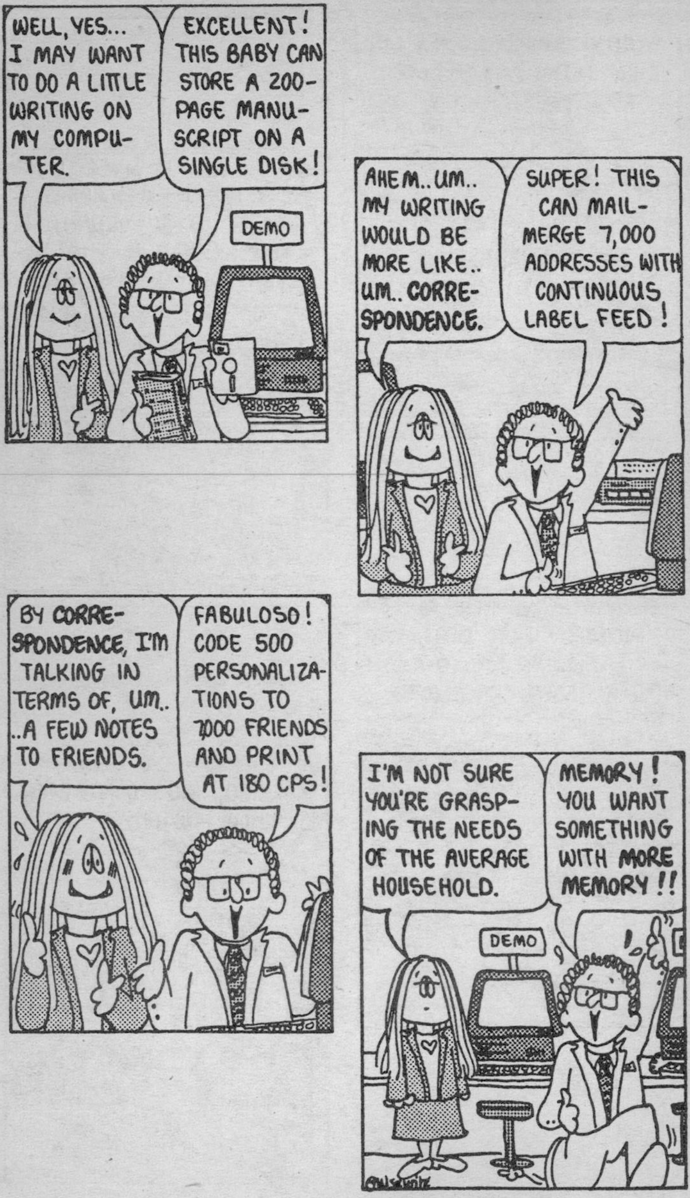
WELL, YES... I MAY WANT TO DO A LITTLE WRITING ON MY COMPUTER.
EXCELLENT! THIS BABY CAN STORE A 200-PAGE MANUSCRIPT ON A SINGLE DISK!
DEMO
AHEM.. UM.. MY WRITING WOULD BE MORE LIKE.. UM.. CORRESPONDENCE.
SUPER! THIS CAN MAIL-MERGE 7,000 ADDRESSES WITH CONTINUOUS LABEL FEED!
BY CORRESPONDENCE, I'M TALKING IN TERMS OF, UM.. ..A FEW NOTES TO FRIENDS.
FABULOSO! CODE 500 PERSONALIZATIONS TO 7000 FRIENDS AND PRINT AT 180 CPS!
I'M NOT SURE YOU'RE GRASPING THE NEEDS OF THE AVERAGE HOUSEHOLD.
MEMORY! YOU WANT SOMETHING WITH MORE MEMORY!!
DEMO

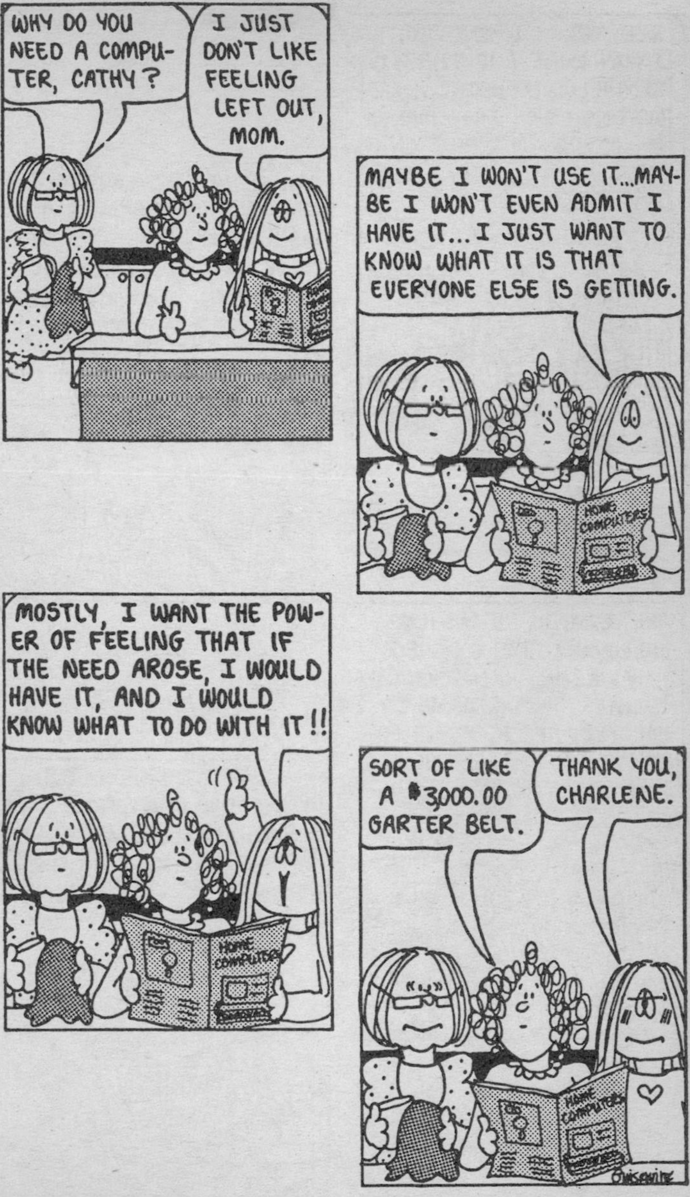
WHY DO YOU NEED A COMPUTER, CATHY?
I JUST DON'T LIKE FEELING LEFT OUT, MOM.
MAYBE I WON'T USE IT... MAYBE I WON'T EVEN ADMIT I HAVE IT... I JUST WANT TO KNOW WHAT IT IS THAT EVERYONE ELSE IS GETTING.
HOME COMPUTERS
MOSTLY, I WANT THE POWER OF FEELING THAT IF THE NEED AROSE, I WOULD HAVE IT, AND I WOULD KNOW WHAT TO DO WITH IT!!
HOME COMPUTERS
SORT OF LIKE A $3,000.00 GARTER BELT.
THANK YOU, CHARLENE.
HOME COMPUTERS

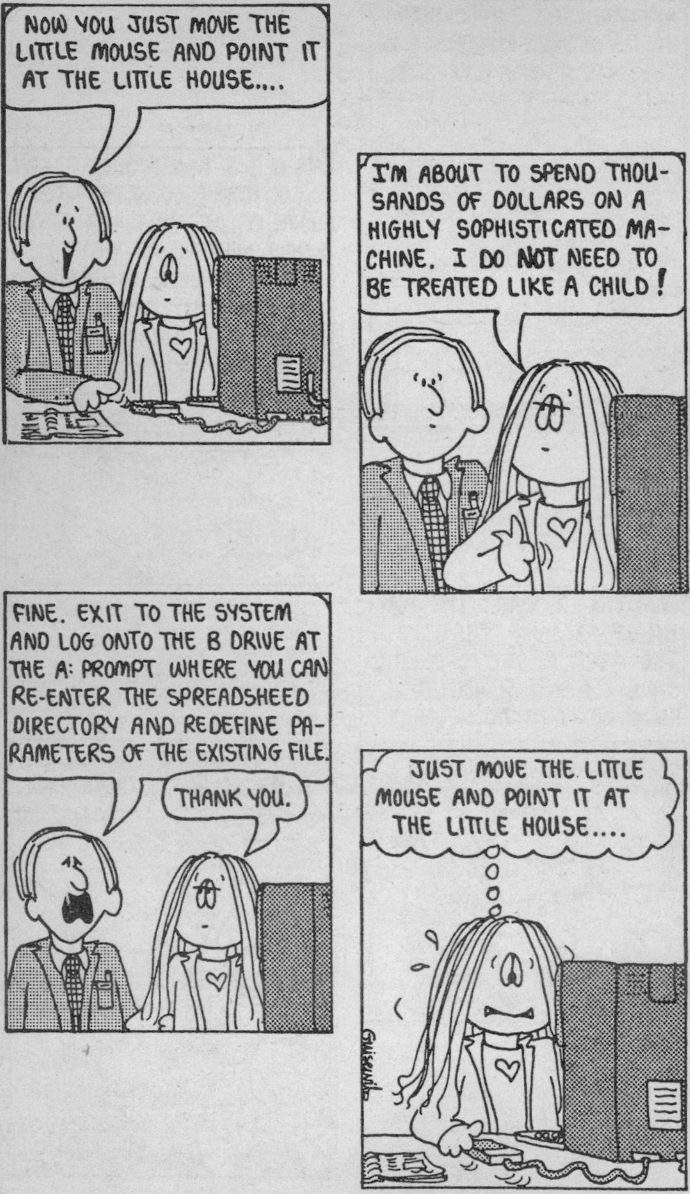
NOW YOU JUST MOVE THE LITTLE MOUSE AND POINT IT AT THE LITTLE HOUSE....
I'M ABOUT TO SPEND THOUSANDS OF DOLLARS ON A HIGHLY SOPHISTICATED MACHINE. I DO NOT NEED TO BE TREATED LIKE A CHILD!
FINE. EXIT TO THE SYSTEM AND LOG ONTO THE B DRIVE AT THE A: PROMPT WHERE YOU CAN RE-ENTER THE SPREADSHEED DIRECTORY AND REDEFINE PARAMETERS OF THE EXISTING FILE.
THANK YOU.
JUST MOVE THE LITTLE MOUSE AND POINT IT AT THE LITTLE HOUSE....
Guisewite

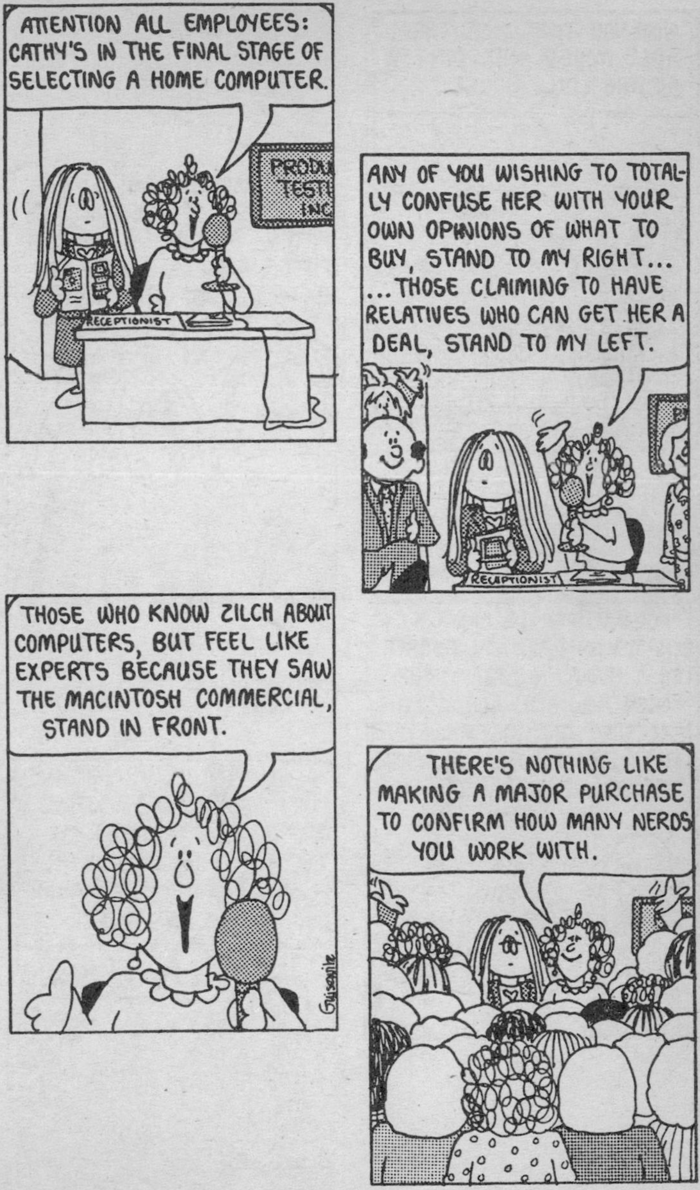
ATTENTION ALL EMPLOYEES: CATHY'S IN THE FINAL STAGE OF SELECTING A HOME COMPUTER.
RECEPTIONIST
ANY OF YOU WISHING TO TOTALLY CONFUSE HER WITH YOUR OWN OPINIONS OF WHAT TO BUY, STAND TO MY RIGHT...
...THOSE CLAIMING TO HAVE RELATIVES WHO CAN GET HER A DEAL, STAND TO MY LEFT.
RECEPTIONIST
THOSE WHO KNOW ZILCH ABOUT COMPUTERS, BUT FEEL LIKE EXPERTS BECAUSE THEY SAW THE MACINTOSH COMMERCIAL, STAND IN FRONT.
Guisewite
THERE'S NOTHING LIKE MAKING A MAJOR PURCHASE TO CONFIRM HOW MANY NERDS YOU WORK WITH.

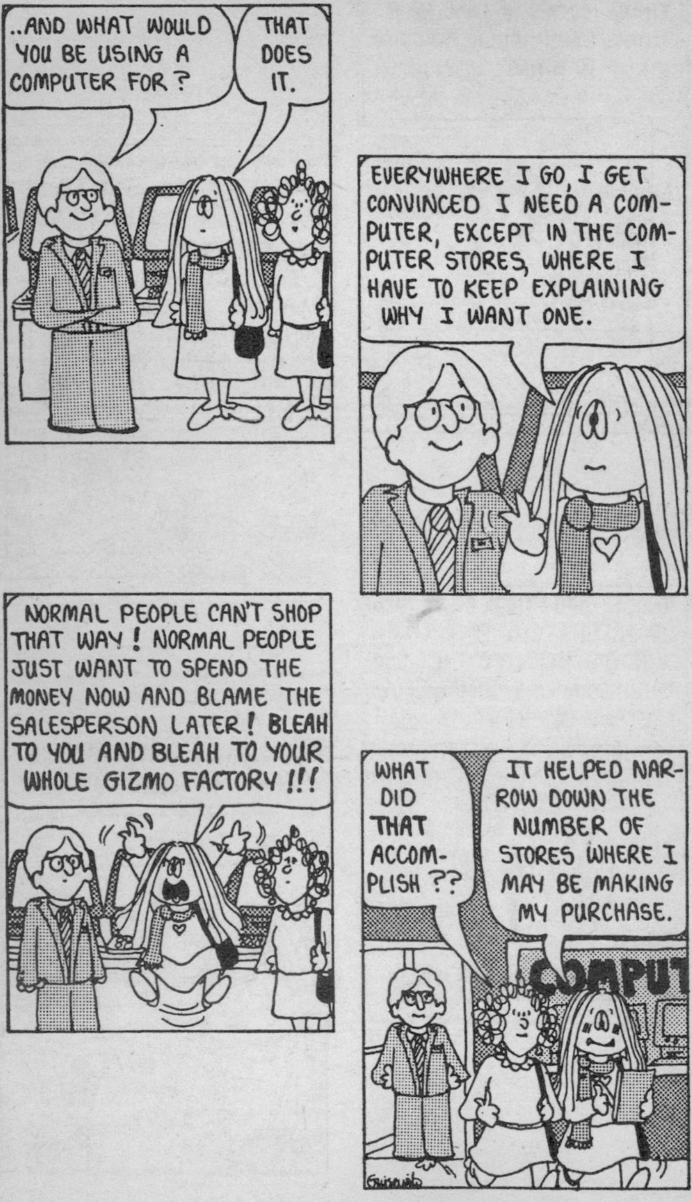
..AND WHAT WOULD YOU BE USING A COMPUTER FOR?
THAT DOES IT.
EVERYWHERE I GO, I GET CONVINCED I NEED A COMPUTER, EXCEPT IN THE COMPUTER STORES, WHERE I HAVE TO KEEP EXPLAINING WHY I WANT ONE.
NORMAL PEOPLE CAN'T SHOP THAT WAY! NORMAL PEOPLE JUST WANT TO SPEND THE MONEY NOW AND BLAME THE SALESPERSON LATER! BLEAH TO YOU AND BLEAH TO YOUR WHOLE GIZMO FACTORY!!!
WHAT DID THAT ACCOMPLISH??
IT HELPED NARROW DOWN THE NUMBER OF STORES WHERE I MAY BE MAKING MY PURCHASE.
COMPUT

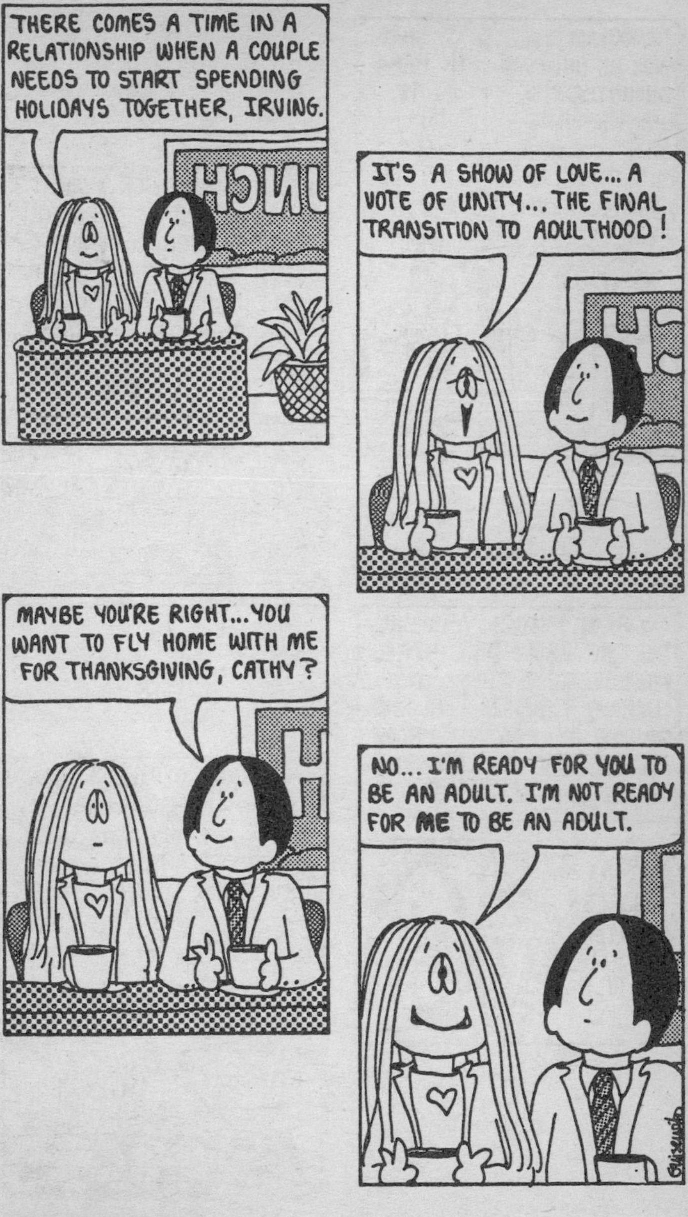
THERE COMES A TIME IN A RELATIONSHIP WHEN A COUPLE NEEDS TO START SPENDING HOLIDAYS TOGETHER, IRVING.
IT'S A SHOW OF LOVE... A VOTE OF UNITY... THE FINAL TRANSITION TO ADULTHOOD!
MAYBE YOU'RE RIGHT... YOU WANT TO FLY HOME WITH ME FOR THANKSGIVING, CATHY?
NO... I'M READY FOR YOU TO BE AN ADULT. I'M NOT READY FOR ME TO BE AN ADULT.
Guisewite

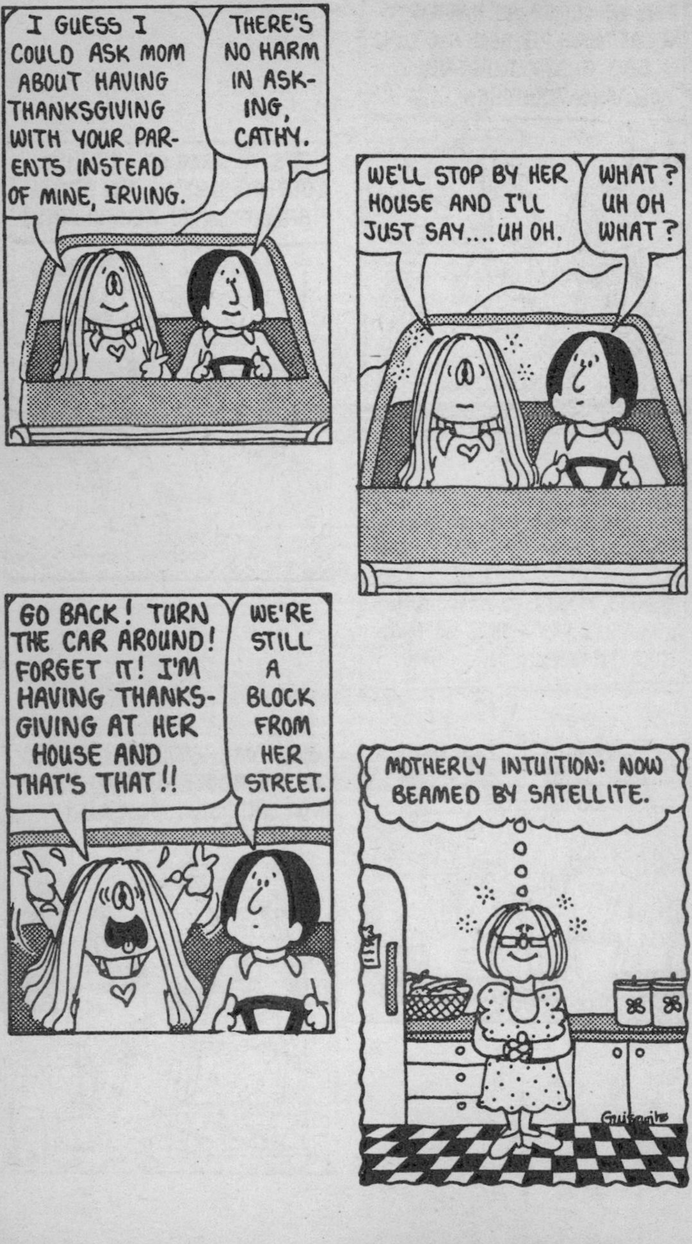
I GUESS I COULD ASK MOM ABOUT HAVING THANKSGIVING WITH YOUR PARENTS INSTEAD OF MINE, IRVING.
THERE'S NO HARM IN ASKING, CATHY.
WE'LL STOP BY HER HOUSE AND I'LL JUST SAY....UH OH.
WHAT? UH OH WHAT?
GO BACK! TURN THE CAR AROUND! FORGET IT! I'M HAVING THANKSGIVING AT HER HOUSE AND THAT'S THAT!!
WE'RE STILL A BLOCK FROM HER STREET.
MOTHERLY INTUITION: NOW BEAMED BY SATELLITE.

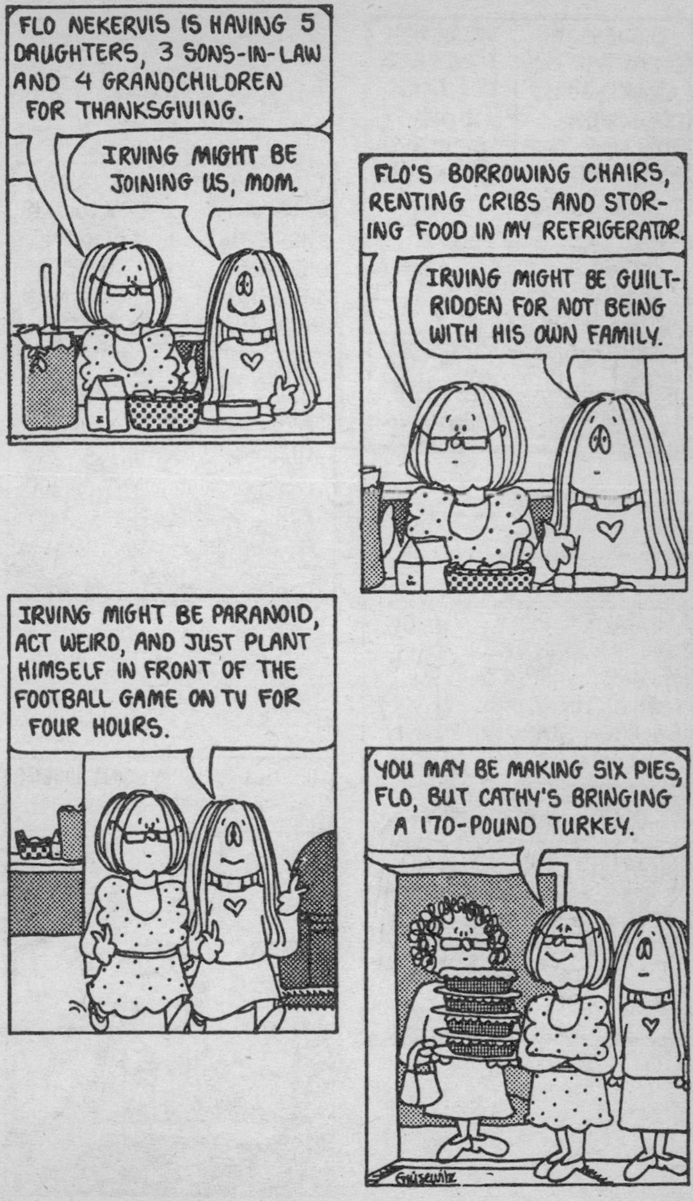
FLO NEKERVIS IS HAVING 5 DAUGHTERS, 3 SONS-IN-LAW AND 4 GRANDCHILDREN FOR THANKSGIVING.
IRVING MIGHT BE JOINING US, MOM.
FLO'S BORROWING CHAIRS, RENTING CRIBS AND STORING FOOD IN MY REFRIGERATOR.
IRVING MIGHT BE GUILT-RIDDEN FOR NOT BEING WITH HIS OWN FAMILY.
IRVING MIGHT BE PARANOID, ACT WEIRD, AND JUST PLANT HIMSELF IN FRONT OF THE FOOTBALL GAME ON TV FOR FOUR HOURS.
YOU MAY BE MAKING SIX PIES, FLO, BUT CATHY'S BRINGING A 170-POUND TURKEY.
Guisewite

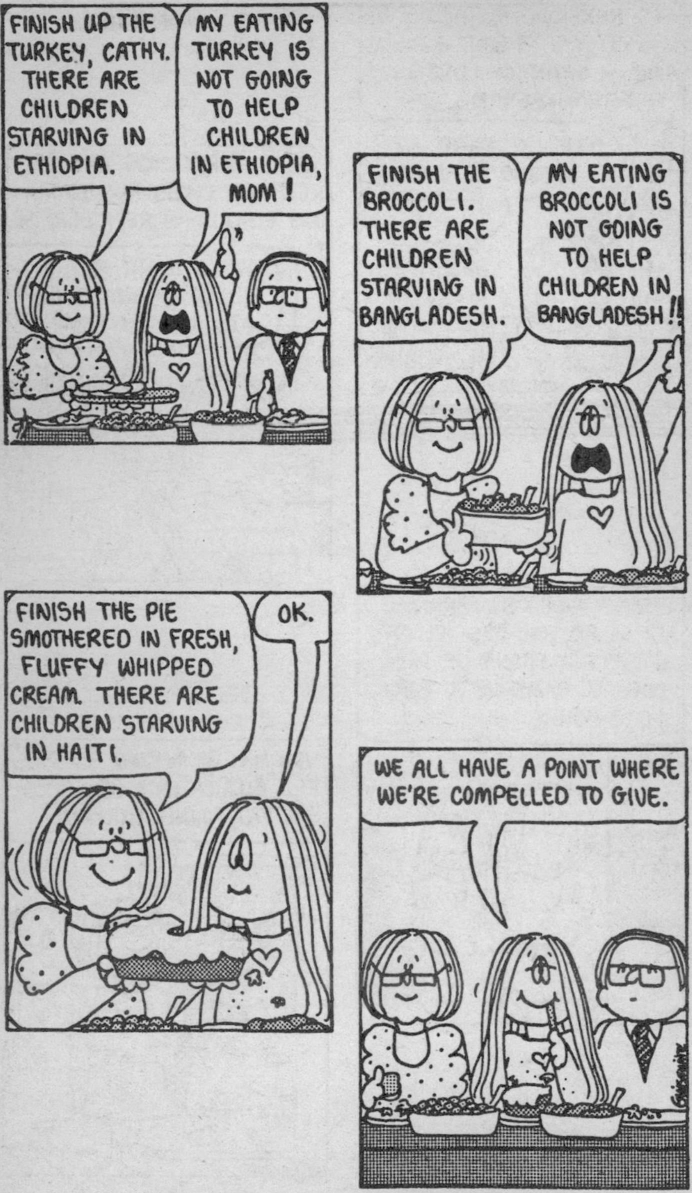
FINISH UP THE TURKEY, CATHY. THERE ARE CHILDREN STARVING IN ETHIOPIA.
MY EATING TURKEY IS NOT GOING TO HELP CHILDREN IN ETHIOPIA, MOM!
FINISH THE BROCCOLI. THERE ARE CHILDREN STARVING IN BANGLADESH.
MY EATING BROCCOLI IS NOT GOING TO HELP CHILDREN IN BANGLADESH!!
FINISH THE PIE SMOTHERED IN FRESH, FLUFFY WHIPPED CREAM. THERE ARE CHILDREN STARVING IN HAITI.
OK.
WE ALL HAVE A POINT WHERE WE'RE COMPELLED TO GIVE.

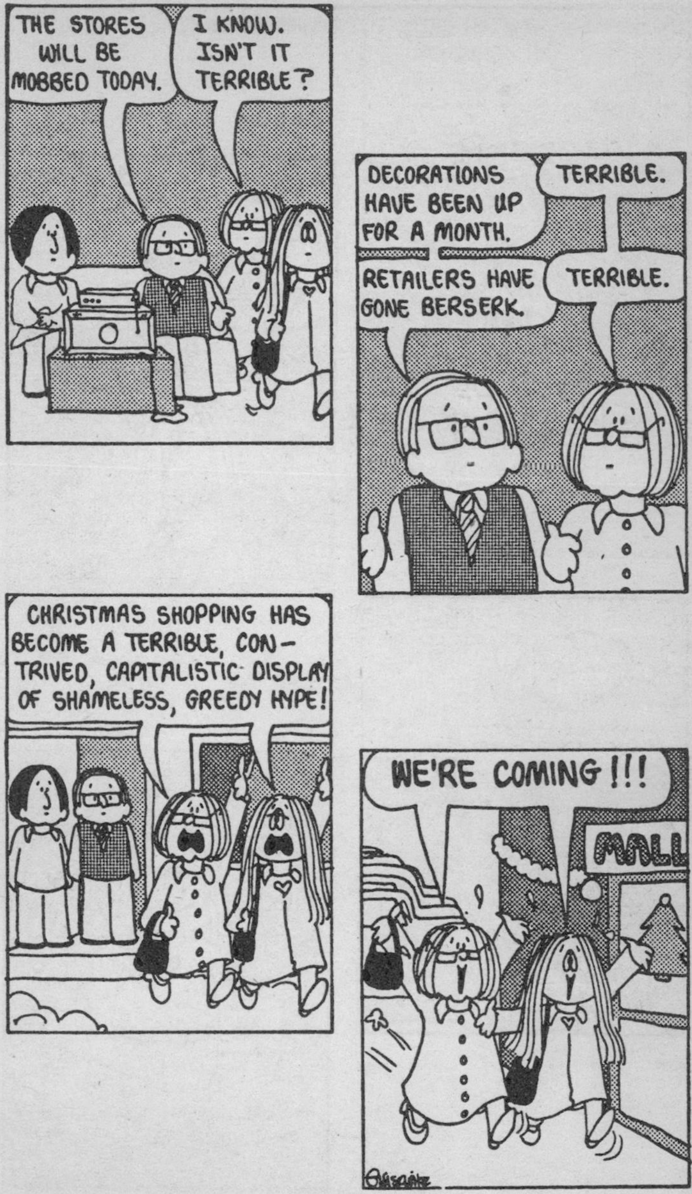
THE STORES WILL BE MOBBED TODAY.
I KNOW. ISN'T IT TERRIBLE?
DECORATIONS HAVE BEEN UP FOR A MONTH.
TERRIBLE.
RETAILERS HAVE GONE BERSERK.
TERRIBLE.
CHRISTMAS SHOPPING HAS BECOME A TERRIBLE, CON-TRIVED, CAPITALISTIC DISPLAY OF SHAMELESS, GREEDY HYPE!
WE'RE COMING!!!
MALL

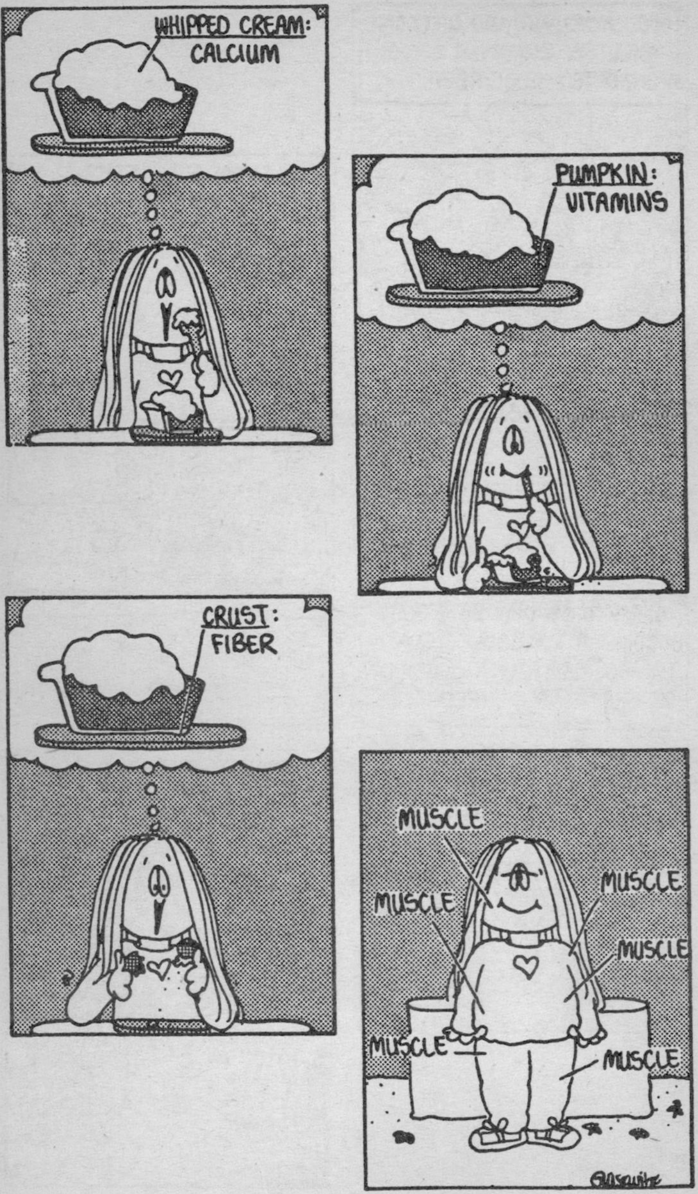
WHIPPED CREAM:
CALCIUM
PUMPKIN:
VITAMINS
CRUST:
FIBER
MUSCLE
MUSCLE
MUSCLE
MUSCLE
MUSCLE
MUSCLE
MUSCLE

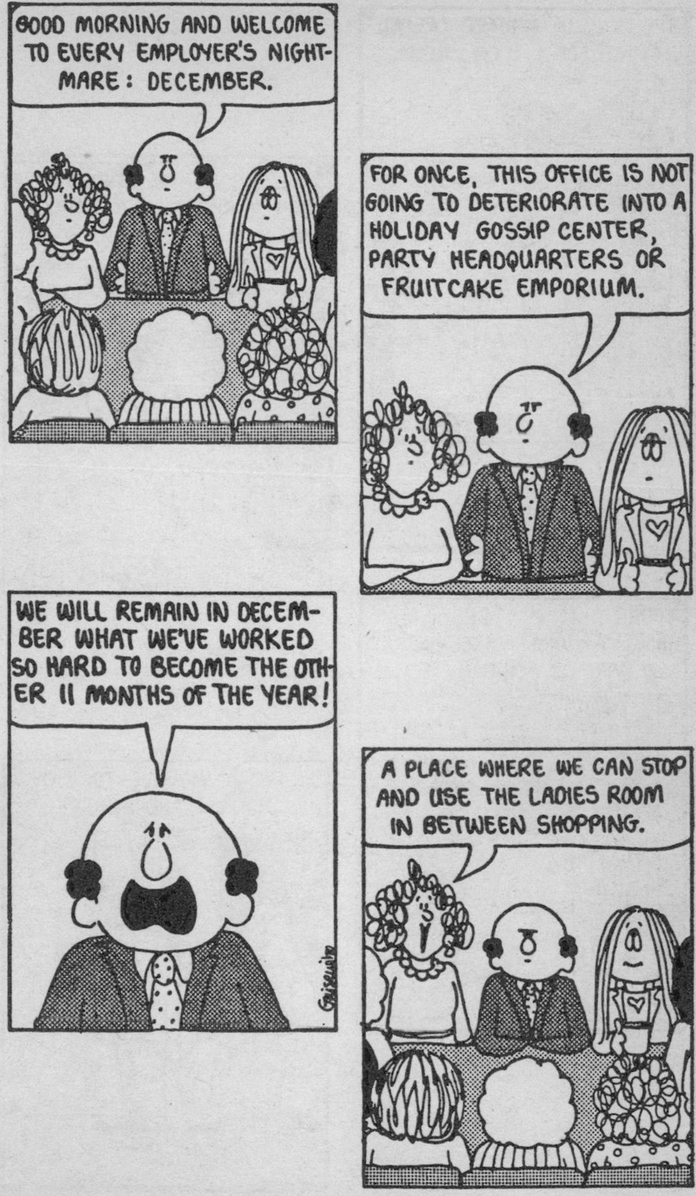
GOOD MORNING AND WELCOME TO EVERY EMPLOYER'S NIGHTMARE: DECEMBER.
FOR ONCE, THIS OFFICE IS NOT GOING TO DETERIORATE INTO A HOLIDAY GOSSIP CENTER, PARTY HEADQUARTERS OR FRUITCAKE EMPORIUM.
WE WILL REMAIN IN DECEMBER WHAT WE'VE WORKED SO HARD TO BECOME THE OTHER 11 MONTHS OF THE YEAR!
A PLACE WHERE WE CAN STOP AND USE THE LADIES ROOM IN BETWEEN SHOPPING.

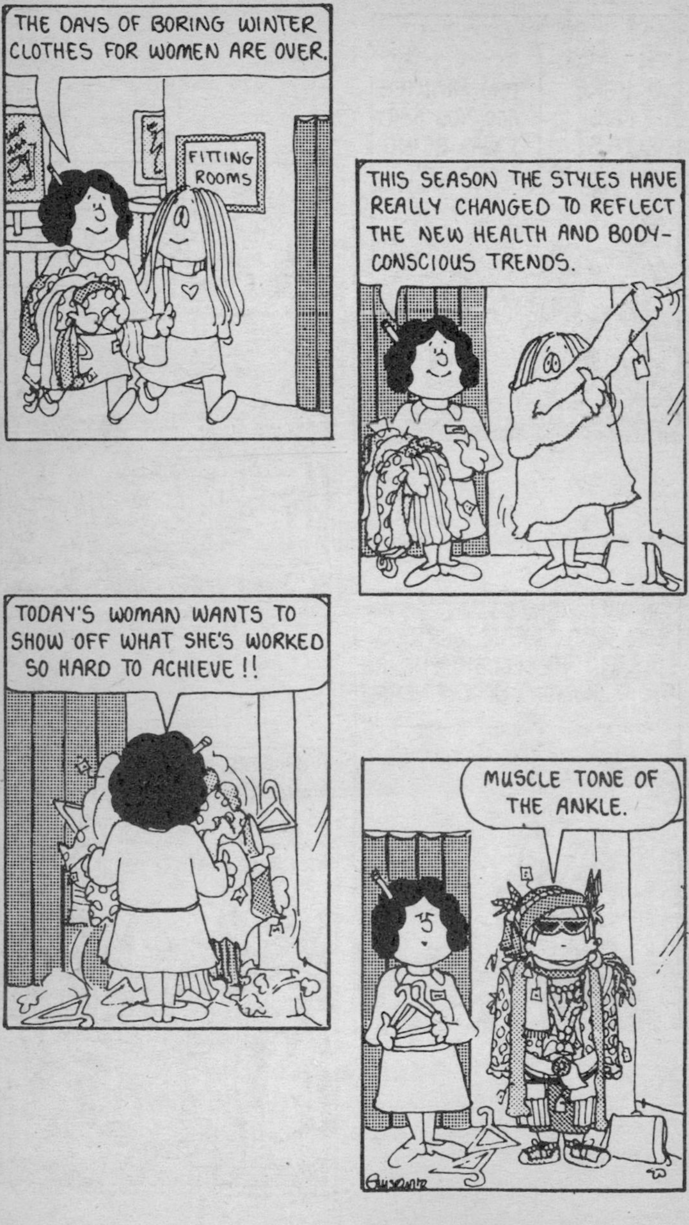
THE DAYS OF BORING WINTER CLOTHES FOR WOMEN ARE OVER.
FITTING ROOMS
THIS SEASON THE STYLES HAVE REALLY CHANGED TO REFLECT THE NEW HEALTH AND BODY-CONSCIOUS TRENDS.
TODAY'S WOMAN WANTS TO SHOW OFF WHAT SHE'S WORKED SO HARD TO ACHIEVE!!
MUSCLE TONE OF THE ANKLE.

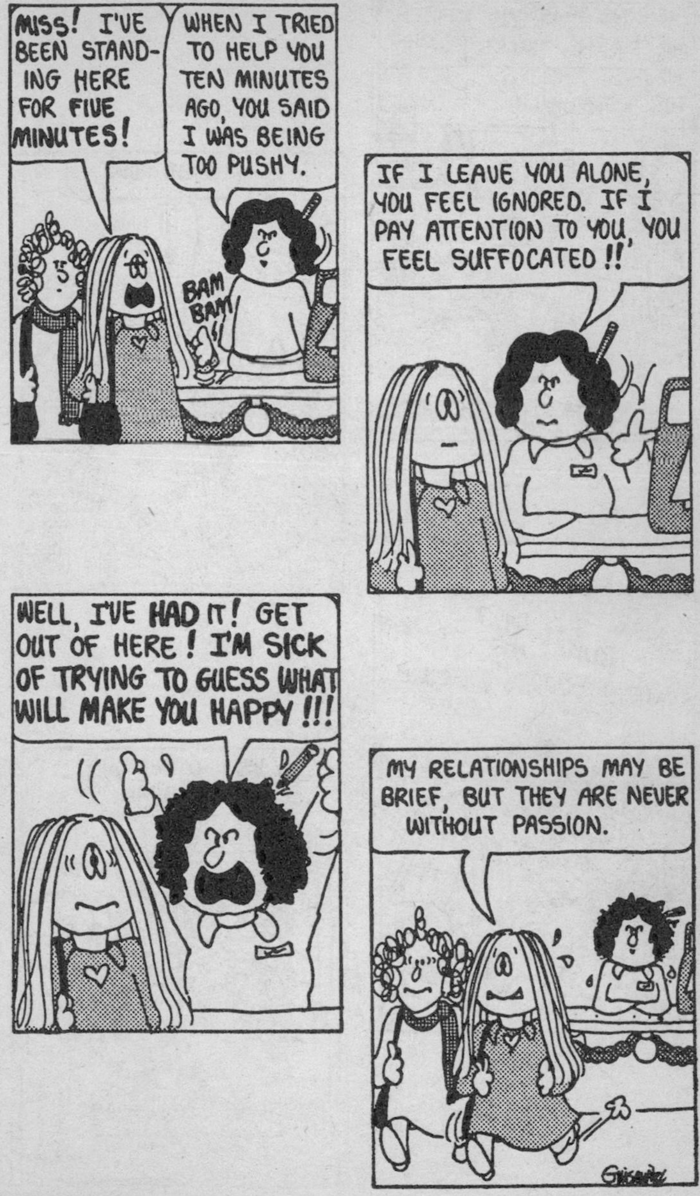
MISS! I'VE BEEN STANDING HERE FOR FIVE MINUTES!
WHEN I TRIED TO HELP YOU TEN MINUTES AGO, YOU SAID I WAS BEING TOO PUSHY.
BAM BAM
IF I LEAVE YOU ALONE, YOU FEEL IGNORED. IF I PAY ATTENTION TO YOU, YOU FEEL SUFFOCATED!!
WELL, I'VE HAD IT! GET OUT OF HERE! I'M SICK OF TRYING TO GUESS WHAT WILL MAKE YOU HAPPY!!!
MY RELATIONSHIPS MAY BE BRIEF, BUT THEY ARE NEVER WITHOUT PASSION.

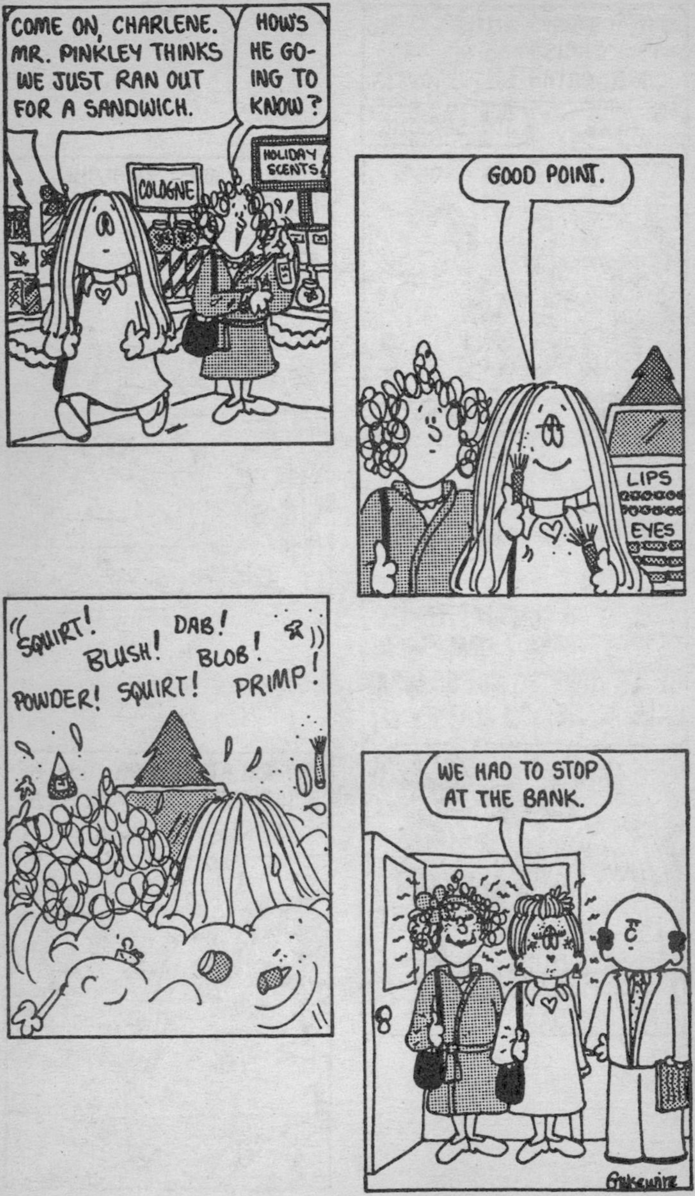
COME ON, CHARLENE. MR. PINKLEY THINKS WE JUST RAN OUT FOR A SANDWICH.
HOW'S HE GOING TO KNOW?
COLOGNE
HOLIDAY SCENTS
GOOD POINT.
LIPS
EYES
SQUIRT! DAB! BLUSH! BLOB! POWDER! SQUIRT! PRIMP!
WE HAD TO STOP AT THE BANK.
Guisewite

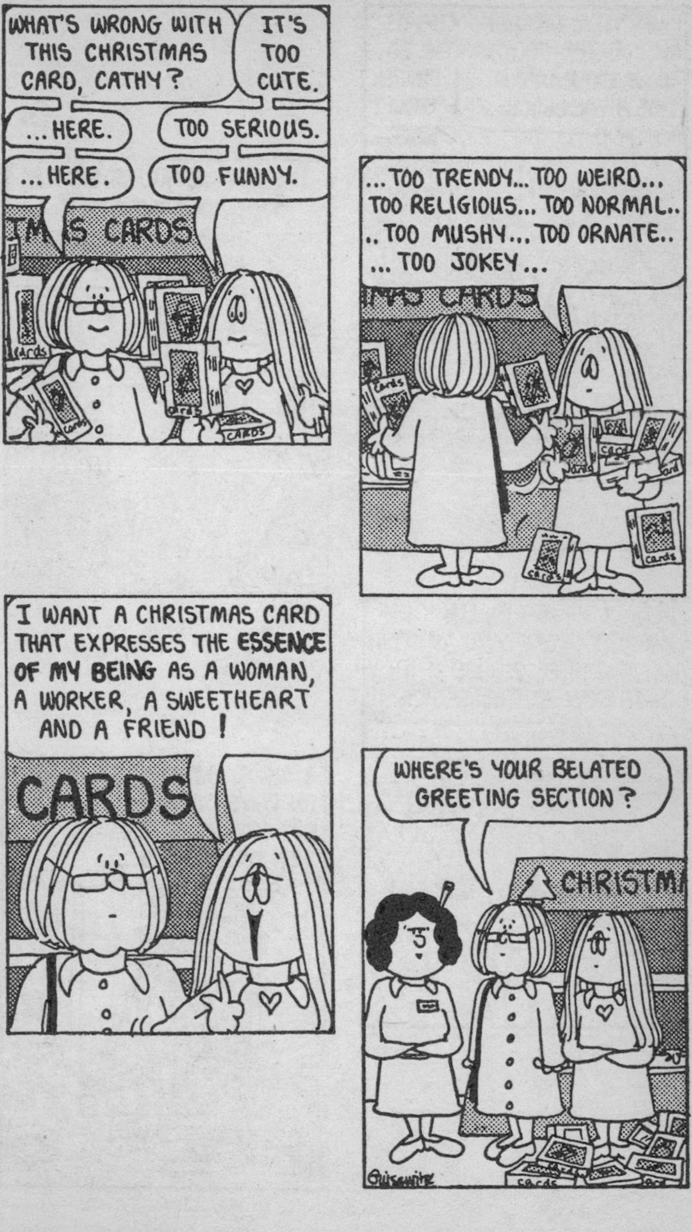
WHAT'S WRONG WITH THIS CHRISTMAS CARD, CATHY?
IT'S TOO CUTE.
...HERE.
TOO SERIOUS.
...HERE.
TOO FUNNY.
...TOO TRENDY... TOO WEIRD... TOO RELIGIOUS... TOO NORMAL.. ..TOO MUSHY... TOO ORNATE.. ... TOO JOKEY...
I WANT A CHRISTMAS CARD THAT EXPRESSES THE ESSENCE OF MY BEING AS A WOMAN, A WORKER, A SWEETHEART AND A FRIEND!
CARDS
WHERE'S YOUR BELATED GREETING SECTION?
CHRISTM
Guisewite

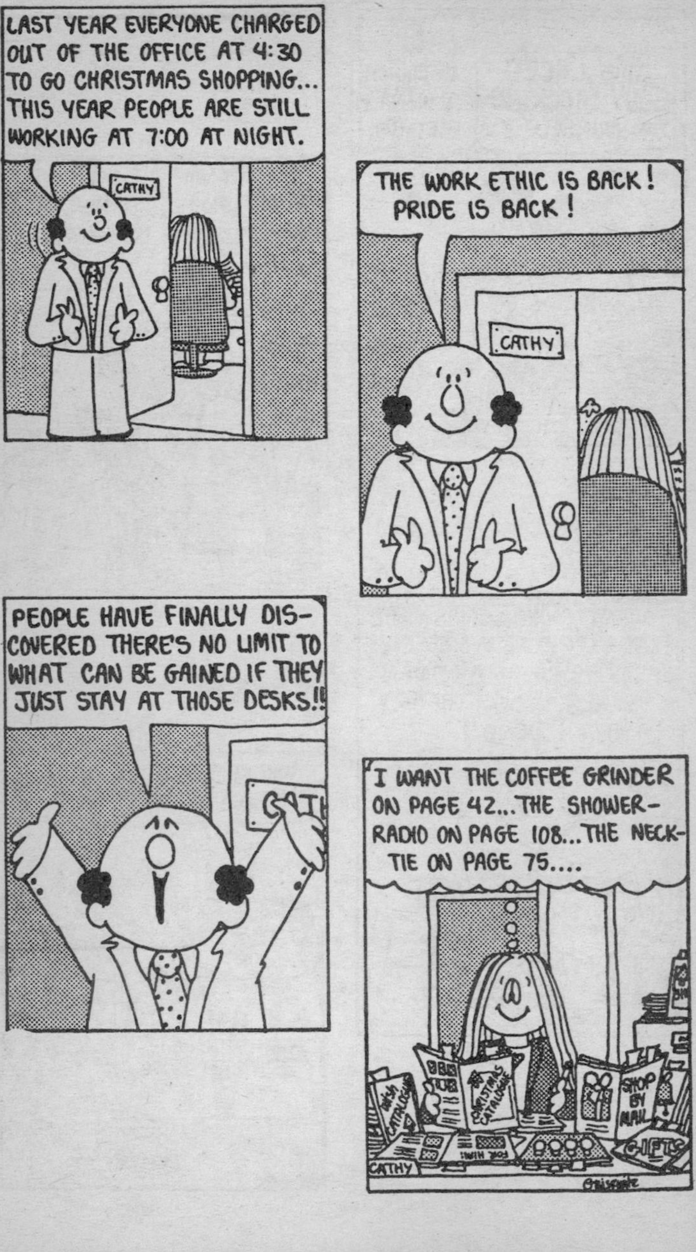
LAST YEAR EVERYONE CHARGED OUT OF THE OFFICE AT 4:30 TO GO CHRISTMAS SHOPPING... THIS YEAR PEOPLE ARE STILL WORKING AT 7:00 AT NIGHT.
CATHY
THE WORK ETHIC IS BACK! PRIDE IS BACK!
CATHY
PEOPLE HAVE FINALLY DISCOVERED THERE'S NO LIMIT TO WHAT CAN BE GAINED IF THEY JUST STAY AT THOSE DESKS!!
I WANT THE COFFEE GRINDER ON PAGE 42... THE SHOWER-RADIO ON PAGE 108... THE NECKTIE ON PAGE 75....
CHRISTMAS CATALOGUE
SHOP BY MAIL
GIFTS
CATHY

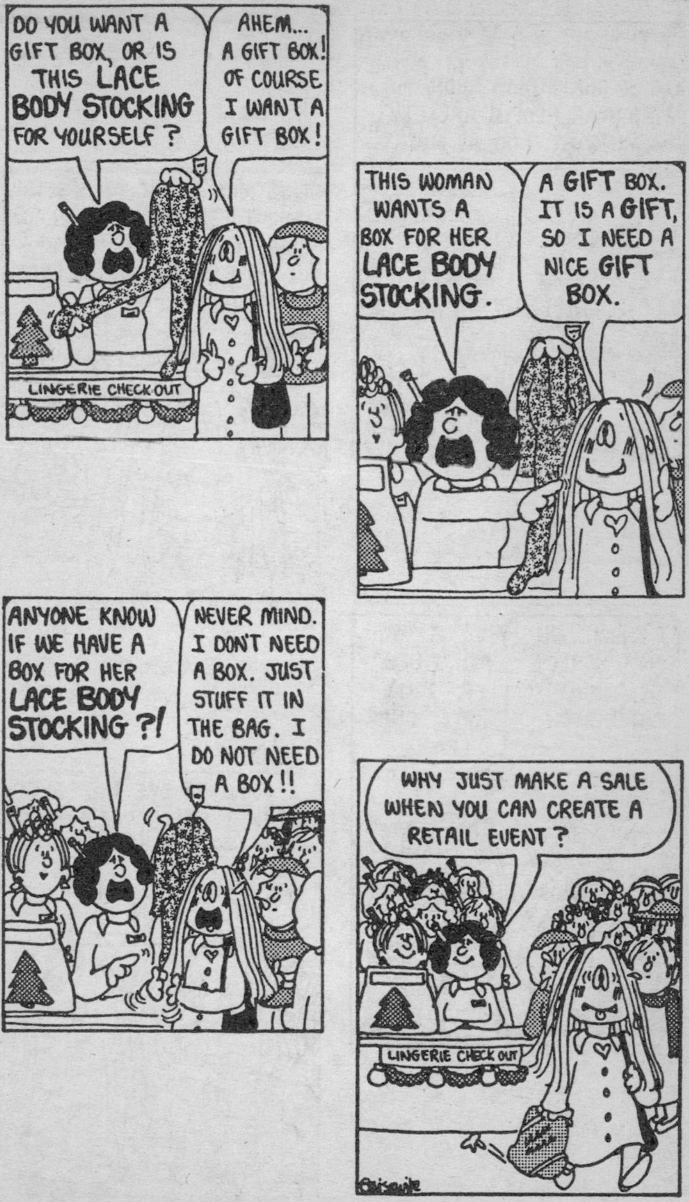
DO YOU WANT A GIFT BOX, OR IS THIS LACE BODY STOCKING FOR YOURSELF?
AHEM... A GIFT BOX! OF COURSE I WANT A GIFT BOX!
LINGERIE CHECK OUT
THIS WOMAN WANTS A BOX FOR HER LACE BODY STOCKING.
A GIFT BOX. IT IS A GIFT, SO I NEED A NICE GIFT BOX.
ANYONE KNOW IF WE HAVE A BOX FOR HER LACE BODY STOCKING?!
NEVER MIND. I DON'T NEED A BOX. JUST STUFF IT IN THE BAG. I DO NOT NEED A BOX!!
WHY JUST MAKE A SALE WHEN YOU CAN CREATE A RETAIL EVENT?
LINGERIE CHECK OUT

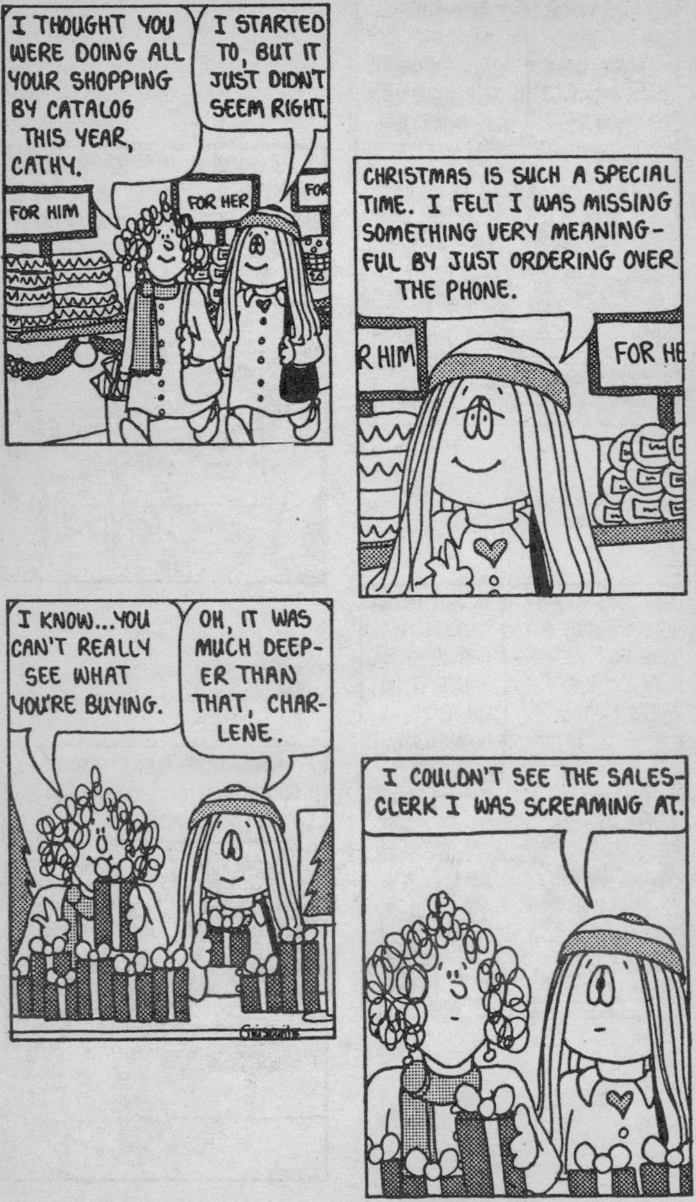
I THOUGHT YOU WERE DOING ALL YOUR SHOPPING BY CATALOG THIS YEAR, CATHY.
I STARTED TO, BUT IT JUST DIDN'T SEEM RIGHT.
FOR HIM
FOR HER
CHRISTMAS IS SUCH A SPECIAL TIME. I FELT I WAS MISSING SOMETHING VERY MEANINGFUL BY JUST ORDERING OVER THE PHONE.
I KNOW...YOU CAN'T REALLY SEE WHAT YOU'RE BUYING.
OH, IT WAS MUCH DEEPER THAN THAT, CHARLENE.
I COULDN'T SEE THE SALESCLERK I WAS SCREAMING AT.

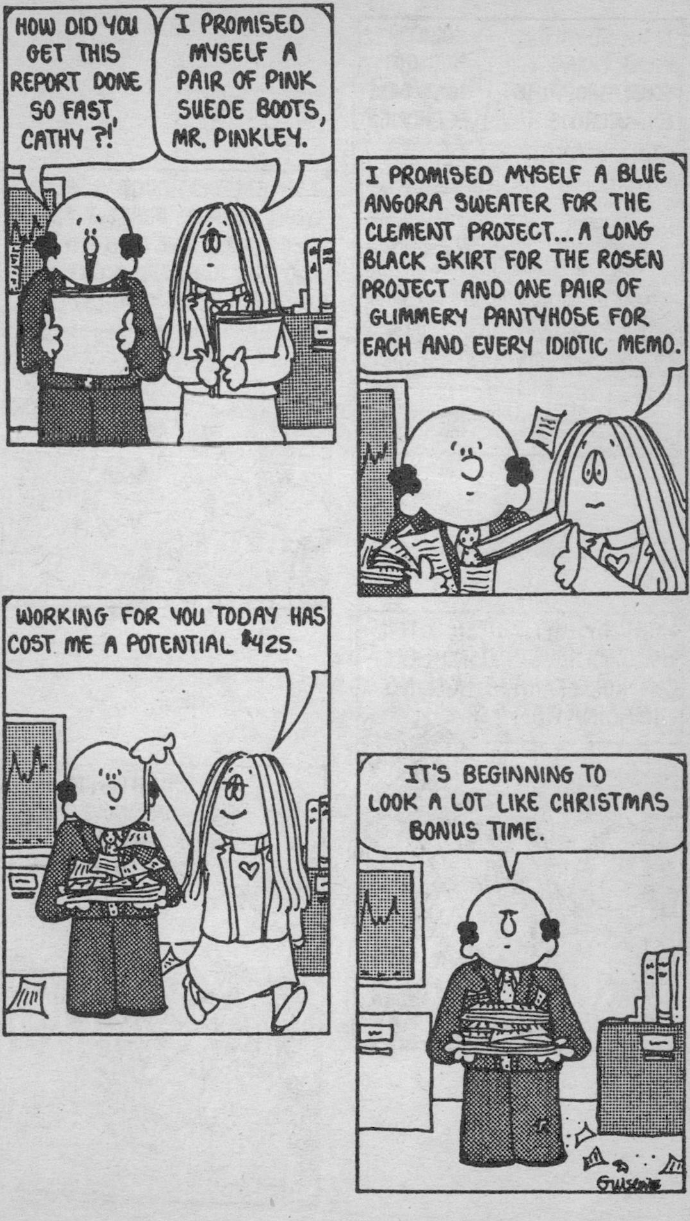
HOW DID YOU GET THIS REPORT DONE SO FAST, CATHY ?!
I PROMISED MYSELF A PAIR OF PINK SUEDE BOOTS, MR. PINKLEY.
I PROMISED MYSELF A BLUE ANGORA SWEATER FOR THE CLEMENT PROJECT... A LONG BLACK SKIRT FOR THE ROSEN PROJECT AND ONE PAIR OF GLIMMERY PANTYHOSE FOR EACH AND EVERY IDIOTIC MEMO.
WORKING FOR YOU TODAY HAS COST ME A POTENTIAL $425.
IT'S BEGINNING TO LOOK A LOT LIKE CHRISTMAS BONUS TIME.
GUISEWITE

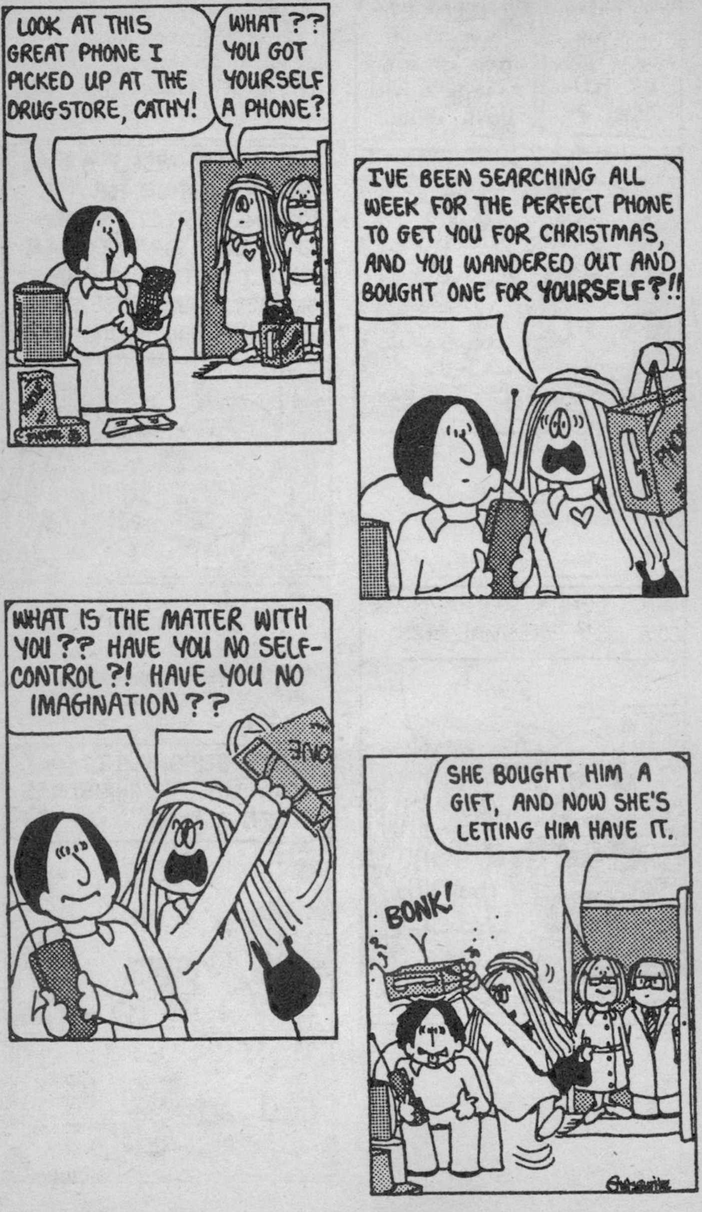
LOOK AT THIS GREAT PHONE I PICKED UP AT THE DRUGSTORE, CATHY!
WHAT?? YOU GOT YOURSELF A PHONE?
I'VE BEEN SEARCHING ALL WEEK FOR THE PERFECT PHONE TO GET YOU FOR CHRISTMAS, AND YOU WANDERED OUT AND BOUGHT ONE FOR YOURSELF?!!
WHAT IS THE MATTER WITH YOU?? HAVE YOU NO SELF-CONTROL?! HAVE YOU NO IMAGINATION??
SHE BOUGHT HIM A GIFT, AND NOW SHE'S LETTING HIM HAVE IT.
BONK!

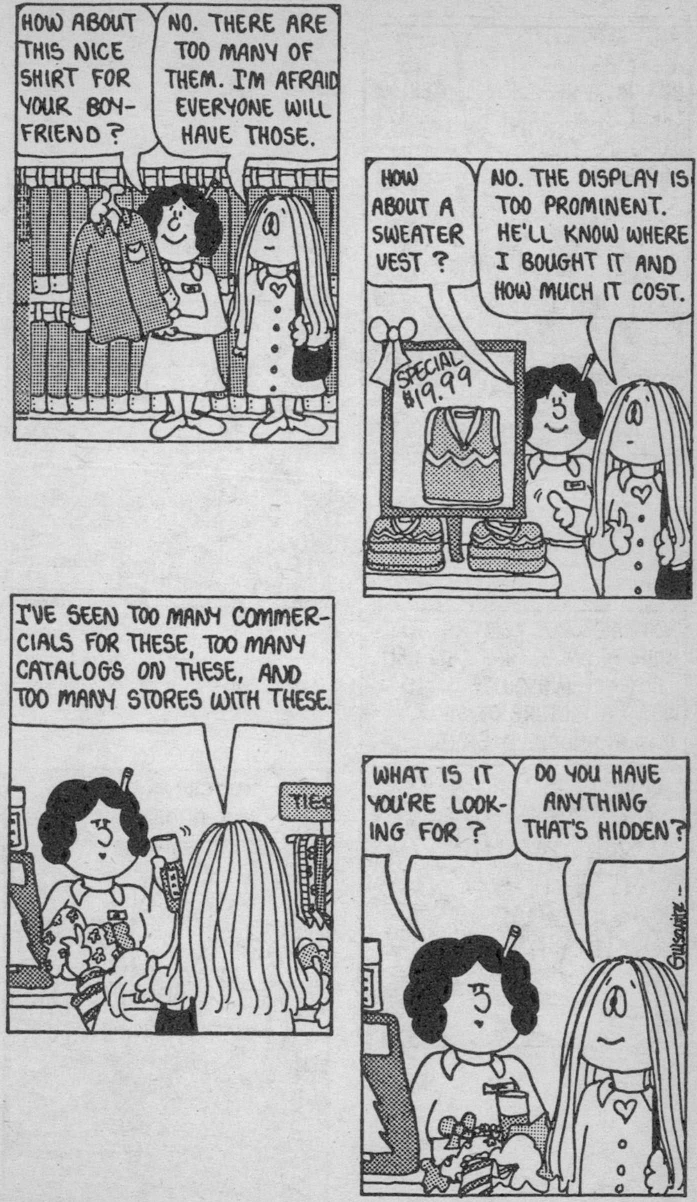

HOW ABOUT THIS NICE SHIRT FOR YOUR BOY-FRIEND?
NO. THERE ARE TOO MANY OF THEM. I'M AFRAID EVERYONE WILL HAVE THOSE.
HOW ABOUT A SWEATER VEST?
NO. THE DISPLAY IS TOO PROMINENT. HE'LL KNOW WHERE I BOUGHT IT AND HOW MUCH IT COST.
SPECIAL $19.99
I'VE SEEN TOO MANY COMMER-CIALS FOR THESE, TOO MANY CATALOGS ON THESE, AND TOO MANY STORES WITH THESE.
WHAT IS IT YOU'RE LOOK-ING FOR?
DO YOU HAVE ANYTHING THAT'S HIDDEN?

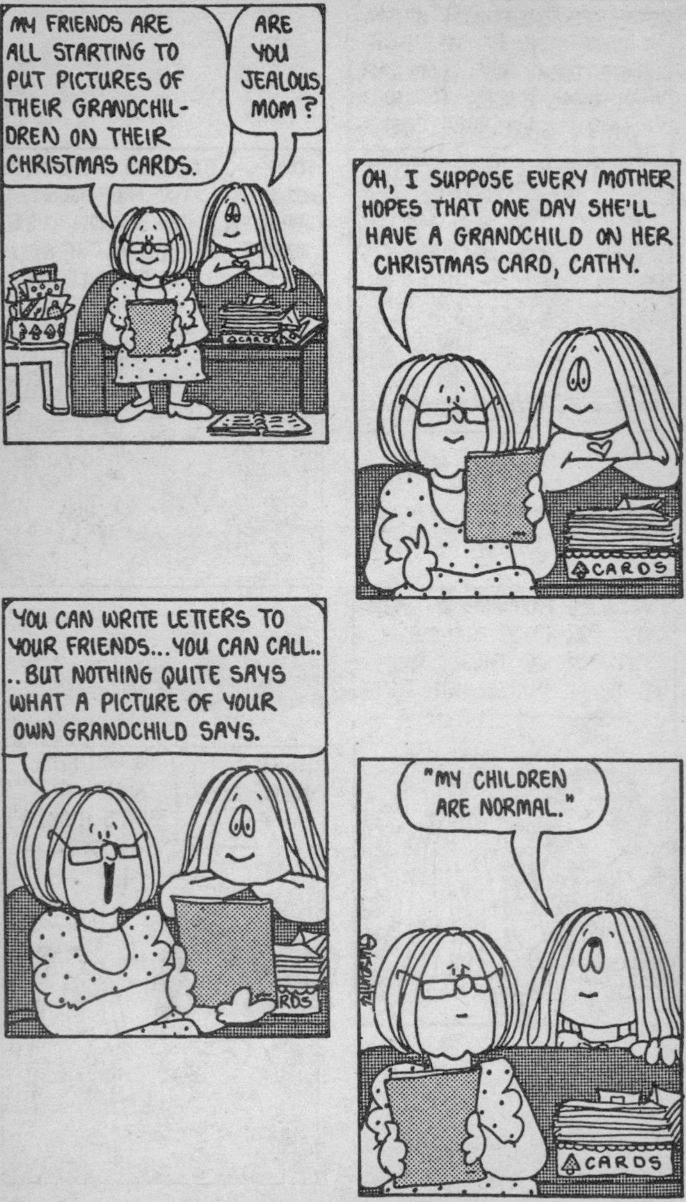
MY FRIENDS ARE ALL STARTING TO PUT PICTURES OF THEIR GRANDCHILDREN ON THEIR CHRISTMAS CARDS.
ARE YOU JEALOUS, MOM?
CARDS
OH, I SUPPOSE EVERY MOTHER HOPES THAT ONE DAY SHE'LL HAVE A GRANDCHILD ON HER CHRISTMAS CARD, CATHY.
CARDS
YOU CAN WRITE LETTERS TO YOUR FRIENDS... YOU CAN CALL.. ..BUT NOTHING QUITE SAYS WHAT A PICTURE OF YOUR OWN GRANDCHILD SAYS.
"MY CHILDREN ARE NORMAL."
CARDS

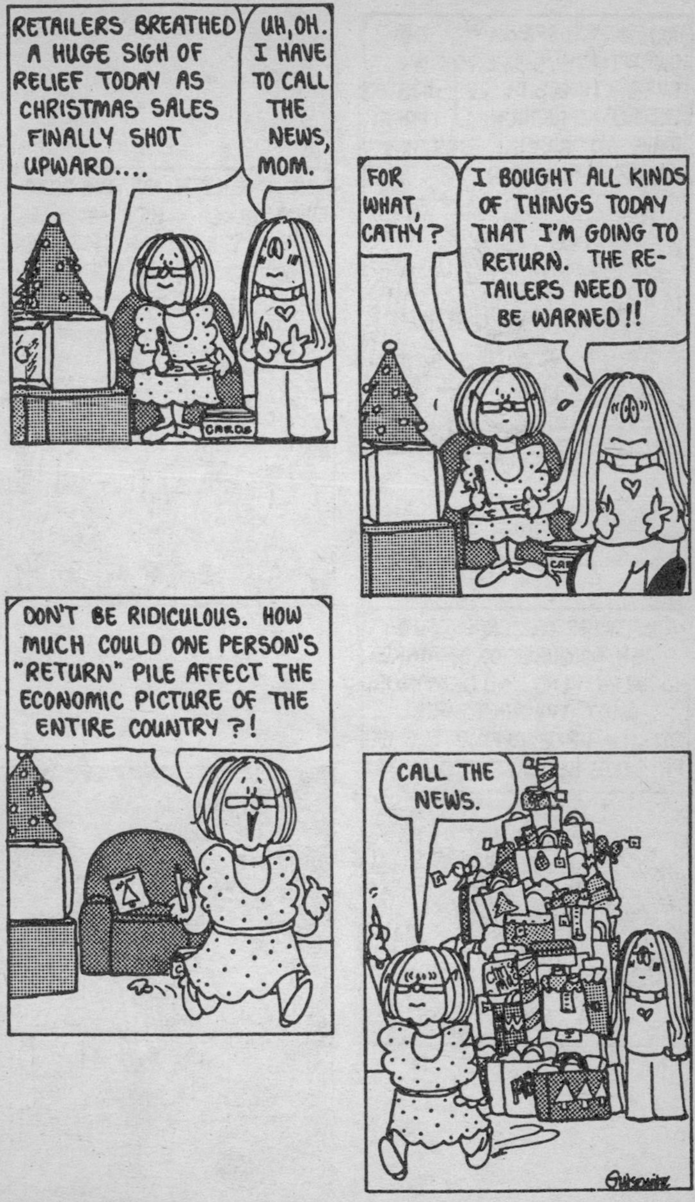
RETAILERS BREATHED A HUGE SIGH OF RELIEF TODAY AS CHRISTMAS SALES FINALLY SHOT UPWARD....
UH, OH. I HAVE TO CALL THE NEWS, MOM.
CARDS
FOR WHAT, CATHY?
I BOUGHT ALL KINDS OF THINGS TODAY THAT I'M GOING TO RETURN. THE RETAILERS NEED TO BE WARNED!!
DON'T BE RIDICULOUS. HOW MUCH COULD ONE PERSON'S "RETURN" PILE AFFECT THE ECONOMIC PICTURE OF THE ENTIRE COUNTRY?!
CALL THE NEWS.

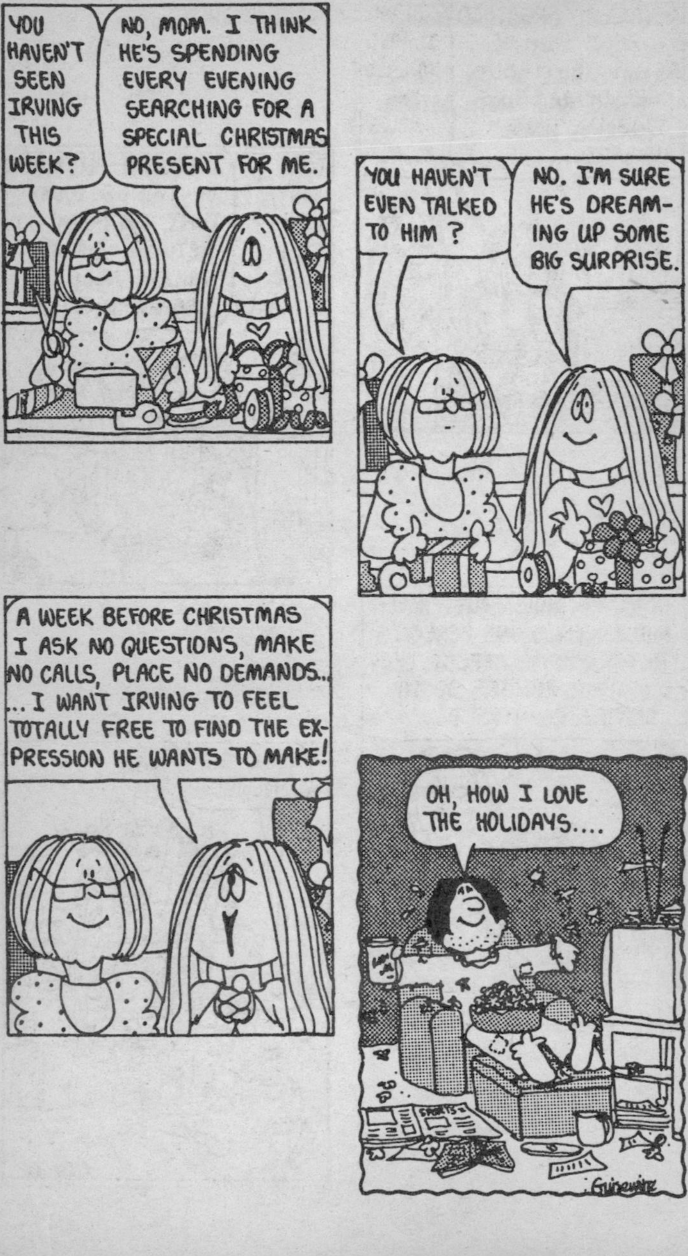
YOU HAVEN'T SEEN IRVING THIS WEEK?
NO, MOM. I THINK HE'S SPENDING EVERY EVENING SEARCHING FOR A SPECIAL CHRISTMAS PRESENT FOR ME.
YOU HAVEN'T EVEN TALKED TO HIM ?
NO. I'M SURE HE'S DREAMING UP SOME BIG SURPRISE.
A WEEK BEFORE CHRISTMAS I ASK NO QUESTIONS, MAKE NO CALLS, PLACE NO DEMANDS...
... I WANT IRVING TO FEEL TOTALLY FREE TO FIND THE EXPRESSION HE WANTS TO MAKE!
OH, HOW I LOVE THE HOLIDAYS....

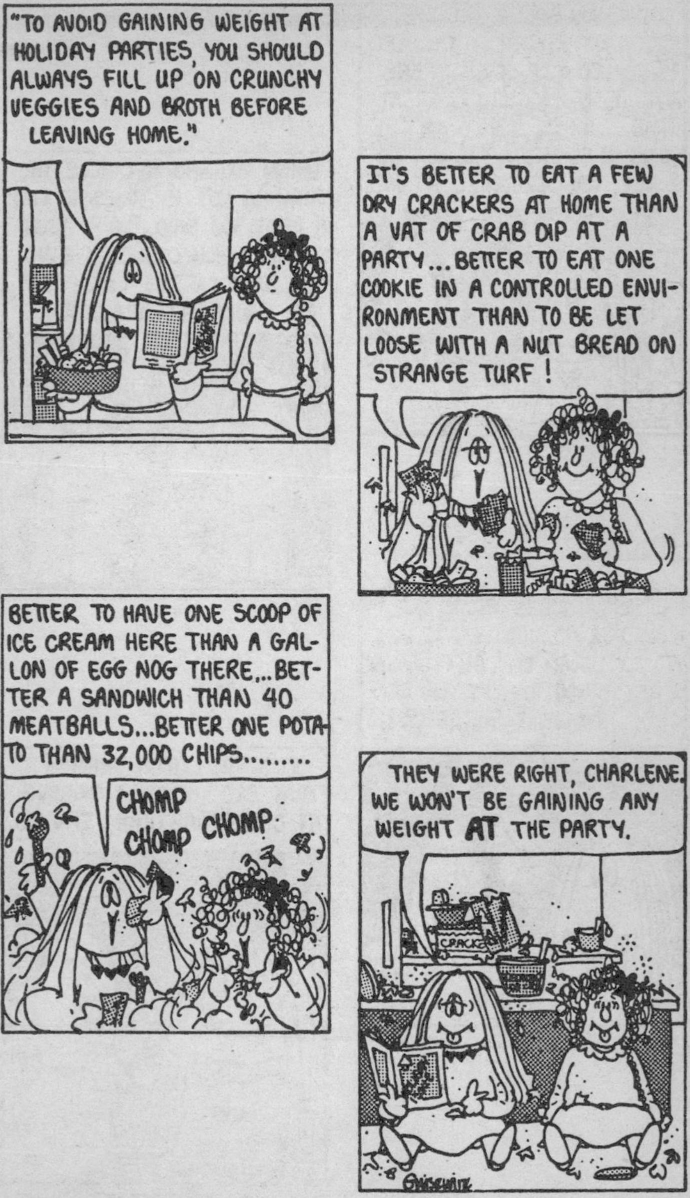
"TO AVOID GAINING WEIGHT AT HOLIDAY PARTIES, YOU SHOULD ALWAYS FILL UP ON CRUNCHY VEGGIES AND BROTH BEFORE LEAVING HOME."
IT'S BETTER TO EAT A FEW DRY CRACKERS AT HOME THAN A VAT OF CRAB DIP AT A PARTY... BETTER TO EAT ONE COOKIE IN A CONTROLLED ENVIRONMENT THAN TO BE LET LOOSE WITH A NUT BREAD ON STRANGE TURF!
BETTER TO HAVE ONE SCOOP OF ICE CREAM HERE THAN A GALLON OF EGG NOG THERE... BETTER A SANDWICH THAN 40 MEATBALLS... BETTER ONE POTATO THAN 32,000 CHIPS........
CHOMP
CHOMP CHOMP
THEY WERE RIGHT, CHARLENE. WE WON'T BE GAINING ANY WEIGHT **AT** THE PARTY.
CRACK

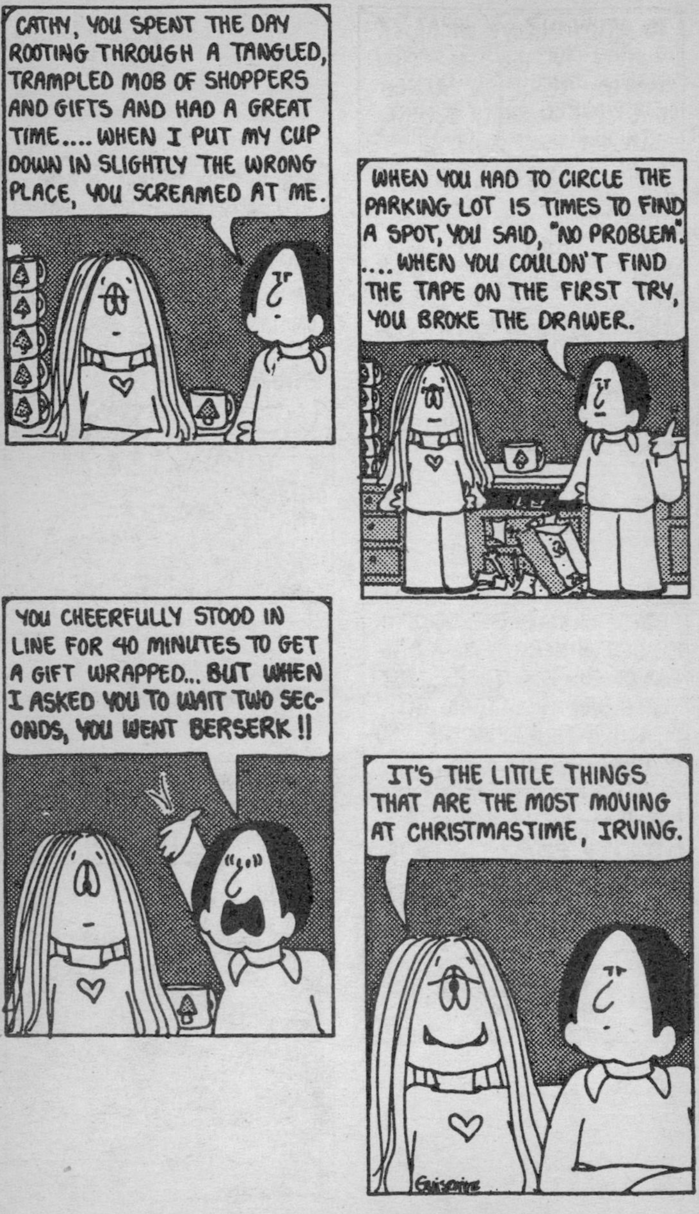

CATHY, YOU SPENT THE DAY ROOTING THROUGH A TANGLED, TRAMPLED MOB OF SHOPPERS AND GIFTS AND HAD A GREAT TIME.... WHEN I PUT MY CUP DOWN IN SLIGHTLY THE WRONG PLACE, YOU SCREAMED AT ME.
WHEN YOU HAD TO CIRCLE THE PARKING LOT 15 TIMES TO FIND A SPOT, YOU SAID, "NO PROBLEM".... WHEN YOU COULDN'T FIND THE TAPE ON THE FIRST TRY, YOU BROKE THE DRAWER.
YOU CHEERFULLY STOOD IN LINE FOR 40 MINUTES TO GET A GIFT WRAPPED... BUT WHEN I ASKED YOU TO WAIT TWO SECONDS, YOU WENT BERSERK !!
IT'S THE LITTLE THINGS THAT ARE THE MOST MOVING AT CHRISTMASTIME, IRVING.
Guisewite

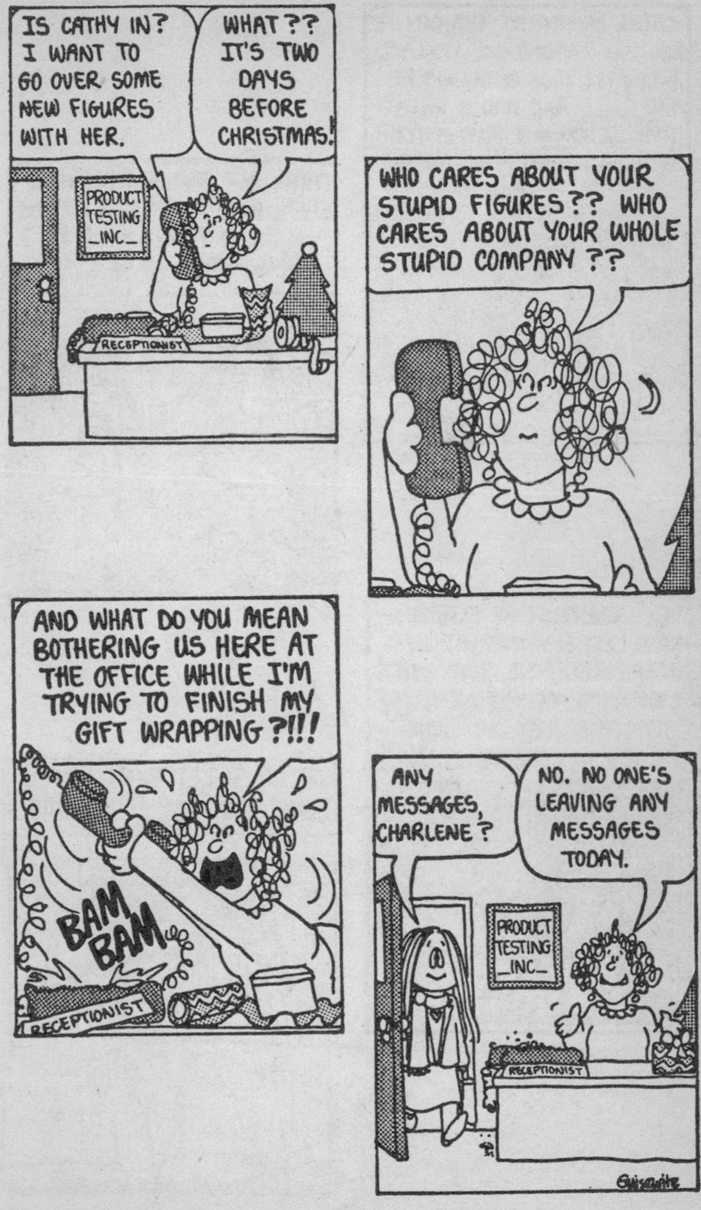
IS CATHY IN? I WANT TO GO OVER SOME NEW FIGURES WITH HER.
WHAT?? IT'S TWO DAYS BEFORE CHRISTMAS!
PRODUCT TESTING INC
RECEPTIONIST
WHO CARES ABOUT YOUR STUPID FIGURES?? WHO CARES ABOUT YOUR WHOLE STUPID COMPANY??
AND WHAT DO YOU MEAN BOTHERING US HERE AT THE OFFICE WHILE I'M TRYING TO FINISH MY GIFT WRAPPING?!!!
BAM BAM
RECEPTIONIST
ANY MESSAGES, CHARLENE?
NO. NO ONE'S LEAVING ANY MESSAGES TODAY.
PRODUCT TESTING INC
RECEPTIONIST
Guisewite

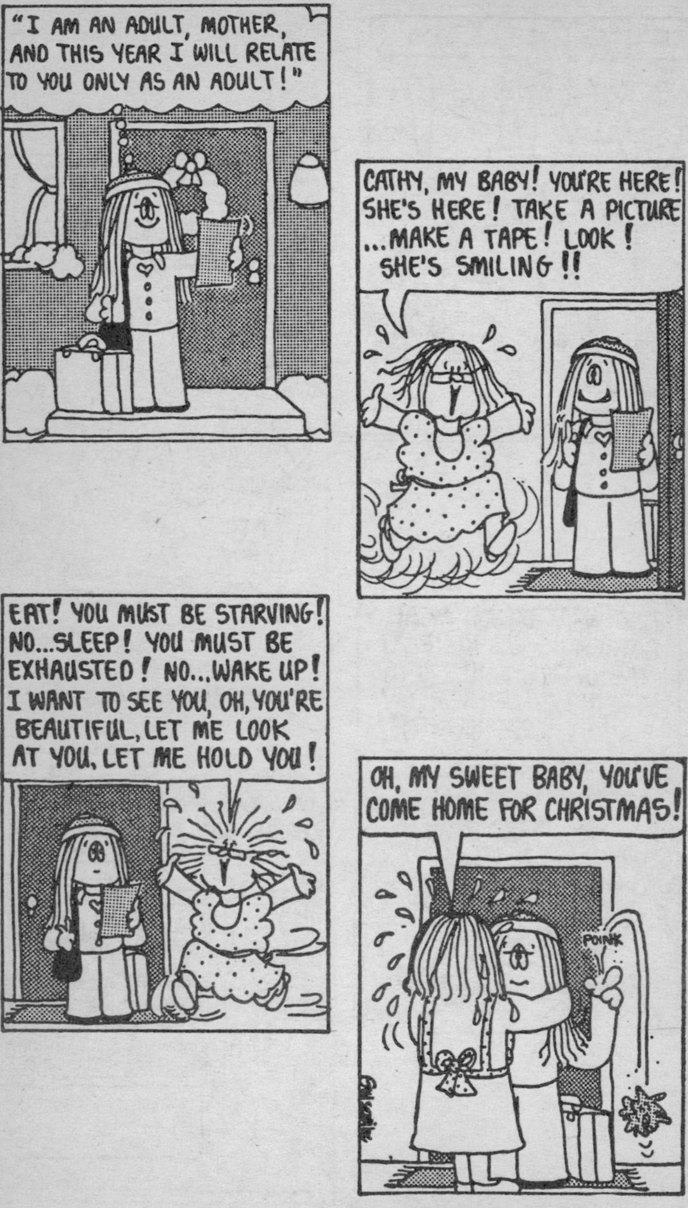
"I AM AN ADULT, MOTHER, AND THIS YEAR I WILL RELATE TO YOU ONLY AS AN ADULT!"
CATHY, MY BABY! YOU'RE HERE! SHE'S HERE! TAKE A PICTURE ...MAKE A TAPE! LOOK! SHE'S SMILING!!
EAT! YOU MUST BE STARVING! NO...SLEEP! YOU MUST BE EXHAUSTED! NO...WAKE UP! I WANT TO SEE YOU, OH, YOU'RE BEAUTIFUL, LET ME LOOK AT YOU, LET ME HOLD YOU!
OH, MY SWEET BABY, YOU'VE COME HOME FOR CHRISTMAS!
POINK

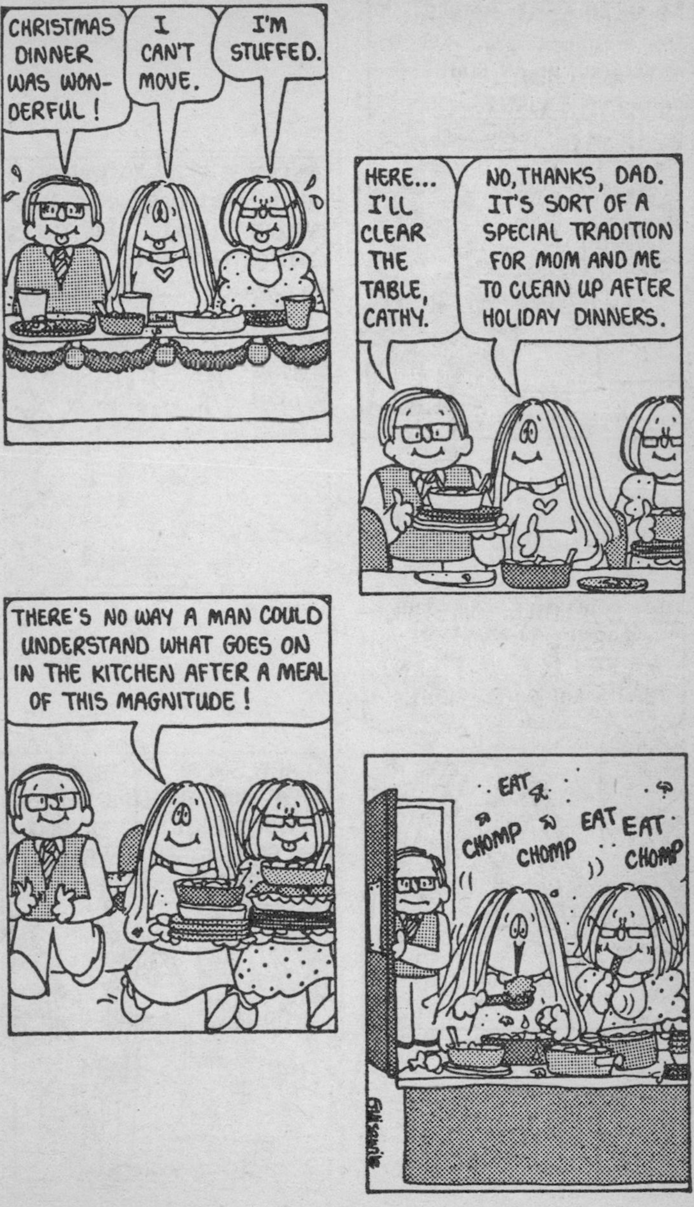
CHRISTMAS DINNER WAS WONDERFUL!
I CAN'T MOVE.
I'M STUFFED.
HERE... I'LL CLEAR THE TABLE, CATHY.
NO, THANKS, DAD. IT'S SORT OF A SPECIAL TRADITION FOR MOM AND ME TO CLEAN UP AFTER HOLIDAY DINNERS.
THERE'S NO WAY A MAN COULD UNDERSTAND WHAT GOES ON IN THE KITCHEN AFTER A MEAL OF THIS MAGNITUDE!
EAT
CHOMP
CHOMP
EAT
EAT
CHOMP

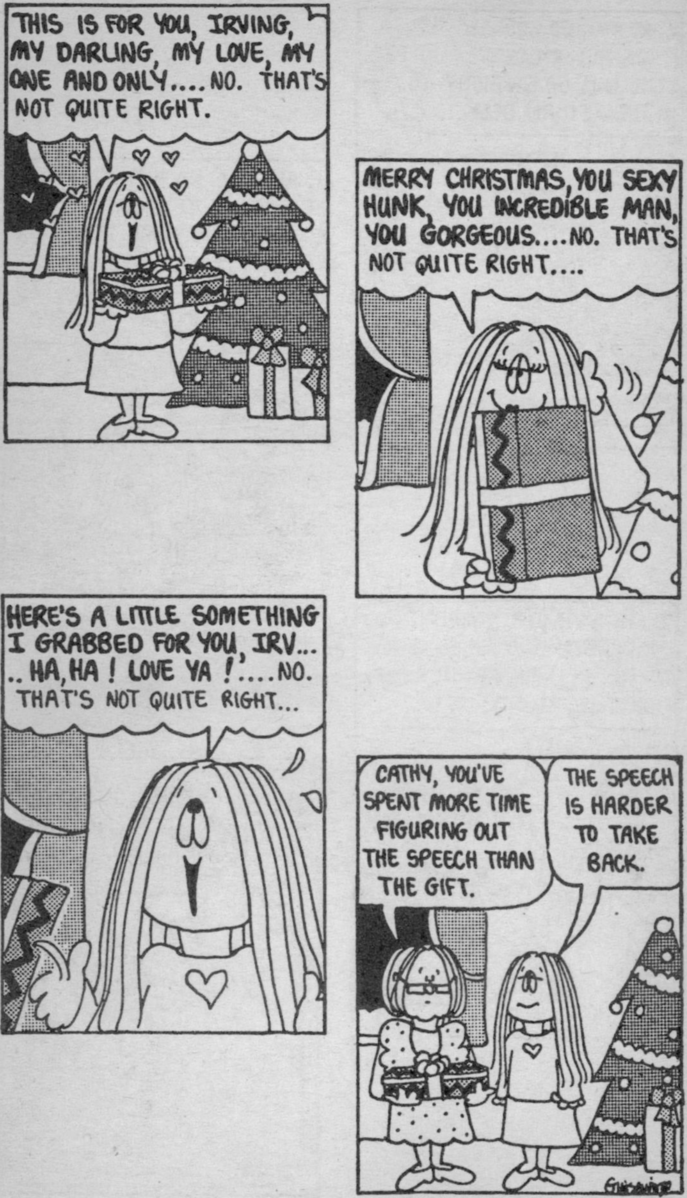
THIS IS FOR YOU, IRVING, MY DARLING, MY LOVE, MY ONE AND ONLY.... NO. THAT'S NOT QUITE RIGHT.
MERRY CHRISTMAS, YOU SEXY HUNK, YOU INCREDIBLE MAN, YOU GORGEOUS.... NO. THAT'S NOT QUITE RIGHT....
HERE'S A LITTLE SOMETHING I GRABBED FOR YOU, IRV... .. HA, HA ! LOVE YA !.... NO. THAT'S NOT QUITE RIGHT...
CATHY, YOU'VE SPENT MORE TIME FIGURING OUT THE SPEECH THAN THE GIFT.
THE SPEECH IS HARDER TO TAKE BACK.

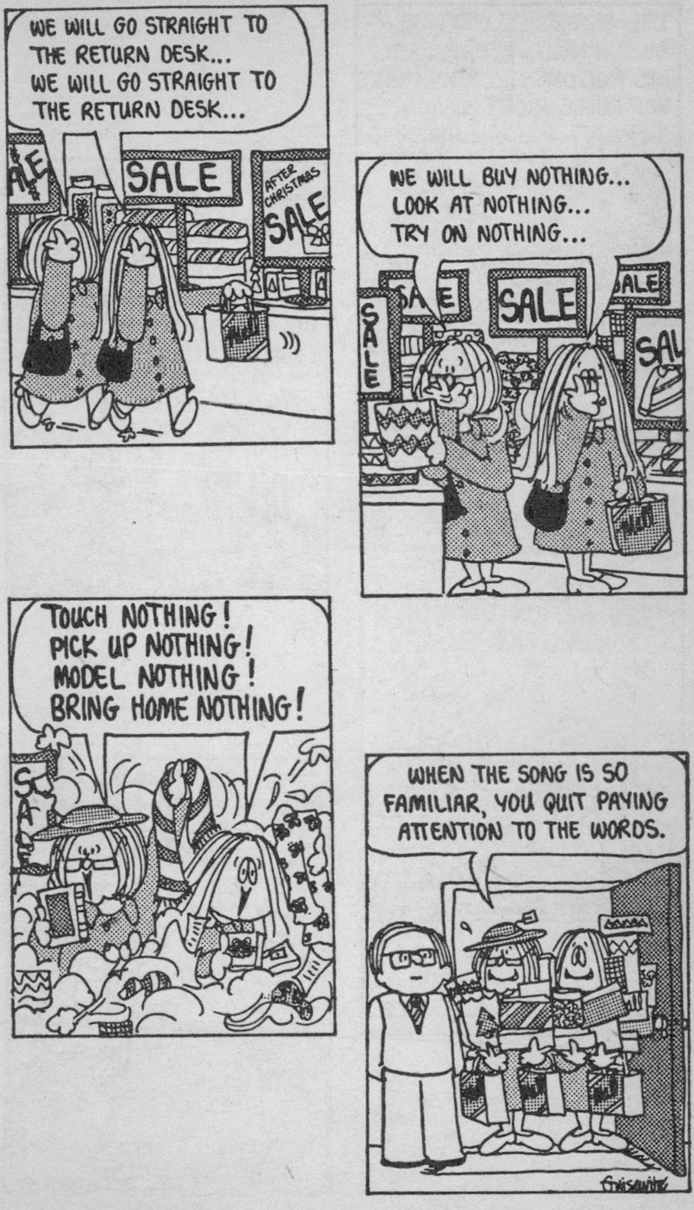
WE WILL GO STRAIGHT TO THE RETURN DESK... WE WILL GO STRAIGHT TO THE RETURN DESK...
SALE
AFTER CHRISTMAS SALE
WE WILL BUY NOTHING... LOOK AT NOTHING... TRY ON NOTHING...
SALE
SALE
TOUCH NOTHING! PICK UP NOTHING! MODEL NOTHING! BRING HOME NOTHING!
WHEN THE SONG IS SO FAMILIAR, YOU QUIT PAYING ATTENTION TO THE WORDS.

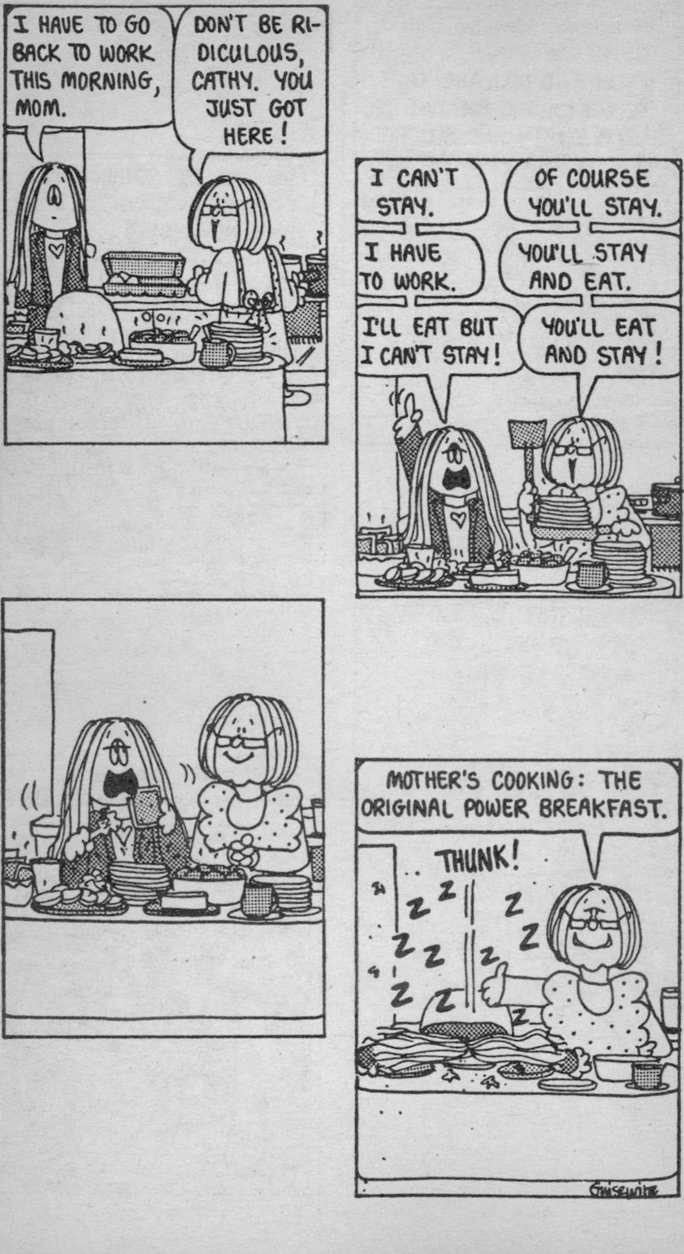

I HAVE TO GO BACK TO WORK THIS MORNING, MOM.
DON'T BE RIDICULOUS, CATHY. YOU JUST GOT HERE!
I CAN'T STAY.
OF COURSE YOU'LL STAY.
I HAVE TO WORK.
YOU'LL STAY AND EAT.
I'LL EAT BUT I CAN'T STAY!
YOU'LL EAT AND STAY!
MOTHER'S COOKING: THE ORIGINAL POWER BREAKFAST.
THUNK!
Z Z Z Z Z Z Z Z Z
Guisewite

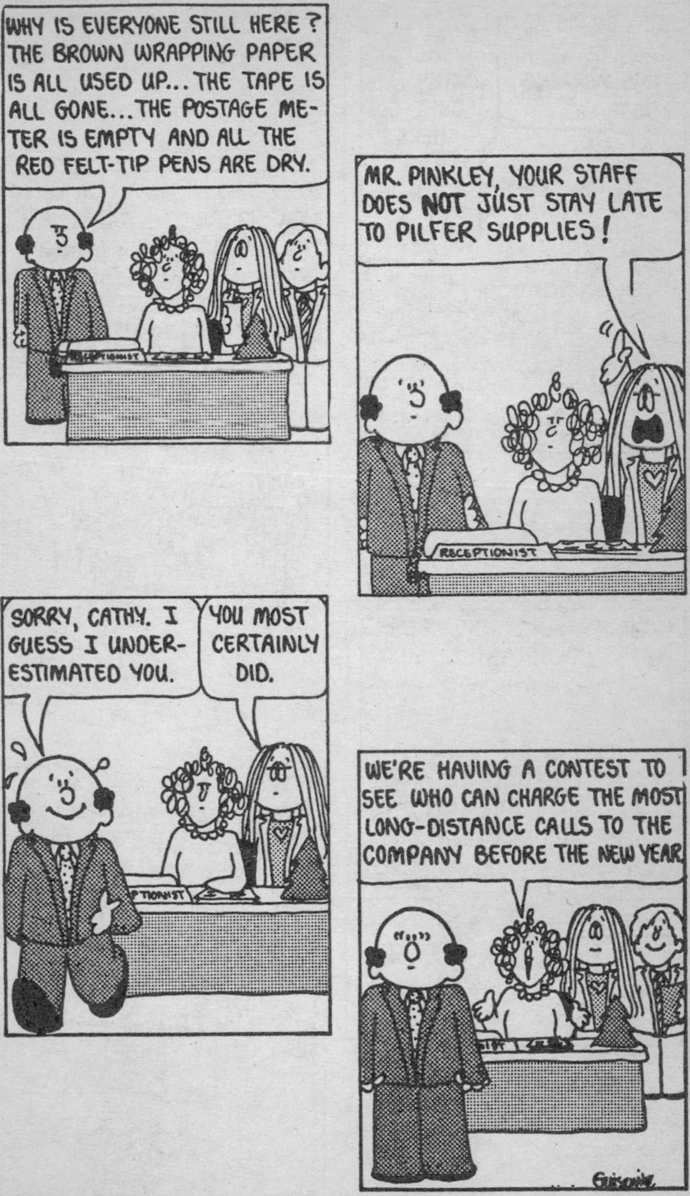
WHY IS EVERYONE STILL HERE? THE BROWN WRAPPING PAPER IS ALL USED UP... THE TAPE IS ALL GONE... THE POSTAGE METER IS EMPTY AND ALL THE RED FELT-TIP PENS ARE DRY.
MR. PINKLEY, YOUR STAFF DOES NOT JUST STAY LATE TO PILFER SUPPLIES!
RECEPTIONIST
SORRY, CATHY. I GUESS I UNDERESTIMATED YOU.
YOU MOST CERTAINLY DID.
WE'RE HAVING A CONTEST TO SEE WHO CAN CHARGE THE MOST LONG-DISTANCE CALLS TO THE COMPANY BEFORE THE NEW YEAR.

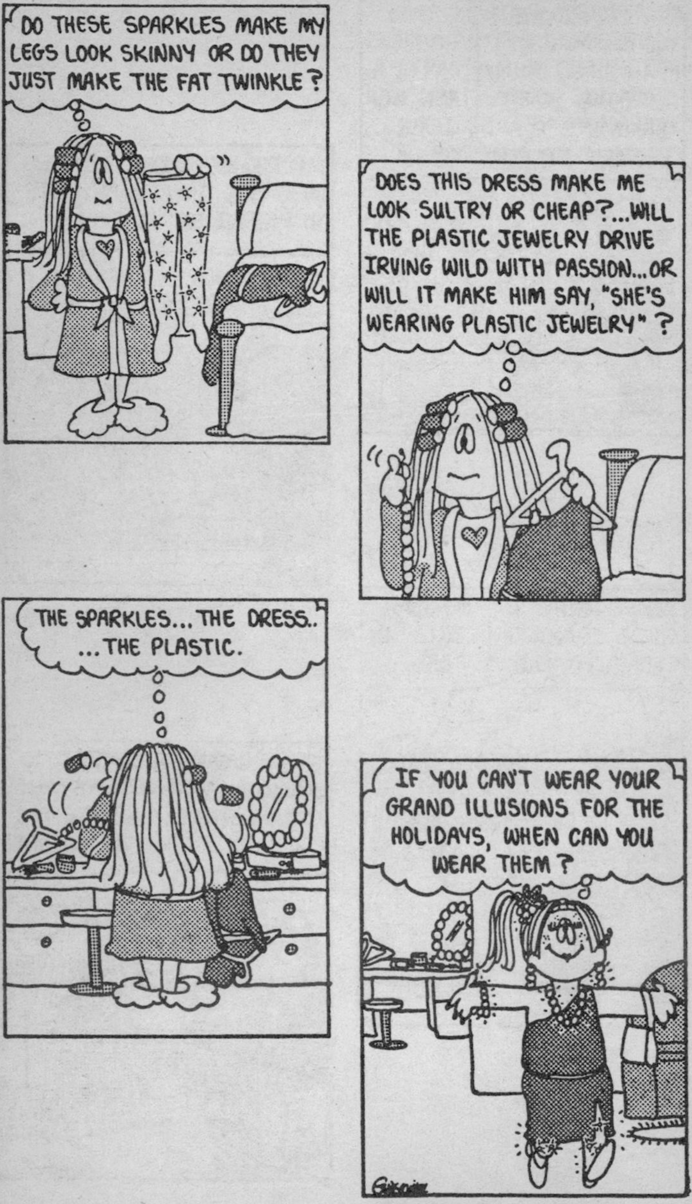
DO THESE SPARKLES MAKE MY LEGS LOOK SKINNY OR DO THEY JUST MAKE THE FAT TWINKLE?
DOES THIS DRESS MAKE ME LOOK SULTRY OR CHEAP?...WILL THE PLASTIC JEWELRY DRIVE IRVING WILD WITH PASSION...OR WILL IT MAKE HIM SAY, "SHE'S WEARING PLASTIC JEWELRY"?
THE SPARKLES... THE DRESS.. ...THE PLASTIC.
IF YOU CAN'T WEAR YOUR GRAND ILLUSIONS FOR THE HOLIDAYS, WHEN CAN YOU WEAR THEM?

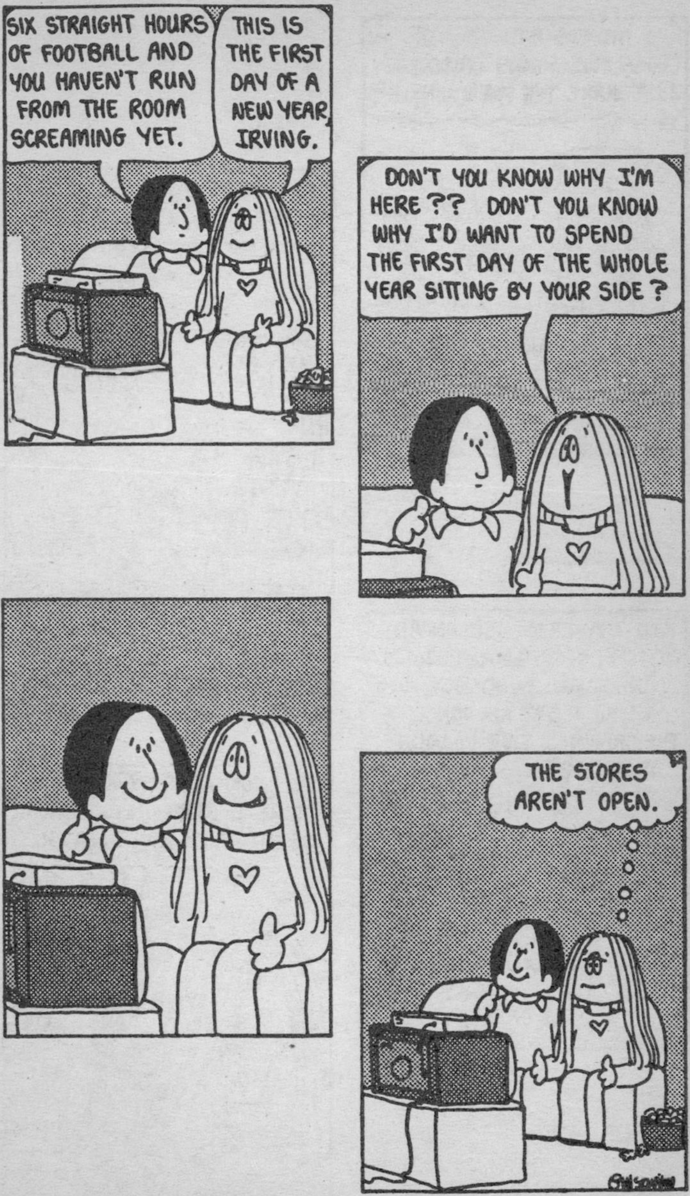
SIX STRAIGHT HOURS OF FOOTBALL AND YOU HAVEN'T RUN FROM THE ROOM SCREAMING YET.
THIS IS THE FIRST DAY OF A NEW YEAR, IRVING.
DON'T YOU KNOW WHY I'M HERE?? DON'T YOU KNOW WHY I'D WANT TO SPEND THE FIRST DAY OF THE WHOLE YEAR SITTING BY YOUR SIDE?
THE STORES AREN'T OPEN.

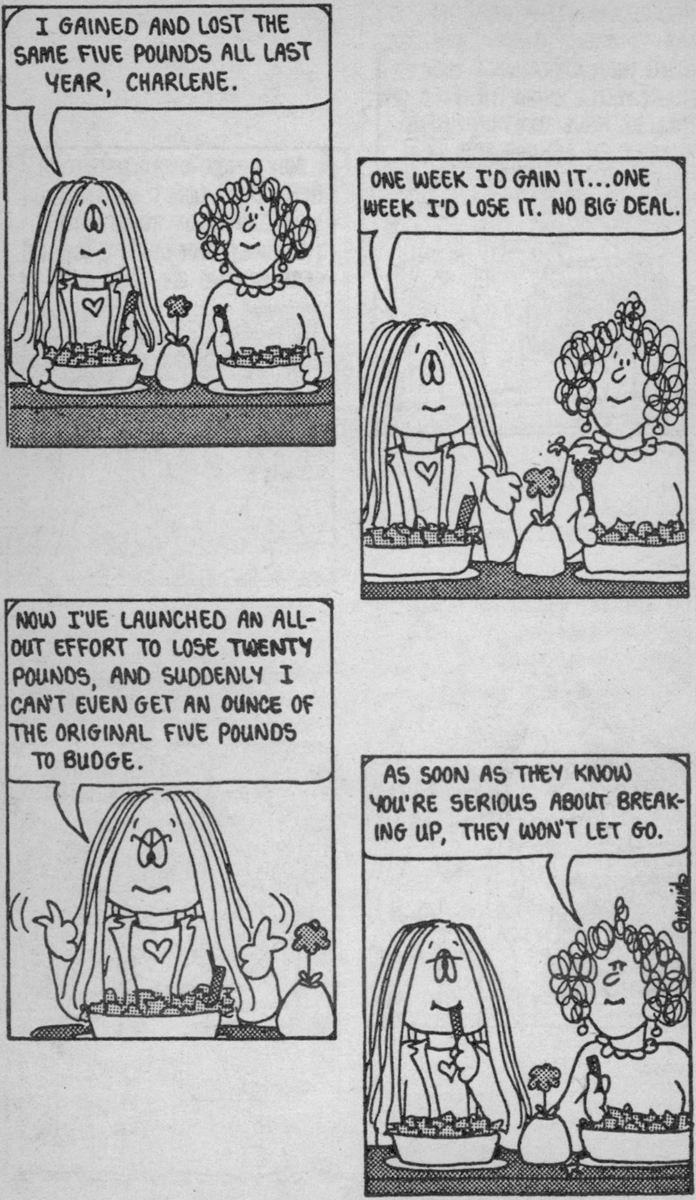

I GAINED AND LOST THE SAME FIVE POUNDS ALL LAST YEAR, CHARLENE.
ONE WEEK I'D GAIN IT...ONE WEEK I'D LOSE IT. NO BIG DEAL.
NOW I'VE LAUNCHED AN ALL-OUT EFFORT TO LOSE TWENTY POUNDS, AND SUDDENLY I CAN'T EVEN GET AN OUNCE OF THE ORIGINAL FIVE POUNDS TO BUDGE.
AS SOON AS THEY KNOW YOU'RE SERIOUS ABOUT BREAKING UP, THEY WON'T LET GO.

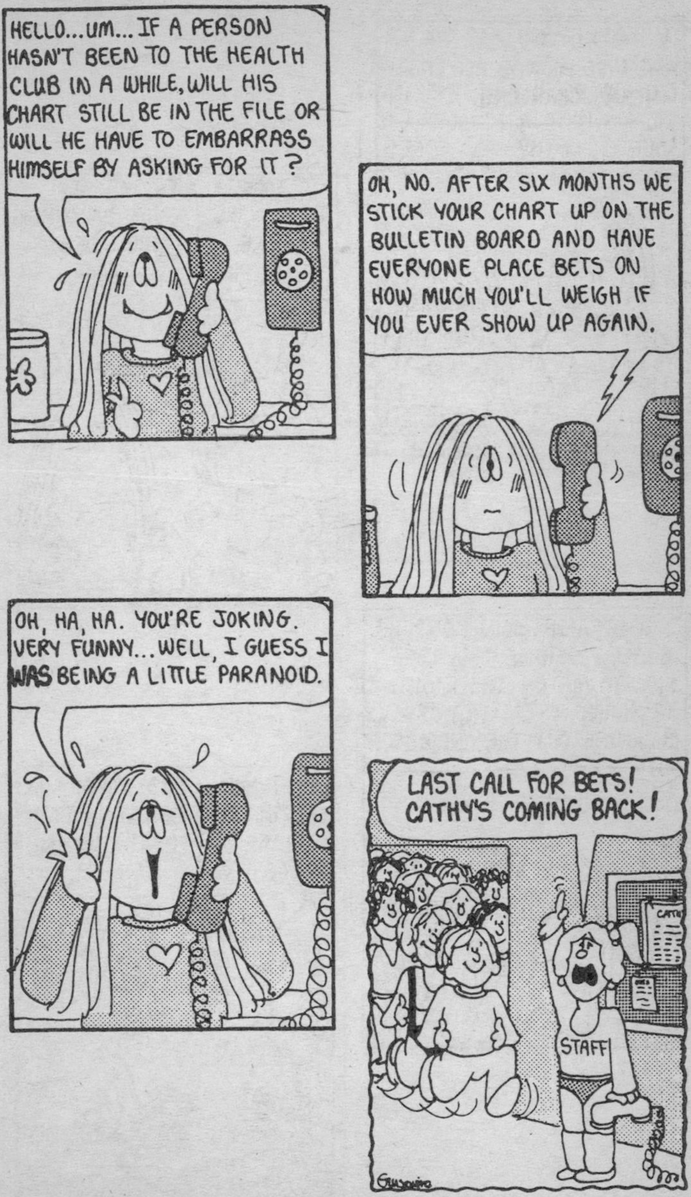
HELLO...UM... IF A PERSON HASN'T BEEN TO THE HEALTH CLUB IN A WHILE, WILL HIS CHART STILL BE IN THE FILE OR WILL HE HAVE TO EMBARRASS HIMSELF BY ASKING FOR IT?
OH, NO. AFTER SIX MONTHS WE STICK YOUR CHART UP ON THE BULLETIN BOARD AND HAVE EVERYONE PLACE BETS ON HOW MUCH YOU'LL WEIGH IF YOU EVER SHOW UP AGAIN.
OH, HA, HA. YOU'RE JOKING. VERY FUNNY... WELL, I GUESS I WAS BEING A LITTLE PARANOID.
LAST CALL FOR BETS! CATHY'S COMING BACK!
STAFF

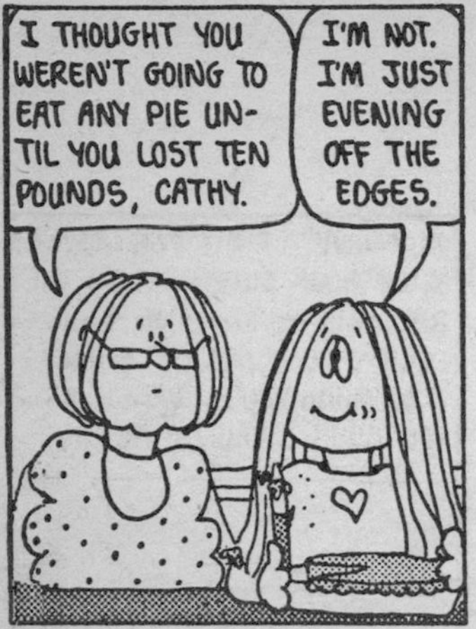

I THOUGHT YOU WEREN'T GOING TO EAT ANY PIE UNTIL YOU LOST TEN POUNDS, CATHY.
I'M NOT. I'M JUST EVENING OFF THE EDGES.

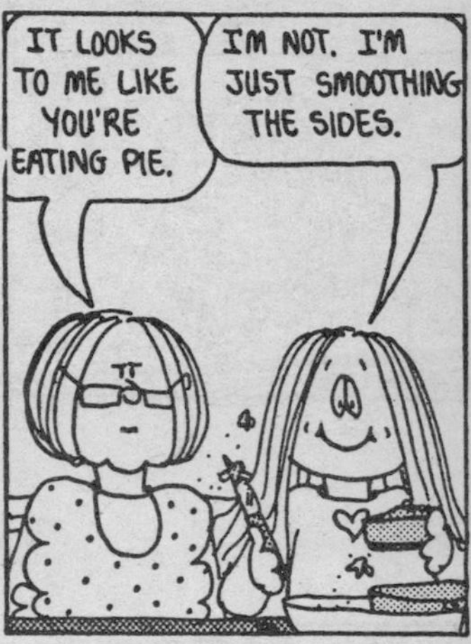

IT LOOKS TO ME LIKE YOU'RE EATING PIE.
I'M NOT. I'M JUST SMOOTHING THE SIDES.

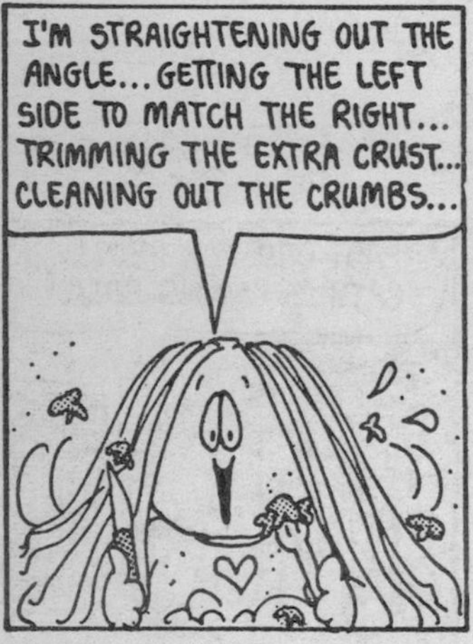

I'M STRAIGHTENING OUT THE ANGLE... GETTING THE LEFT SIDE TO MATCH THE RIGHT... TRIMMING THE EXTRA CRUST... CLEANING OUT THE CRUMBS...

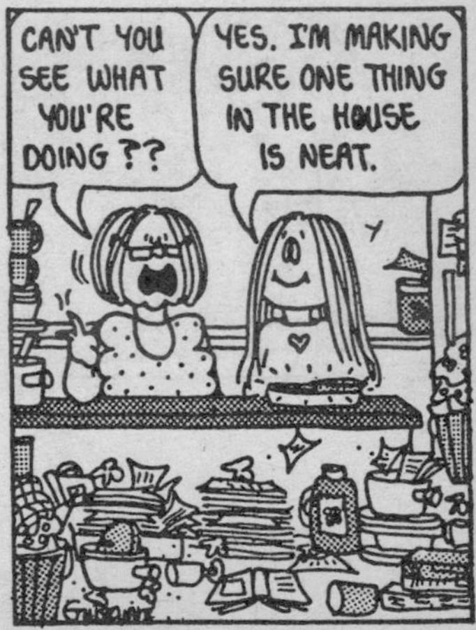

CAN'T YOU SEE WHAT YOU'RE DOING ??
YES. I'M MAKING SURE ONE THING IN THE HOUSE IS NEAT.

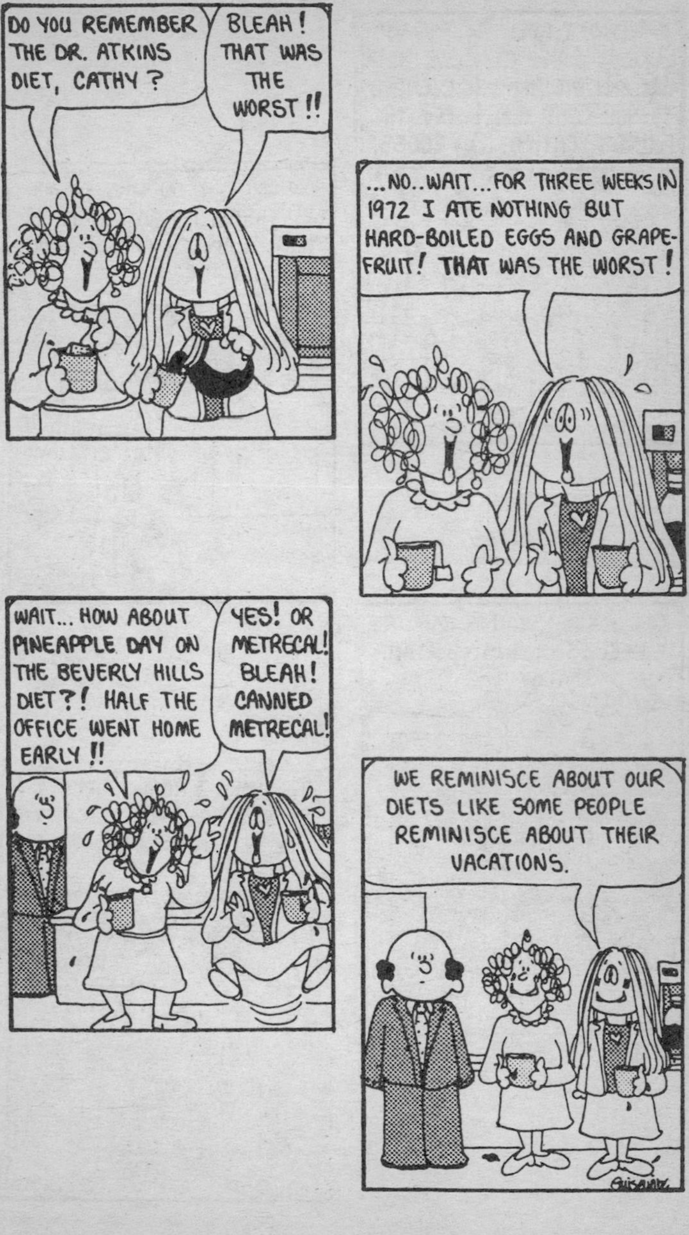
DO YOU REMEMBER THE DR. ATKINS DIET, CATHY?
BLEAH! THAT WAS THE WORST!!
...NO..WAIT...FOR THREE WEEKS IN 1972 I ATE NOTHING BUT HARD-BOILED EGGS AND GRAPE-FRUIT! THAT WAS THE WORST!
WAIT... HOW ABOUT PINEAPPLE DAY ON THE BEVERLY HILLS DIET?! HALF THE OFFICE WENT HOME EARLY!!
YES! OR METRECAL! BLEAH! CANNED METRECAL!
WE REMINISCE ABOUT OUR DIETS LIKE SOME PEOPLE REMINISCE ABOUT THEIR VACATIONS.

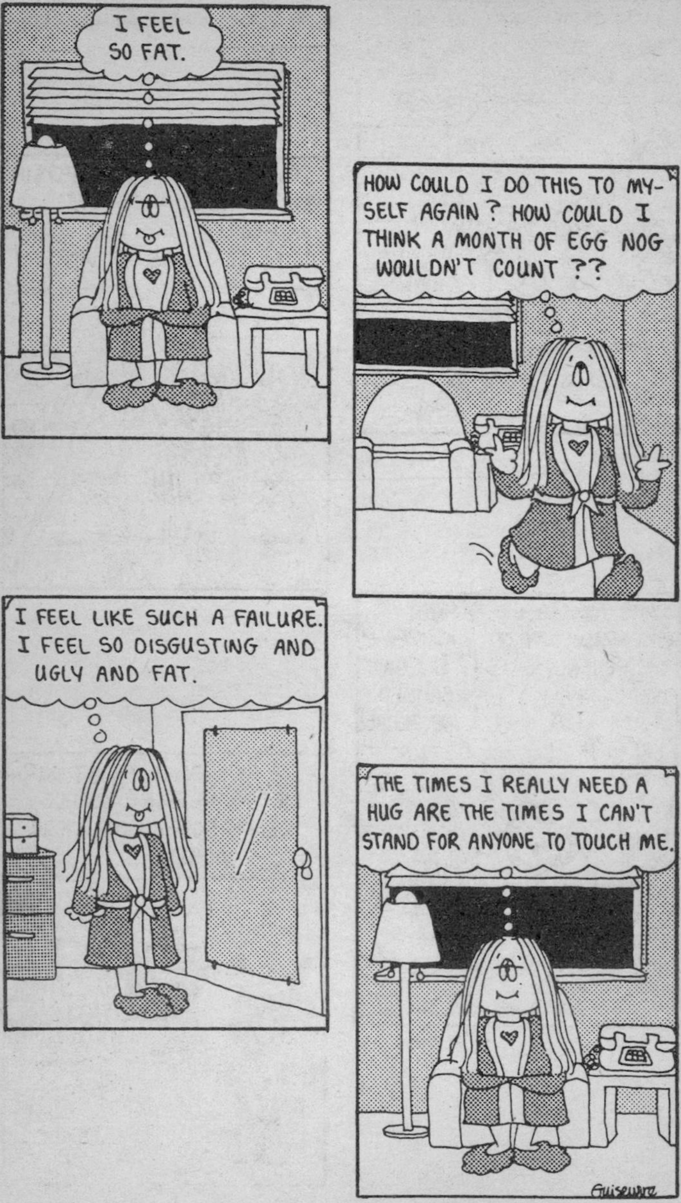
I FEEL SO FAT.
HOW COULD I DO THIS TO MYSELF AGAIN? HOW COULD I THINK A MONTH OF EGG NOG WOULDN'T COUNT??
I FEEL LIKE SUCH A FAILURE. I FEEL SO DISGUSTING AND UGLY AND FAT.
THE TIMES I REALLY NEED A HUG ARE THE TIMES I CAN'T STAND FOR ANYONE TO TOUCH ME.
Guisewite